Steamers, Saddles & Scalpels

The Life, Times, and Legacy of E. F. Guyon

by

Peter Guyon
a grandson

Biographies are but the clothes and buttons of the man—the biography of the man himself cannot be written.
— Mark Twain, *Autobiography*

TABLE OF CONTENTS

ACKNOWLEDGMENTS

I have found valuable insights and information about my grandfather's life in two short published biographical sketches, both of which I have used as primary sources and outlines for this biography. The most recent, which also contains the most information, is found in Hiram T. French's *History of Idaho*, published in 1914 (the "French Biography").

In December 2008, I became aware of a second biographical review in *An Illustrated History of the State of Idaho*, published by the Lewis Publishing Company of Chicago in 1899 and compiled by Richard Z. Johnson (the "Johnson Biography"). It is shorter and less detailed than the French Biography, but preceded it by approximately fifteen years.

Whether Grandpa Guyon contributed to either biography is unknown. Both contain details that support the idea that he was interviewed or, at the very least, consulted. There is no known record of his contesting the contents of either, although there are inconsistencies between them.

Using the general biographical information from the abridged biographies as an outline, I have added information from other sources, including oral history passed down to me in my family, documents and correspondence that my grandfather created or collected himself, newspaper articles, and books and other publications consulted and collected by me. I gleaned other important information from conversations over time with my uncle Edwin Fenimore Guyon, including an interview on September 14–15, 1990, in Victor, Idaho. Edwin Fenimore's crystal-clear recollections of events transpiring more than seventy years in the past provided an otherwise unattainable perspective to parts of this biography.

I must also acknowledge that during the course of writing this biography I have been aided and prompted in ways I cannot explain entirely. Particularly where writing about occurrences unsupported by documents, I have felt guided to alter statements or observations I had already written, almost as if someone was looking over my shoulder. After making the suggested changes, I was always rewarded with a subtle—but unmistakable—confirmation that the altered statement was factually accurate.

I owe a debt of gratitude to Margaret Guyon Brown Grainger, who befriended me many years ago and allowed me to copy a treasure trove of personal letters between Grandpa Guyon and her mother Maud and others. Without that correspondence, many of the details of Grandpa Guyon's life in the 20th century would have been impossible to reconstruct.

I express my appreciation to my friends and family members, and especially to my children Elisabeth, Peter Jr., and Catherine, for their words of encouragement during my struggles to write this biography and, in the case of Elisabeth, for her critique of a very rough and difficult-to-read draft and many later suggestions for improvement.

Finally, I acknowledge the assistance of my friend Paul Toscano for his incisive and insightful comments and suggestions.

INTRODUCTION

E. F. Guyon,[1] my paternal grandfather, was an intellectually gifted, enlightened, and remarkably accomplished person who was born in the Deep South before the American Civil War. A singularly eclectic individual, he began his working life as a farm laborer in rural Oregon in 1865 at the tender age of twelve at the latest, and for the next twenty-plus years followed many different vocations: schoolteacher, Indian agent, blacksmith, storekeeper, farm laborer, United States postmaster, gold miner, cowboy, sheep shearer, debt collector, volunteer Indian fighter, and cattle rancher—and this list may not be exhaustive. In 1891, at the age of thirty-seven, he earned his medical degree from the University of Cincinnati and thereafter served as a general practitioner in Oregon, Idaho, and Wyoming for more than thirty years.[2]

Grandpa Guyon held many positions in the Independent Order of Odd Fellows ("IOOF") in Idaho, including that of Grand Patriarch. As a physician, he gained national and international renown for his knowledge and expertise in the treatment of tuberculosis, and was the author of legislation in Oregon and Idaho designed to improve the quality of medical services for the public at large. Despite his inauspicious location in rural southeastern Idaho, he was called upon in the early years of the 20th century to represent the state of Idaho and the IOOF at national and international conclaves relating to medical and other important humanitarian issues. To his patients in southeast Idaho and elsewhere, he was a respected and trusted medical practitioner whose leanings in favor of conservative treatment were widely known. Last but by no means least, he was a loving husband, father to five children, and patriarch to two separate families.

Grandpa was a contemporary of iconic events of the mid-19th through the early 20th centuries: he was eight at the onset of the American Civil War in 1861; eleven when Lincoln was assassinated and the war ended in 1865; fifteen when the golden spike was driven at Promontory, Utah, in 1869;

---

[1] His full name was Edwin Fernando Guyon, but he almost always identified himself as "E. F. Guyon," even in family correspondence. In this biography I refer to him variously as "Edwin," "Grandpa Guyon," "my grandfather," "Grandpa," "Doc Guyon," or "Doc."

[2] To the public at large, my grandfather was Doc Guyon. In our family he was virtually always referred to as "Grandpa Guyon," although I can remember a few instances where he was more formally referred to as "the Doctor." His influence in our family has lasted long after his death. A chance comment by my father in the late 1950s that my grandfather "always wanted to learn French" kindled in me a desire to study the French language, history, and culture that has burned brightly my entire life. Dr. Guyon's interest prompted the inclusion, in his memory, of the French expressions, quotations, and proverbs in this biography.

twenty-two when General Custer and the men of the Seventh Cavalry met their fates near the Little Big Horn River in Montana in June, 1876; forty-nine when the Wright Brothers achieved sustained flight at Kitty Hawk, North Carolina, in 1903; fifty-eight when the Titanic sank in the North Atlantic in April, 1912; sixty when the Great War began in 1914; days shy of sixty-five when it ended in the fall of 1918; sixty-six when Prohibition became the law of the land via the 18th Amendment on January 16, 1920; almost seventy-six when the stock market crash of Black Tuesday ushered in the Great Depression on October 29, 1929; and eighty when the 21st Amendment repealed Prohibition on December 5, 1933.

I cannot escape visualizing my grandfather as Doc Adams, played by the actor Milburn Stone, in the long-running television series *Gunsmoke*. The older, mustached, irascible, well-respected, and knowledgeable medical icon of Dodge City of the Old West, always dressed in a suit, tie, and vest with a handy pocket-watch on a chain across the front, always available to the needy, and always motivated by his sense of humanity and altruism rather than money, fits well my grandfather's mold as I see him, from the office accessed by a flight of stairs from the street to the roll-top desk filled with sundry documents and scraps of paper. Doc Adams in the *Gunsmoke* series would have practiced medicine some twenty years before my grandfather even graduated from medical school, but in my mind the western frontier in Kansas of the 1870s is not that far removed from the reality of the western frontier in Oregon of the 1890s, where my grandfather, like Doc Adams, traveled by horse and buggy and removed the occasional bullet from various victims of violence.

The title to this biography includes three images that represent important sequences of events in my grandpa's life: (1) the steamships that carried him as a very young child from his beginning in the South to his life in the West; (2) the ubiquitous saddle treasured by the cowboy whose mold he came to fit (if only temporarily) during his early life in Pendleton and Pilot Rock; and (3) the scalpel, emblematic of the balance of his life as a physician and surgeon in Oregon, Idaho, and Wyoming.

To document and append the "Times" portion of this biography I utilize several devices: I discuss various historical events and circumstances that occurred concurrently with or in some way may have affected his life; I add background information where the biography's perspective seems to require enhancement or the information itself seems especially interesting; and I posit possibilities where plausible alternatives to probable, but unconfirmed, facts seem desirable. In these ways, I hope to broaden the reader's perspective and appreciation of my grandfather's life in its entirety and in its historical context.

My grandfather died more than ten years before I was born, but I can recall stories and comments about him made during my childhood, not only from my family, but also from members of the community in Montpelier, Idaho, where I grew up and where my grandfather had practiced medicine for over thirty years. He was spoken of often, and always with reverence and respect, but I acquired the feeling over time that there was much about him that was not fully known or understood. That feeling has been confirmed from time to time during the course of my efforts to write his biography, and has compelled me to ensure, as much as possible, that he is accurately remembered and portrayed.

Writing this biography has allowed me to engage with a person I never met, but to whom I now feel closely connected. He is no longer a mere name to me, and I hope to convey to the reader a sense of the essence of this very real person.

It is no overstatement that Doc Guyon continues to be a source of positive inspiration, at least to his descendants[3] and perhaps others. Blessed with an exceptional intellect, and having developed the unflagging will, work ethic, and determination to match it, E. F. Guyon was a self-made man in the strictest sense of the word. He was not wealthy materially, partly because of circumstances over which he had no control, and partly because of his personal commitment to serve his fellow man, oftentimes to his own pecuniary disadvantage. His life and legacy in no small way demonstrate the invincible nature of the human spirit and the eternal truth, often forgotten, that there are worthy ideals that far transcend mere money and gain in importance.

E. F. Guyon
(1853–1934)

Part I

—

Origins

Chapter 1.

FRENCH ROOTS
AND
AMERICAN RELATIVES

Le sort fait les parents,
le choix fait les amis.[4]
— Jacques Delille, *Malheur et Pitié*

This chapter introduces all the known characters in my grandfather's immediate family, examines possible genealogical connections to his more remote ancestors, and discusses questionable published conclusions about his family pedigree.

Emily Louise Shattuck Guyon, Courageous Wife and Mother

Emily Louise and Edwin – 1864

My great-grandmother Emily Louise Guyon, née Shattuck ("Emily Louise"), chanced to be in New Orleans, Louisiana, in 1853 during the worst outbreak of yellow fever ever to descend on the population in the city's recorded history. Before the rampaging disease, also colloquially referred to, among other names, as "Yellow Jack" "Bronze John," or "the saffron scourge," had run its course, almost 10 percent of the city's population was dead. Emily Louise, pregnant during the spring and summer of 1853 when the threat of the contagion was highest, was among the survivors. Despite the danger, on Monday, November 7, she gave birth to her first and only child, a healthy baby boy she and her husband named Edwin Fernando Guyon.

---

4 "Fate chooses our relatives, we choose our friends."

Emily Louise was born in Missouri on March 20, 1829, and was twenty-four when she became a mother.[5] She and the infant boy's father, John Guyon, were married circa 1849 (the exact date and location of the marriage remain undiscovered). John Guyon disappeared without a trace in approximately 1854, leaving the new mother to raise their infant son alone.

Not long after her husband's disappearance, Emily Louise left New Orleans with her son and possibly other family members and traveled via the Panama Route[6] to California. There she resettled and married Henry C. Smith in Sacramento on June 10, 1858.[7] Together, the couple raised Emily Louise's son as Edwin Fernando Smith, primarily in Oregon. Emily Louise kept her first marriage to John Guyon a closely guarded secret from Grandpa until 1878 when, on her deathbed, she finally revealed it to him.

Emily Louise died less than three weeks short of her forty-ninth birthday on March 2, 1878, in Pilot Rock, Oregon, from unknown causes. She is buried in the Pilot Rock cemetery next to Mr. Smith under the name of Emily L. Smith.

The Mysterious John Guyon, Erstwhile Husband and Father

John Guyon[8] was a spectral character in Grandpa's life. A native of Jersey City, New Jersey, and a contractor and builder of wharves and bridges, he had come to New Orleans "at an early day"[9] to ply his trade at the mouth of the Mississippi. He was probably born between 1815 and 1829. Nothing is known concerning his training, experience, aspirations, personality, or appearance, and next to nothing is known about his family roots except that he was the eventual product of Huguenot refugees who left France toward the end of the 17th century[10] to escape religious persecution. John Guyon's parents, siblings, other children he may have fathered, and other family connections are entirely unknown.

---

[5] Date of birth, Emily Louise's tombstone in the Pilot Rock Cemetery, Pilot Rock, Oregon; her place of birth from US Census Records, South Salem, Marion County, Oregon, July 31, 1860.
[6] "The Panama Route" refers generally to the path taken across the Isthmus of by travelers from points east to California.
[7] Marriage record, City of Sacramento, California, 10 June 1858.
[8] Edwin's father is identified in the French Biography as Leon John Guyon and in the Johnson Biography as John Guyon. For consistency and to avoid possible confusion, I refer to him as John Guyon.
[9] Hiram T. French, *History of Idaho* (Chicago: Lewis, 1914), 1256.
[10] Ibid.

If John Guyon's disappearance was a monumental disappointment to Emily Louise and her child, the void left by his absence was diminished, if not completely filled, by the infant boy's selfless maternal grandmother, Elizabeth Shattuck. This intrepid woman may well have saved both Emily Louise and her baby from economic ruin, to say nothing of providing moral support in a time of severe emotional crisis.

Elizabeth Shattuck was born in Virginia on August 24, 1789, and died in San Francisco, California, on May 8, 1868, after suffering for months from heart disease and dropsy (i.e., edema, a condition consistent with congestive heart failure). The record of her death is extraordinarily detailed and reports that she died at the age of seventy-eight years, eight months, and fourteen days.[11] The death occurred at 10:00 p.m. in her home at 437 Minna Street, San Francisco. She passed away in the arms of "Frank," possibly her son, and was buried in San Francisco in a rosewood coffin with her name and age on the plate in the Willow section, lot 40, of the old Masonic Cemetery.[12]

Despite the prayers and wishes of grieving family members, friends, and clergy that she rest in peace, the Shattuck family matriarch was not destined to remain in the Masonic Cemetery forever. The thirty acres originally consecrated to hold the mortal remains of deceased human beings eventually became too valuable to justify such a continued unprofitable use. In the 1930s, all its human remains, including those of Elizabeth Shattuck, were exhumed and reinterred elsewhere.[13] Her final resting place is Woodlawn Memorial Park, Colma, California.[14]

---

[11] Mortuary Record of the City and County of San Francisco, 10 May 1868, LDS Archives film #975830.

[12] Julia Lordner (Gardner?) to Emily Louise Smith, 13 May 1868 (misdated 1867); Alphabetical List of Interments, Old Masonic Cemetery, 115, FHL #975837.

[13] The exhumation of the remains of approximately fourteen thousand persons from the Masonic Cemetery was met with stiff resistance by some of their descendants, and was preceded by legal wrangling that began in 1900 and continued for over thirty years. Legal skirmishes eventually resulted in two federal court decisions. The first, *Gamage v. Masonic Cemetery Ass'n, et al.*, 31 F.2d 308 (1929), memorializes a successful attempt on the trial court level by sixteen lot holders in the Masonic Cemetery to temporarily enjoin the City and County of San Francisco from allowing the removal. The second, *Masonic Cemetery Ass'n, et al. v. Gamage, et al.*, 38 F.2d 950 (1930), is an appeal of the lower court decision that reversed the injunction, dismissed the underlying complaint filed by the lot holders, and allowed the governmental entities to proceed with the removal. Other San Francisco cemeteries, including Laurel Hill, Odd Fellows, and Calvary, which contained the remains, respectively, of fifty thousand, fifty thousand, and thirty thousand persons, were similarly affected.

[14] Woodlawn Memorial Park to Dr. J. C. Geiger, Director of Public Health, City and County of San Francisco, 8 May 1934.

In the absence of any requests by next of kin, the headstones of those exhumed from the Masonic Cemetery were used as fill for the land-based approaches to the San Francisco Bay Bridge.[15] It is presumed that Elizabeth Shattuck's headstone met that fate.

Nothing is known about her spouse or spouses, although it is known that besides Emily Louise, Elizabeth Shattuck was the mother of at least two daughters, Eliza and Julia, and possibly one son, Frank. Eliza's married surname in 1852–1853 was Hall, and later on she was known as Eliza Peck. By 1860, Julia's married surname was Uhlrich, but she was also known later as Julia Gardner.[16] Any other siblings are unknown.

Elizabeth Shattuck's maiden name is also unknown, although the possibility it might be Fernando merits consideration. There is no other known family connection with the name Fernando. The fact that my father's middle name is Shattuck, his grandmother's maiden name, may mean that the same custom or pattern determined Grandpa Guyon's middle name. The daguerrotype below, found in his effects after his death, may be the likeness of his maternal grandmother circa 1839.

The scant available information about the life of Elizabeth Shattuck suggests a supportive mother and grandmother at the center of her family. She was present in New Orleans in 1853 when Grandpa Guyon was born and may have accompanied him and his mother to California. In 1857 she appeared in a city directory in Sacramento, California, as head of her own household, of which Emily Louise and Grandpa Guyon were almost certainly members. Three years later, she was identified in the United States Census of 1860 in San Francisco, again as head of her own household, where she lived with her daughter Julia and her probable grandson Henry Hall.[17]

---

[15] "Masonic Cemetery (Defunct)," Find a Grave, accessed July 19, 2016, http//www.findagrave.com/cgi-bin/fg.cgi?page=cr&CRid=1991573.

[16] In a letter of May 8, 1868, to Emily Louise, Julia's handwriting is not altogether legible, and it is possible that her signature "Julia Gardner" may actually be "Julia Lordner."

[17] Approximately twenty years earlier, in 1838 or 1839, the name of "Mrs. Elizabeth Shattuck" appears in Louisville, Kentucky, where she lived over the store of Foster & Lytle, clothiers, No. 11 West Water Street; see G. Collins, *The Louisville Directory for the Years 1838-1839* (Louisville, KY: Louisville Microfilms, [195?]), 21, 38, 93. No other residents are identified. This Elizabeth Shattuck was likely either widowed or divorced, and appears to have had the same living arrangement above a business as Grandpa Guyon's grandmother had in New Orleans in 1853. The surname Shattuck does not appear to have been particularly common in the area, which may be an indicator she is Emily Louise's mother.

Henry and his younger brother Josiah Hall raise several complicating factors in Edwin's family history as explored below.

The Perplexing Riddle of Henry and Josiah Hall

Henry Hall in all probability was Elizabeth Shattuck's grandson, and may have long been thought to be her *only* grandson other than Grandpa Guyon. According to my father, Grandpa Guyon told his children during their youth that he had no living relatives after 1906. Grandpa also told them that prior to 1906 he had but one relative, who had disappeared around the time of the San Francisco earthquake and was never heard from again.[18] Because of the coincidence of the relative's disappearance and the San Francisco earthquake, Grandpa suspected that the relative had been lost *in* the earthquake, but never knew for sure.

Although Grandpa apparently never identified the person by name, there is little doubt that the lost relative he was referring to was Henry Hall, his first cousin,[19] but confirming Henry as Grandpa's sole lost relative is not without uncertainty. According to the United States Census of 1860, Henry, age six, was living in Sacramento with Elizabeth Shattuck, age seventy, the head of the household, and Julia Uhlrich, age thirty-one. We know Julia was Elizabeth's daughter and a sister of Emily Louise. From those facts we might be tempted to assume Henry Hall was Julia's son, although the 1860 census does not reveal familial relationships.

More ambiguity is injected into the equation by the United States Census of 1870. It identifies Henry Hall, age seventeen, living in San Francisco with Josiah Peck, age fifty-seven, Josiah's wife Eliza Peck, age forty-five, and a lad named Josiah Hall, age thirteen. Eliza was also Elizabeth Shattuck's daughter and Emily Louise's sister, but the 1870 census, like the 1860 census, reveals no familial relationships, which raises the additional puzzle of where Josiah Hall fits.

To answer that question, we must fast-forward ten years. In the United States Census of 1880, Josiah Peck, age sixty-seven, was still living with his

---

[18] Unfortunately, the demise of Henry Hall, or Eliza or Julia in any of their known names, cannot be confirmed from the lists of those who are known to have perished in San Francisco in 1906 as a result of the earthquake.

[19] In a letter to my sister Karen dated November 13, 1960, my father related that "Dad's mother also had a sister who came west with [Emily Louise] . . . but [she] must have perished in the 1906 earthquake as Dad never heard from her again after that." The story is too similar to the story of Henry Hall to ignore, but impossible to reconcile with the information I have presently. Whether my father was confused about the issue or whether I have not accurately remembered what he told me are both possibilities — or Grandpa Guyon himself may have been confused about the identity of his lost relatives when he related the story to his children.

wife Eliza Peck, age fifty-five, and Josiah Hall, age twenty-two, who is finally identified as Josiah Peck's stepson.

In summary of the available information, it appears that Henry Hall and Josiah Hall were brothers and Grandpa Guyon's first cousins. Both were born to Emily Louise's sister Eliza—Henry in about 1853 in Louisiana and Josiah in about 1857 in California prior to her marriage to Josiah Peck. This conclusion is inconsistent with Grandpa Guyon's stated belief that he had only one relative before 1906.

Josiah Hall died at the age of fifty-two of a "gunshot wound of the body" on March 28, 1909 in San Francisco.[20] Whether Edwin was aware of the event, or even the existence of Josiah Hall, is uncertain but improbable.

A Henry Hall died on November 10, 1917, in Caddo Parish, Louisiana, at the age of sixty-five, with the estimated birth year of 1852, although there appears to be no way to definitively confirm that he was Grandpa Guyon's first cousin.

The Curious Mystery of "Frank"

The letter of May 13, 1868, from Julia Lordner to Emily Louise identifies Julia and "Sister Eliza" as Emily Louise's sisters and the existence of Frank, although his relationship to the family is not entirely clear. The implication is that he is Elizabeth Shattuck's son and a brother to Julia, Emily Louise, and Eliza. Julia reports in the letter that her mother "died without a struggle in Frank's arms," which suggests Frank was her son or a much-loved son-in-law.

In the 1868 letter Frank is identified only by his first name. Had he been someone outside the immediate family, it seems more probable that his last name would also be mentioned. Julia also states, "I am in deep mourning[;] so is Frank" and "Frank sends his love to all." Those two statements seem to suggest a blood, as opposed to in-law, relationship.

Outside Elizabeth Shattuck, Julia, Emily Louise, Eliza, Frank, Josiah Hall, and Henry Hall, no one else in Dr. Guyon's immediate family has been identified with certainty.[21]

---

[20] San Francisco County Records, 1824-1997, Coroner's Death Register, 1906-1912.

[21] David O. Shattuck, an attorney and district court judge in San Francisco, lived at the "SW cor of Mary and Minna" in 1860, according to the San Francisco Directory of that year (p. 304). The connection with Minna Street, seven years before Elizabeth Shattuck's death, may be entirely coincidental. Another possible relative is Frank W. Shattuck, who had a daughter Frank O. Shattuck, born in 1861 according to the 1880 United States Census in Petaluma, Sonoma, California.

Huguenot Roots

Guyon family tradition, confirmed in both the French Biography and the Johnson Biography, is that Grandpa Guyon descended in the male line from Huguenot[22] refugees who fled religious persecution in France after the revocation of the Edict of Nantes in 1685 (the "Revocation"). The Revocation removed what little protection French Protestants had enjoyed since 1598 to practice their religion and triggered a massive outflow of humanity that by comparison had only trickled prior to 1685.[23]

It is possible that the first Guyons in my grandfather's patriarchal line to flee France came directly to North America; more probably they emigrated first to the British Isles or other locations in Europe before eventually arriving on American shores.

Huguenot Names

The family name itself, at least in its most common variations of Guyon and Guion, lends credence to the family's connection to French protestantism. Both names are clearly of French origin and both are recognized Huguenot family names. Some families with the name of Guyon or Guion are known to have emigrated from France directly to North America, others to the British Isles, and still others to different destinations, but it is not known whether those particular families are the only Guyon or Guion families to leave France after the Revocation, or whether there were others with the same or similar names.[24]

---

[22] The genesis of *Huguenot*, originally a derisive term, has become obscured by the passage of time, and alternative theories have evolved to explain its origins. One is that it was derived from Besançon Hugues, a Swiss politician and leader of the Geneva Eidgenossen. Literally "oath fellows," the German word *Eidgenossen* may refer to Protestants bound to each other by an oath of secrecy. Another possible explanation is that its pattern was Hughes Capet, the founder of the French royal house. Yet another is that it is a mixture of *Hughes*, *Eidgenossen*, and *Huisgenooten* (a Dutch word meaning "house mates" or "roommates," reminiscent of Protestants meeting and living in secret to study their religion). Still another theory is that it is a corruption of *Eidgenosse*: due to the difficulty of its pronunciation for French speakers, *Eidgenosse* became *Eignot* in Swiss-German, hence Huguenot.

[23] The Huguenot diaspora was a movement spawned by religious intolerance in France that took place over a period of more than one hundred years and involved the emigration of hundreds of thousands of adherents to the teachings of John Calvin. I believe an understanding of it provides meaningful insight into my grandfather's family, cultural, and religious background. With that objective in mind, I offer an abbreviated summary and discussion of the movement in Appendix I for what enlightenment it may contain.

[24] There are numerous possible variations of the name, including Guyant, Gaynon, Guyan, Goyon, Guye, Gui, Gaien, Dion, and Doyon.

What is missing in Grandpa Guyon's patriarchal line is a specific connection between John Guyon and his father, grandfather, and so on. The sparse information presently available about John Guyon does not allow the identification by name of any of the individuals in the generations that preceded him.

The French Biography states that Grandpa Guyon's ancestors left France after 1685, but neither biography avers when they actually arrived in North America. This lack of even a general suggestion of the time of their arrival compounds the difficulty in tracing actual, identifiable Guyon ancestors after the Revocation.

Assuming that Grandpa Guyon's French Huguenot ancestors left France in 1685 or thereabouts, and their descendant John Guyon was born in New Jersey during the first quarter of the 19th century (roughly between 1800 and 1825), we are left with 115–140 years unaccounted for in the Guyon line just since the Revocation. Presuming approximately twenty-five years per generation, five generations of Guyon ancestors would have been born after 1685 in John Guyon's ancestral line. Since we do not know when John Guyon's forebears came to New Jersey, or from where they immediately came, we can only speculate. Fortunately, the history of the Huguenot movement in general provides some clues that may allow the identification of possibilities, if not probabilities.

Aunis, the Birthplace of Many American Huguenots

One such clue may be found in the fact that a large percentage of Huguenot immigrants finding their way to Boston, New York, Jamestown, and Charleston via England and Holland in the fading years of the 17th century came from the French seaboard provinces of Poitou, Saintonge, and Aunis.[25] The area encompassed in these provinces between the Loire and Gironde rivers was largely Protestant prior to the Revocation; in fact, the tiny Aunis is known as the birthplace of American Huguenots.[26] Comprised of only seven hundred square miles of territory, Aunis was originally part of Saintonge. In the fourteenth century, Charles V (known as Charles le Sage;[27] b. 1337–d. 1380; reigned 1364–1380) appended the

---

[25] Charles W. Baird, *History of the Huguenot Emigration to America* (New York: Dodd, Mead & Company, 1885), 1:262.
[26] Ibid., 1:264.
[27] English translation: "Charles the Wise."

little district to the city of La Rochelle as a reward to the citizens of that city for their fidelity and loyalty during his wars with the English.[28]

Ancestral possibilities in Grandpa Guyon's line can be found in Aunis. Louis Guion, a resident of Mauzé, a small town in Aunis, is known to have emigrated to England shortly after the Revocation. Sparse records establish that by August 21, 1694, he, along with his wife Marie Morin, was in London on the occasion of the baptism of their son, also named Louis, in the French church on Glasshouse Street.[29]

A different Louis Guion, who may have been related to the Louis Guion from Mauzé, given the identity of names, bought land in New Rochelle, New York, in 1690. According to family tradition of the second Louis, his son, also Louis, was twelve years old in 1698, and was born at sea shortly after the Revocation.[30]

Another possibility is Jacques Guion *fils*, who was in New York City as early as 1701 with his wife Anne Vigneau. No actual relationship between Grandpa and either Louis Guion is known.[31]

Possible Guyon Family Ties in the United States

A book originally published in 1893 identifies seven generations of the Guyon family beginning with Louis Guyon, Ecuyer,[32] born in La Rochelle circa 1630.[33] His genealogical line may intersect with that of the Louis Guyon whose son was born at sea shortly after the Revocation, but this cannot be confirmed due to inconsistencies in dates. The name John Guyon appears in the third, fourth, fifth, and sixth generations as a child, but no verifiable connections to Dr. Guyon's family are evident from the lists of descendants.

---

28 Baird, *History of the Huguenot Emigration*, 1:264.
29 Ibid., 301.
30 Ibid.
31 Morgan H. Seacord, *Biographical Sketches and Index of the Huguenot Settlers of New Rochelle 1687-1776* (New Rochelle, NY: Huguenot and Historical Association of New Rochelle, 1941), 28.
32 Ecuyer is a French title approximating that of squire in England; a social rank above a gentleman and below a knight.
33 Thomas P. Hughes, *American Ancestry: Giving the Name and Descent, in the Male Line, of Americans Whose Ancestors Settled in the United States Previous to the Declaration of Independence, A. D. 1776* (Baltimore: Genealogical Publishing, 1968), 1:34-35.

Possible Guyon Connections to Ireland

In addition to those Guion families that came to the east coast of North America near the end of the 17th century and the Louis Guion family from Mauzé, other Huguenot families with the name Guyon or Guion went to the British Isles.[34] A publication called *Irish Pedigrees, Volume 2*, originally published in Dublin in 1892 by John O'Hart, reveals three tables of Huguenot names of individuals and families who settled in Ireland and Great Britain. No Guion or Guyon families prior to 1685 are identified, but Table II contains the names of settlers during the reign of Louis XIV (1643–1715) and includes both the names Guion and Guyon. Table III contains the names of French refugees who were naturalized by letters patent, irrespective of dates of settlement, and includes both the names Guion and Guyon.

The possibility that John Guyon's ancestors settled first in the British Isles before making their way to North America is compelling for several reasons. First, it might account for some or all of the five "lost" generations of the Guyon family between 1685 and 1825 and might explain the apparent lack of documents available from sources in the United States. Second, it is known historically that many French refugees went straightaway from France to the British Isles and settled there, some temporarily and some permanently, which could well have included predecessors in John Guyon's ancestral line. Third, there is a possible DNA connection with the British Isles—specifically Ireland—that might provide missing links in the genealogical chain of the Guyon family.

DNA Puzzles

In 2011, my sister Kathleen and I discovered genetic genealogy, which raised the possibility of finding ancestors through DNA testing.[35] It is

---

[34] Although *Guyon* and *Guion* are the spellings that may be most obviously traced from generation to generation, efforts were made to trace the family name in all of its known variations.

[35] DNA testing involves identifying various different locations (called "markers") on the Y chromosome, which are then given specific names. As an example from my test, the name DYS388 stands for DNA Y-chromosome segment 388. Each marker has several repeating segments of DNA called Short Tandem Repeats ("STRs"), which are counted (in my case twelve at DYS388), and given a value called an "allele." The combination of the alleles from every marker tested produces an individual's Y_DNA Profile, which is also referred to as a "haplotype." Haplotypes are indicative of more recent common ancestry, whereas "haplogroups" are indicative of more ancient ancestral groupings. My particular haplogroup is identified as R1b1b2a-M269, which, I am told, "is found at very high frequencies (50-80%) throughout western Europe, particularly in Ireland, Wales, Scotland, England, Portugal, France, Germany, and northern Italy." The objective

based upon the fact that each individual's DNA contains a complete record of his or her ancestral history. In the direct maternal line, each female inherits mitochondrial DNA from her mother, who inherited it from her mother, who inherited it from her mother, and so on. A male inherits a Y chromosome from his father, who inherited it from his father, who inherited it from his father, and so on.

Through DNA testing, in addition to the frequency of my haplogroup in western Europe, I was able to determine that there are indications of common ancestry many generations back in Ireland. However, my haplotype is not common among indigenous Irish people. The significance of this discovery (presuming it is true) is its consistency with the idea that Grandpa Guyon's Huguenot forebears first emigrated to the British Isles, specifically Ireland, stayed there for generations, married, had children, and then left, eventually coming to the United States.[36]

American Indian Relatives?

A persistent but not widely-known rumor that Grandpa Guyon had American Indian ancestry has circulated in the shadows in the immediate and extended family and beyond. The suggestion appears to be baseless for lack of evidence. There is nothing apparent in my haplotype, the French Biography, the Johnson Biography, or Grandpa's effects that is supportive of such a connection. When, where, and why the rumor began are unknown, but it would not be surprising that Grandpa's black hair and dark complexion during his youth provided the grist for the mill that produced this particular rumor at a time when having American Indian relatives was a decidedly negative attribute.

---

of the DNA Y chromosome testing is to determine whether people alive today have a common male ancestor and, if so, the proximity of that common ancestor, measured by generations. For example, my first comparison with other people in the existing database revealed a common male ancestor approximately seventeen generations in the past. The idea, of course, is to contact the people with whom you have a common ancestor to determine how close the relationship actually is. Although DNA testing purports to be a science, it seems to be far from an exact one.

[36] Much of the science of DNA testing involves probabilities, likelihoods, and statistical analysis, not to mention the reality of mutations to markers from generation to generation. The *most* that can be said about the relationship between two people living today is whether or not it is likely that they share a common ancestor. The ability to identify such people will increase as the databases containing such information grow. It is hoped that that likelihood will eventually lead to the discovery of additional information concerning the Guyon line.

A public twenty-six-page document entitled "Descendants of Leon John Guyon" dated March 24, 2008 (the "Leon Guyon Report") contains information about "the pioneers that came into the Walla Walla Valley Area, as a starter for those doing their family genealogy."[37]

Much of the Leon Guyon Report may be accurate, but it contains a number of statements and conclusions that I feel compelled to dispute, the most significant of which is the identification of the individual named Leon Guyon as Grandpa Guyon's father.[38]

The Leon Guyon Report seems to presume that Leon Guyon is Edwin's father, likely because of the similarity in names and because he, like John Guyon, lived in Jersey City, New Jersey. That fact alone, amplified by the reality so little is known about Edwin's father, seems compelling, and it is tempting to simply conclude that the elusive John Guyon is found. Such a conclusion does not, however, take into account the disappearance of John Guyon in the mid-1850s, his connections with New Orleans, or his trade, all matters of record. These three important issues create a serious discrepancy in the Leon Guyon Report. Considered with the following additional incongruities, the identification of this particular Leon Guyon as Edwin's father is in grave doubt.

The information in the Leon Guyon Report purports to come from the 1895 New Jersey State Census, which describes him as a male, "other" nationality, and thirty to sixty years old. I have not considered the minor variation in spelling between Guyon and Guion because it may well be that

---

[37] My grandfather and his first family had ties to the Walla Walla Valley. "Descendants of Leon John Guyon," accessed September 6, 2016, http://museum.bmi.net/PicnicPeopleAL/Guyon, Leon John.htm.

[38] Although other inaccuracies are possible, some of the more important ones are found on page 3: it is incorrectly stated (although admittedly consistent with the incorrect information in the French Biography) that Dr. Guyon graduated from Walla Walla College in 1874 with a BA, whereas he attended Whitman Academy — not Walla Walla College — and did not receive a degree. Neither was he a member of the National Guard, at least as we know it today, and neither did he "chase Chief Joseph." His involvement in the Bannock Indian War in 1878 as a volunteer is discussed in detail below. Neither was the Medical College of Ohio known as Miami Medical College when Dr. Guyon attended it. Miami Medical College was founded in 1852 by Reuben Mussey, a disgruntled former faculty member of the Medical College of Ohio. The Miami Medical College and the Medical College of Ohio were separate entities and competitors through the 19th century, including in 1889–1891 when Edwin attended the latter. In 1896 the Medical College of Ohio merged with the University of Cincinnati, and the Miami Medical College did the same in 1909. This created the Ohio-Miami Medical College of the University of Cincinnati. Its name was changed in 1920 to the College of Medicine of the University of Cincinnati.

the two spellings were used interchangeably. Presuming for purposes of this discussion that the 1895 New Jersey census records are accurate and accurately stated in the Leon Guyon Report, Leon Guyon could have been born as early as 1835 and as late as 1865. As we know with certainty, Emily Louise was born in 1829. If Leon Guyon were her husband, she would have been at the very least six years older than he. It is possible that she married a man six years or more her junior, but it seems more likely that she would have married someone her own age or older.

Edwin's father could have married a second time, but the couple in 1895 Jersey City also is reported to have had two sons, Leon and William, each under five years of age. The presence of the young children is highly indicative that Mary was much closer to thirty age-wise than sixty in 1895. It does not necessarily mean that Leon Guyon was also closer in age to thirty, but it seems more likely.

The *coup de grâce* is the statement in the New Jersey census that both Leon Guyon and his wife Mary were of "other" nationality, presumably meaning other than American. The French Biography clearly states that Dr. Guyon's father was a native of Jersey City, which would exclude Leon Guyon on that basis alone.

It may be possible that Leon Guyon is Grandpa Guyon's father, but it is more likely that he is not. The Leon Guyon in the New Jersey census, even if he was as old as sixty in 1895, would have been only seventeen years old in 1852, a year prior to Grandpa Guyon's birth. There is enough overlap in ages to allow for the *possibility* that this individual is Dr. Guyon's father, but those same overlaps are more suggestive of improbability.

Even if it is likely that the Leon Guyon in 1895 Jersey City was not Dr. Guyon's father, it does not follow that he was not related at all. Presuming Leon Guyon was born nearer the 1860s, he could easily be a nephew of John Guyon or some other relative. Consequently, he remains a "possible" on the list of relatives of Dr. Guyon.

Chapter 2.

AT HOME
IN
ANTEBELLUM NEW ORLEANS

circa 1853–1855

A baby is an inestimable blessing and bother.
— Mark Twain

This chapter examines the location and environment of Grandpa Guyon's birth and infancy in New Orleans, supplies a more detailed discussion of the disappearance of John Guyon, and discusses the considerations and circumstances that led to Emily Louise's decision to leave the Crescent City and make a new life in California.

The Birth of Edwin Fernando Guyon

Edwin's birth in New Orleans on November 7, 1853, cannot be confirmed through any known public or official documents. Guyon family lore, supported by Grandpa Guyon's own statement in a letter to his daughter Maud in later life, confirms the event and probably the exact location:

> I would like to have you see New Orleans where I was born. I was born not far from the old St. Charles Hotel near corondolet [sic] st.[39]

In 1853, Elizabeth Shattuck maintained a residence near the St. Charles Hotel in New Orleans at 107 Carondelet Street.[40] In the absence of any other information to the contrary, it seems more likely than not that Elizabeth Shattuck's home is the location mentioned by Grandpa Guyon in his letter to Maud. It seems likely that Emily Louise, along with her husband, gravitated to her mother's hearth and home in the weeks—and

---

[39] E. F. Guyon to Maud Brown, 27 March 1928.
[40] *Cohen's 1853 New Orleans directory, including Jefferson City, Carrollton, Gretna, Algiers and M'Donogh* (Woodridge, Connecticut: Research Publications, 1980), 239.

perhaps months—before and after Grandpa Guyon's birth to enable the grandmother to help her daughter through her confinement and childbirth and to bond with the new baby.

Emily Louise in New Orleans

How long Emily Louise was in New Orleans before Grandpa Guyon's birth is unknown, but evidence from an unlikely source raises the possibility that she had been there for at least two years. A published list of unclaimed letters in New Orleans in November 1851 identifies a "mrs Emily Gaynon" as a recipient.[41] More than a year later, in July 1853, a similar notice was given to "mrs Emily Guion."[42]

The Carondelet Street Neighborhood

New Orleans was the commercial center of the Old South, partly because of its physical location at the mouth of the well-traveled Mississippi, but also because of its hot summers and balmy winters, which encouraged year-round business. During the 1850s it had the largest slave-trading market in the United States[43] and forty-five percent of the total cotton crop of the nation,[44] not to mention the tremendous amounts of sugar, tobacco, and other commodities, passed through the docks, wharves, and warehouses near Carondelet Street.[45]

On a modern map, Elizabeth Shattuck's address is located southwest of the corner of Carondelet and Canal Streets. Carondelet Street itself, a one-way street eastbound, stretches from Robert Street in the Garden District to Canal Street, where its extension becomes the well-known Bourbon Street.

The agreeable weather that attracted businessmen and travelers of all kinds also had its drawbacks, not the least of which was a high incidence of tropical diseases, including yellow fever.

---

[41] *New Orleans Times-Picayune*, November 14, 1851, p. 4.
[42] *New Orleans Times-Picayune*, July 9, 1853, p. 5.
[43] Robert C. Reinders, *End of an Era, New Orleans, 1850–1860* (New Orleans: Pelican, 1989), 25.
[44] Ibid., 37.
[45] "Carondelet Street," Wikipedia, accessed August 7, 2016, http://en.wikipedia.org/wiki/Carondelet_Street

The 1853 Appearance of Yellow Fever

New Orleans has had a long and intimate relationship with yellow fever that predates the official founding of the city in the early 1700s, but it did not begin to be confirmed by reliable records until 1817. Since then, history has regularly recorded numerous manifestations of the disease. One markedly virulent appearance in 1847 caused the death of more than 2,300 inhabitants,[46] but even the 1847 outbreak was a relatively minor one compared to the full-blown epidemic that occurred in 1853, the year of Grandpa Guyon's birth.

The 1853 appearance of the disease holds the dubious distinction as the most devastating yellow fever outbreak ever to alight upon New Orleans. During that summer and fall, from June through October, approximately 40,000 of the city's inhabitants developed cases of yellow fever. Of that number, roughly 9,000 are acknowledged to have perished from the disease. Approximately another 2,000 died during that same period from fevers that could not be specifically identified as yellow fever.[47]

That yellow fever was spread by the common mosquito *Aedes aegypti* was unknown at the time. The incorrect consensus was that the disease somehow had its genesis in the glut of decaying dead animals, "night soil" (a more delicate term for human excrement), and garbage that accumulated in the streets. Ignorant of the reality that its hot and humid conditions created an almost petri dish environment for mosquitoes, New Orleans was lucky in 1853 not to have lost even more of its inhabitants to the disease than actually perished.

There are wide variations in estimates of the population of New Orleans at the height of the catastrophe in the summer of 1853, but it is probable that roughly 100,000 people stayed in the city through the entire epidemic.[48] The loss during a period of five months of more than ten percent of the city's population to yellow fever and other unknown fevers underscores but one of the dangers of living in New Orleans in 1853.

New Orleans Authorities Downplay the Severity of the Disease

Yellow fever outbreaks were not uncommon during the summers in New Orleans in the 1850s. Minor ones were tolerated as annoyances,

---

[46] "Yellow Fever Deaths in New Orleans, 1817–1905," accessed August 7, 2016, http://www.nutrias.org/facts/feverdeaths.htm.
[47] John Duffy, *Sword of Pestilence: The New Orleans Yellow Fever Epidemic of 1853* (Baton Rouge: Louisiana State University Press, 1966), 167.
[48] Ibid.

nuisances, or inconveniences, but businessmen and travelers were reluctant to come to New Orleans in the face of any appearance of the disease that they perceived as a serious threat to their personal health or safety. Their collective absence, along with that of their money earmarked to be spent in New Orleans, would have a decidedly negative effect on the local economy.

As reports of yellow fever infections started to appear during the summer of 1853, along with the inevitable death notices and funerals, the response on the part of city officials, with the connivance of the newspapers, was passivity. To avoid tarnishing the image of the Crescent City in the eyes of businessmen and travelers, the newspapers were prone to understate, if not completely deny, the existence of an actual epidemic—that is, until the numbers of sick, dying, and dead could no longer be explained away or ignored.[49]

When the city fathers finally acted, it was with reluctance, and the ineffectiveness of their gingerly response was exceeded only by its absurdity: the city government arranged for the firing of cannons into the air and the burning of tar in the streets in an effort to somehow disrupt the stranglehold of the disease. Skepticism naturally followed, although many doubters of the effectiveness of cannon firing laughingly acknowledged that it would probably do no harm.[50]

Emily Louise Braves the Dangers of Yellow Fever

Emily Louise was likely present in New Orleans during the entire period the epidemic ran its course, and apparently completely escaped its wrath. As a bonus, she gave birth to a healthy baby boy almost immediately after the yellow fever juggernaut had ground to a halt.[51] The danger to her is highlighted by the fact that in the Fourth District alone, at least 144 children lost both parents.[52] Neither were infants and children in general safe from the disease, which in some cases decimated entire families.[53]

The Disappearance of John Guyon

The actual circumstances and events surrounding John Guyon's disappearance are not known. The French Biography merely states that he

---

49 Ibid., *passim.*
50 Ibid., 74.
51 Ibid., 112.
52 Ibid., 78.
53 Ibid., 67.

"disappeared and no trace of him was ever found" without hazarding a reason or other explanation. The discussion that follows raises several possibilities that might explain his sudden absence.

Guyon Family Mythology[54]

At least two slightly varying theories have circulated in the Guyon family. The first is that one day Emily Louise became anxious because her husband had not returned from work at the accustomed time. To allay her fears, she stepped outside their home and looked up the street for him. She saw him walking toward home and went back inside to wait, but he never arrived. In the other version, Emily Louise did not see her husband walking toward home, but rather saw his footprints in the snow near their home after he failed to appear, indicating he was on his way to his family and had almost arrived when he disappeared. Neither version informs us whether there was evidence of a scuffle at the location of his disappearance.

The idea of snow in New Orleans at first seems improbable; however, although very rare, snow in New Orleans is not unknown. Since 1850, it has snowed about seventeen times in fourteen seasons. Actual accumulations occurred only in 1881, 1895, 1899, 1958, 1963, and 2008; trace amounts appeared thirty-eight different times, but didn't linger.[55] Noticeable amounts, regardless of whether they were accumulations or not for purposes of measurement, tend to validate the otherwise apocryphal story of footprints in the snow.

Both versions of the family theory suggest John Guyon was waylaid close to home by forces or persons unknown, but do not exclude the possibility that he simply changed his mind about returning home, and went elsewhere. Little is known about the relationship between Emily Louise and John Guyon, although Edwin told his children that his mother was "bad tempered." If that same description also applied to his father, it was unknown to the infant Edwin. Without additional information, the

---

[54] On the theory that family lore and legend, often based in fact, sometimes run amok in the course of retelling over generations, my personal inclination is to consider all possibilities, whether recognized by family theories or not.

[55] Carolyn Kolb, "When It Snowed in New Orleans," *New Orleans Magazine*, accessed August 9, 2016, http://www.myneworleans.com/New-Orleans-Magazine/January-2013/When-It-Snowed-in-New-Orleans/.

explanation that Edwin's father may have abruptly left the marriage because of conflicts with his spouse seems inadequate.

Was John Guyon a Yellow Fever Victim?

According to the Johnson Biography, John Guyon died of yellow fever when Edwin was a child. It seems curious that the Johnson Biography is the only known source of this statement, but it is tempting to embrace it because it explains the seemingly inexplicable. If John Guyon did not die of yellow fever or meet some other fate over which he had no control, then we must entertain the possibility that he intentionally abandoned his wife and infant son.

It may be more than coincidental that he disappeared during the 1853 yellow fever epidemic. It is easy to conclude, circumstantially, that he was a victim of the fever. On the other hand, the lists of those who met their deaths as a result of that epidemic do not appear to include the name or any variation of the name of Grandpa Guyon's father, although his absence on the rolls of the dead is itself inconclusive.

It is highly likely that the records of the victims do not identify all who perished. Those who succumbed in hospitals would be more likely identified from hospital records or newspaper accounts, while those who died at home or in some other private place might not. Even in the absence of a full-blown epidemic, it would have been relatively easy for John Guyon to die from yellow fever in complete anonymity.

Was John Guyon a Victim of Crime?

It is also possible that John Guyon met with foul play in the Crescent City. New Orleans was the fifth largest city in the United States in 1850, with a population of 116,375.[56] Its population had increased historically from 12,000 in 1806[57] to 41,000 in 1820[58] and 46,310 in 1830.[59] During the bustling winter seasons of the mid-1850s, the estimated population exceeded 150,000, although of that number approximately 35,000 were transients.[60]

---

[56] Reinders, *End of an Era*, 7.
[57] Ibid., 5.
[58] Ibid., 6.
[59] Ibid.
[60] Duffy, *Sword of Pestilence*, 167.

Predictably, the prevalence of crime in New Orleans rose commensurately with its population, giving it one of the highest crime rates in the United States in that era[61] and making it a very dangerous place to live. Numerous factors contributed to its dubious notability as a haven for criminals, but the city's lack of an effective police force was probably the most important single factor that contributed to the phenomenon.

The New Orleans Police Force Struggles

The New Orleans police force in the 1850s numbered between 250 and 300, giving the city a police-to-citizen ratio of approximately 1:388,[62] which was not out of line in the same era with Boston's (250 officers for a population of approximately 137,000) at 1:548.[63]

The *size* of the New Orleans police force was arguably adequate for the city's population, but the same cannot be said for its *effectiveness*. This disparity was due in large part to systemic political and organizational factors not directly related to actual law enforcement.

The police department in the first half of the decade of the 1850s was largely ineffectual in detecting and fighting crime because it lacked "an intelligent and regular system of control by municipal officials."[64] In other words, there was no central headquarters that coordinated and controlled all the city's policemen and to which the policemen reported.

Each municipality in New Orleans had its own separate police force, with little centralized control overall. The result was a lack of accountability between the City of New Orleans and the various semi-autonomous municipal police organizations within its boundaries. This fragmented system encouraged petty squabbles over territorial jurisdiction, lack of cooperation between organizations supposedly on the same side of the law, and little or no citywide control over police corruption. Time, resources, and energies were expended on non-law-enforcement issues, leaving the detection and prevention of crime as secondary considerations. The New Orleans police force itself included a small staff of detectives, but was mostly composed of patrolmen who walked a beat, although a twelve-man river patrol was organized in 1854. The average New Orleans

---

[61] Reinders, *End of an Era*, 65.
[62] Ibid., 63.
[63] "The Official Website of the Boston Police Department," accessed March 1, 2017, bpdnews.com/history/
[64] Ibid.

police officer generally worked long hours and was paid $45 per month, although not necessarily regularly.[65]

Low wages and the uncertainty of payment forced policemen to make up deficiencies in other ways. A favorite was surreptitiously unleashing animals required by law to be leashed. Having himself set the animal free, the policeman then took the unleashed animal to the pound, where he claimed one-half the $2.50 fee paid by the worried and angry owner for the return of the animal. Another was bringing in an allegedly runaway slave for the $10 reward when the slave had not been a runaway at all, but had been on a legitimate errand when apprehended by the policeman. Neither were policemen immune from bribes or opportunities for collaboration with owners of brothels and gambling houses, along with other forms of corruption.[66]

Political wrangling eventually gave way to effective mayoral control over the disjointed police force, but that did not occur until 1856. This contributed to improvement of the police force in the mid- to late 1850s,[67] but had little effect earlier.

Police corruption was not the only reason for the high crime rate in New Orleans. A class of domestic and foreign professional criminals from colder climes, primarily swindlers of all kinds, followed legitimate travelers to New Orleans to fleece them while simultaneously taking advantage of the mild winter weather. Those swindlers, it is said, were at the top of the criminal food chain, closely followed by forgers and counterfeiters, whose craft was simplified by the fact that each bank issued its own currency.

Dangers along the Mississippi Waterfront

The waterfront in 1850s New Orleans was particularly susceptible to criminal activity of all kinds. A person could easily be robbed, beaten, drugged and shanghaied, or even murdered. Due in no small part to the ineptitude and ineffectiveness of the police force, there was a good chance that serious crimes, including murder, would go undetected and unpunished. A murderer, even if caught and convicted in New Orleans, had a very small chance of receiving a death sentence for the crime,[68] although that punishment was not uncommonly meted out elsewhere.

---

[65] Ibid., 64–65.
[66] Ibid.
[67] Ibid., 63.
[68] Ibid., 68.

Thievery was rampant on the wharves of New Orleans, where cotton, tobacco, sugar, and other goods of all kinds were temporarily stored. Nighttime presented an almost perfect opportunity for those bent on stealing.[69] With no real artificial light to speak of, and particularly during the "witching hour" between the time the night watchmen went home and the day watchmen reported for duty, light-fingered larcenists could move about virtually undetected.

Bales of cotton, cases of champagne, sacks of coffee, and almost anything else were fair game, as were the cargos of steamboats not yet unloaded. Fully laden steamboats were irresistible prey to river pirates.[70] Traveling in swift-moving skiffs, these fearless nocturnal foragers had easy access to the steamboats' decks, which were barely above water level due to the weight of their cargos. Once onboard, the robbers quickly subdued any luckless watchman who might be in their way. The booty from these midnight excursions would then be sold on the black market, either in the city or at nearby plantations. The tiny force of river police was almost entirely ineffective in preventing or solving such crimes.[71]

John Guyon's occupation as a bridge and wharf builder necessarily brought him into proximity with the dangerous waterfront environment. He could easily have been murdered or shanghaied with no clue left by the perpetrator(s) to make known his fate or mark his final resting place.

The Decision to Move West

In the mid-1850s, after hopes had dwindled that John Guyon would ever return, Emily Louise decided to move to California, and it seems unlikely she would make the trip without another adult at least. We know that by 1857 Elizabeth Shattuck was a resident of Sacramento,[72] and it is possible, but unconfirmed, that she, Emily Louise, and Edwin traveled to California together. Grandpa Guyon's cousin Henry Hall and his aunt Julia Uhlrich were also in California by at least 1860, but whether they arrived there before Emily Louise and her child, or accompanied them, is not known.

---

[69] Ibid.

[70] Not uncommonly, the river pirates were respectable citizens of the Third District or Algiers by day, who used their knowledge of the area and available booty to enrich themselves by night.

[71] Reinders, *End of an Era*, 67.

[72] I. N. Irwin, *1857/58 Sacramento Directory and Gazetteer* (Woodridge, CT: Research Publications, 1980), 86; Marriage record, City of Sacramento, 10 June 1858.

There are several possible reasons for the family's decision to move to California. Emily Louise and Elizabeth Shattuck and possibly other family members, having just experienced and survived yellow fever, may have simply wanted to escape the possibility—or probability, if they stayed in New Orleans—of tangling with the disease again.

Their change in location could also have been motivated by social and political forces. The gathering anger against slavery that would ultimately lead to its disappearance from the American landscape within ten years may have warned them that dangerous changes were afoot over which they would have no control. They were not entirely ignorant of the ever-increasing North-South conflicts over slavery and states' rights, and may have felt unsafe because of them.

The family members may have sensed greater opportunities in the West, where populations were smaller, open spaces were bigger, and new arrivals could live their lives free from many of the traditions and institutions of the East and the Old South.

The Family's Brush With Manifest Destiny

This family's move to California can be said to be part of what is known in American history as Manifest Destiny. This 19th-century ideal appeared in the national psyche to justify virtually everything from the expansion of settlements westward (oblivious to the claims of the indigenous people and others already there) to the war with Mexico in the mid-1840s that resulted in the Americanization of the whole of the Great Southwest. Its irresistible force gave form to the perceived special virtues of the American people and their institutions. It also created justification for the idea that America's mission was to redeem the world and remake it in her own image, all under the direction of the Almighty.

The arrogance implicit in Manifest Destiny can hardly be overstated; yet it was a reality, and it cannot be denied that its power shaped the American West in very significant ways. This is not to say that Emily Louise and her traveling companions were aware of the energies collectively described as Manifest Destiny, or that they willingly participated in its embodiment. However, the idea that so many people were on the move, for whatever reason, may well have encouraged them to take the risk of moving west. If nothing more, it may have created in the family a feeling of belonging to a larger community, also on its way west. America's muscles were flexing, and the rippling effect on the populace in general, and on this family in particular, must have been as exciting as it was irresistible.

32

The forces that began to push or pull Americans westward in the early to mid-1840s were eclipsed by the discovery of gold in California at Sutter's Mill on January 24, 1848. That event triggered a tide of adventurers and would-be gold miners (not to mention those whose professions were to mine the miners) that would change the landscape of California and the West forever. During the twenty years from the discovery of gold in 1848 to the completion of the transcontinental railroad in 1869, more than 400,000 souls made the journey to California over the Isthmus of Panama; roughly 250,000 moved overland to California and other locations on the West Coast.

The Panama Route and the Overland Route, as they were respectively called, presented very different obstacles and considerations to the traveler wishing to go to the west coast of North America, not the least of which were cost, time of travel, and danger from Indians, animals, and disease.

After the discovery of gold in 1848, the demand for access to the California gold fields fueled public and private attempts to provide steamship accommodations to the flood of individuals who would soon stream through the Isthmus of Panama. New Orleans newspapers clamored to attract passengers for steamship lines.[73] Emily Louise may

---

[73] See, for example, *New Orleans Times-Picayune*, February 27, 1853, p. 1; November 8, 1853, p. 1.

have been influenced to make the journey by advertisements such as the one above, which appeared on Friday, September 4, 1855 in the *Times-Picayune.*

The timing of the Guyon family's move during the California gold rush was probably coincidental. It seems unlikely that women travelling alone with a small child in tow had any interest whatsoever in gold prospecting or mining. Even so, it must have been exhilarating to travel along with the tide of humanity, though their objectives, destinations, and aspirations were altogether different.

Part II

—

Steamers and Saddles

Chapter 3.

THE JOURNEY TO CALIFORNIA
VIA
THE ISTHMUS

circa 1855–1858

Boast not thyself of to-morrow; for
thou knowest not what a day may bring forth.
— Proverbs 27:1

This chapter considers and discusses the travel options Emily Louise faced in the mid-1850s and offers plausible scenarios surrounding her eventual journey, likely via steamship from New Orleans to Central America; routes she may have taken overland across the Isthmus of Panama to reach the Pacific side; and her ensuing voyage, again probably via steamship, to San Francisco.

Inherent Uncertainties

It would not be surprising if Emily Louise was filled with trepidation and anxiety over the impending move to California. She was a woman in transition: a relative stranger in a man's world whose marital status was ambiguous, with a small child, traveling to far-off California in the embrace of a tide of humanity making up the greatest migration ever to occur in North America.

Before leaving New Orleans, Emily Louise may have changed her mind about relocating to California, perhaps many times. The process of grieving over the disappearance of her husband likely was exacerbated by her lack of knowledge of his fate. What if he were still alive? What if he were to resurface in New Orleans to find her gone? Those questions, and others, doubtless occupied Emily Louise's mind as she contemplated moving west. Despite what her unresolved feelings may have been, she was able to overcome them, demonstrating in no small way her personal strength and courage in the face of great adversity.

The magnitude of the decision to move from New Orleans to San Francisco was not lost on Emily Louise and her mother. It was common knowledge in the 19th century that transcontinental distances were vast and travel was slow, dangerous, and notoriously unreliable. Until 1869 and the completion of the transcontinental railroad, a traveler wishing to make the trip from New Orleans to California had only three options: (1) the Overland Route from St. Louis or Council Bluffs to San Francisco and other locations on the West Coast; (2) "'round the Horn," meaning around the southern tip of South America by sailing ship; and (3) the Panama Route, namely across the Isthmus of Panama to a ship on the Pacific side and then north to San Francisco. Each option apposite to Emily Louise is discussed immediately below.[74]

The Overland Route

The Overland Route from St. Joseph, Independence, or Council Bluffs offered a number of "trail" options along the way, primarily the Oregon Trail, California Trail, and Mormon Trail.

Already conveniently on the Mississippi, Emily Louise could easily have taken a stern-wheeler to St. Joseph or some other northern point. Once there, she could have arranged to travel overland all the way to California.

Traveling overland meant walking, riding in a wagon, or riding on the back of a horse or mule. Most travelers appeared to glide across the sea-like expanse of the prairie in single-file trains of canvas-covered prairie schooners. Some of these wagons were as long as fifteen feet, and they were typically drawn by two or more pairs of oxen, although mules were not uncommon. The advantages of wagon trains were many; one of the primary benefits was safety in numbers, both for protection and for assistance.

Not surprisingly, most emigrants preferred walking to riding in dusty, bumpy wagons, which had nothing akin to modern shock absorbers to lessen the impact of rough roads and terrain. The prospect of traveling under such conditions with a small child—and likely her mother—must have seemed overwhelming and ill-advised to Emily Louise.

---

[74] Because the Panama Route was almost certainly chosen by Emily Louise as her way to California, I have included as Appendix II additional background information concerning its development and importance.

The actual distance to California varied somewhat by the route taken, but was approximately 2,000 miles. The distance from Council Bluffs to San Francisco was advertised to be 2,161 miles.[75]

A gazetteer of the era advised travelers that the distance to California could be covered "with wagons drawn by mules or oxen in from 60 to 90 days at an expense of not over $100 for each passenger."[76] Simple arithmetic and common sense demonstrate the statement to be grossly over-optimistic, if not an outright falsehood. To complete the trip from Council Bluffs to San Francisco in sixty days, the traveler had to cover more than thirty-six miles a day on average. To complete the journey in ninety days, the wagons had to average twenty-three miles a day.

The unpleasant facts were that there were no improved roads on the prairie and through the mountains, and nothing approaching high speed was possible. Discounting the inevitability of accidents, bad weather, sickness, and disease to hamper the travelers' progress, and without taking into account wash days or rest days, a much more realistic speed for the typical wagon drawn by oxen was eleven to seventeen miles per day. This meant that the journey necessarily took from four to six months.[77]

The 1853 gazetteer also underestimated the cost of overland travel. Supplies alone easily cost $200 or more for travelers without their own wagons and gear. Those already owning wagons and supplies paid less.

Civilization as it was known in the East, with all its comforts, was virtually nonexistent in the West, and that included, for the most part, the way west. Accommodations such as hotels or roadhouses were unknown in all but larger settlements, and living in wagons and sleeping on the ground increased the travelers' vulnerability to dangerous animals, insects, disease, and the weather.

Unfriendly Indians were a perceived source of danger for many emigrants, although actual conflicts resulting in emigrant fatalities were rare. It is estimated that hostile Indians accounted for only 362 emigrant deaths on the Great Plains between 1840 and 1860.[78]

---

75 Ibid.

76 John Hayward, "Routes to California and Oregon," in *A Gazetteer of the United States of America* (Hartford, CT: Case, Tiffany, and Company, 1853), RailsandTrails.com, accessed August 9, 2016, http://www.railsandtrails.com/gazetteer/1853/routeCA-OR.htm.

77 "Oregon Trail," FamilySearch Wiki, accessed August 9, 2016, https:// familysearch.org/ wiki/en/Oregon_Trail.

78 "Frequently Asked Questions," National Historic Oregon Trail Interpretive Center, accessed November 30, 2016, https://www.blm.gov/or/oregontrail/history-faqs.php#question9.

By far the greatest dangers to emigrants were those created by themselves. Accidents and deaths resulting from mishandling firearms and tools like axes and saws were not uncommon. Even seemingly innocuous cuts and scrapes could result in life-threatening infections. Knowledge of sanitation in the 1850s was rudimentary at best. Each particular group of emigrants might take the time to specify areas to dispose of human-created waste in all its forms, but it is unlikely that there was any consistent enforcement of such designations if they existed in the first place.

There would have been little motivation on the part of emigrants whose primary concern was survival to worry about human waste on the vastness of the Great Plains. The cumulative effect of the roughly 250,000 travelers between 1848 and 1869 created conditions very favorable to the proliferation of waterborne and other diseases and infections, not the least of which was the dreaded cholera.[79]

Taking into account all the inherent dangers and uncertainties, Emily Louise's concern for the comfort and safety of her baby boy alone could have excluded the Overland Route as a possible way to California, even if her own comfort and safety were of little or no concern to her.

Around the Horn of South America

Emily Louise's second option was to travel by wind-powered ship around the southern tip of South America and then north to California. Typically, a sailing ship bound for California began its journey on the East Coast of the United States, usually in New York. It stopped for passengers at various ports along the way, mainly Savannah, Charleston, and New Orleans, and then navigated south around Cape Horn or, more probably, through the less tempestuous Strait of Magellan. Once on the Pacific side, the ship followed the western coastline of North and South America to San Francisco. This journey was more than 14,000 miles in length and required at least six months to complete.[80]

---

[79] Cholera was the most common killer of emigrants on the prairie, particularly along the Platte River in Nebraska. Between 1849 and 1855, the disease accounted for 3 percent of all emigrant deaths, which approximated 6,000 to 12,500 individuals. It is an intestinal disease caused by the bacterium *Vibrio cholerae*, usually found in contaminated water or food sources, that causes diarrhea, vomiting, and leg cramps. The disease attacks with varying severity; only one in twenty gets the severe form of the disease. Death can occur in a matter of hours from rapid dehydration caused by profuse, watery diarrhea and shock. It is unlikely to be transferred by direct contact between persons.

[80] The duration of ocean voyages, particularly those on wind-propelled ships, was necessarily approximate. The vicissitudes of wind and weather made it impossible to predict arrival at one's

Even though the distance was daunting, the sea voyage likely appeared more attractive to Emily Louise than making the journey overland. Not only was the prospect of walking 2,000 miles absent in a sea journey, but travelers by sea were also spared confrontations with dangerous animals and unfriendly Indians along with diseases and discomforts created by the accumulation of human waste.

Travel under sail had its own dangers and discomforts. Aside from dangerous weather conditions, limited space made cramped quarters and lack of privacy inevitable, and hundreds of people confined so closely together created their own environmental opportunities for disease and infections that could quickly spread through the ship's population. An outbreak of influenza, which could prove fatal, especially to the very young and the very old, was possible, as was cholera, typically through the ingestion of spoiled food. In the lower latitudes, malaria was always a significant concern.

The Panama Route

The third alternative, and only other option available to Emily Louise, was the Panama Route, so called because travelers went across the Isthmus of Panama from a steamship or sailing ship on the Atlantic side to a (hopefully) waiting second steamship or sailing ship bound for San Francisco on the Pacific side. After 1849 a fleet of steamships carried passengers between Central America and the west coast of the United States, principally San Francisco.

Typically, steamers bound for Panama began their journeys at New York City, just like their wind-driven counterparts, and made calls along the way to pick up mail and passengers at various ports, including Savannah, Charleston, and New Orleans.

A world map readily exposes the time and distance advantages of the Panama Route over the Cape Horn route. The distance from New York to San Francisco via Cape Horn is approximately 14,700 miles; over the Panama Route 5,750 miles.[81] Depending on the availability of means of travel across the Isthmus and connections with ships on the Pacific side, the Panama Route could cut the time around the Horn by half.

Trans-Panama steamer travelers, particularly those in steerage, were plagued by the same cramped quarters and lack of privacy as those on

---

destination with any reasonable degree of certainty. Ships were often forced to deviate many miles from their anticipated routes in search of favorable winds.
[81] Hayward, "Routes to California and Oregon."

wind-driven ships. Luckily, the steamer travelers had to endure them for a much shorter time: roughly three months from New York to San Francisco, and even less for those like Emily Louise, who would have joined the journey at New Orleans.

The Panama to San Francisco segment usually took two to four *weeks*. Because of the shorter time, many of the problems associated with extended sea voyages, such as disease, boredom, cramped quarters, lack of privacy, and the like, were diminished.

Another consideration may well have been the fact that Emily Louise and her child were already conveniently (a relative term) located for travel to California across the Isthmus. Compared with the relatively short trip by land via the Panama Route, the prospect of traveling up the Mississippi to St. Louis or some other gateway to the Overland Route—before she could even start the journey of 2,000 miles overland—must have made no sense to her.

Havana and Central America

All things considered, Emily Louise's best alternative was to travel to California via the Isthmus of Panama. The first leg of the journey required her to travel from New Orleans to the eastern coast of Central America, a distance of approximately 1,400 miles, or 1,650 miles if her ship stopped in Havana along the way.[82] Once at her destination, she was obliged to find her way across the Isthmus. When she reached its western shore, her objective was to board a ship to San Francisco, approximately 3,260 miles to the north.[83]

There were three commonly used destinations on the Atlantic side of the Isthmus,[84] each of which provided an alternative way of crossing: Chagres, Panama; Aspinwall, Panama (also known as Colón); and San Juan de Nicaragua, Nicaragua (also known as either San Juan del Norte or Greytown).

In 1855–1856, at least eleven different steamers, and possibly others, brought passengers from New York City to Aspinwall, Chagres, and San

---

[82] Ibid.

[83] It was by no means certain that a ship would be waiting on the Pacific side of the isthmus to ferry the travelers to California; waits of days or even weeks were not uncommon.

[84] To be entirely accurate, there was a fourth possible route to the Pacific over the Isthmus of Tehuantepec (Mexico), which had been used during colonial times, but I have ignored it as a possible route for purposes of this biography because in the 19th century it was open only for about one year during 1858–1859, and Emily Louise was already in California and remarried by June 10, 1858.

Juan de Nicaragua,[85] although it is not always possible to determine whether New Orleans was an intermediate port of call. The *SS George Law* made the trip from New York City to Aspinwall on January 5, 1855; March 5, 1855; April 5, 1855; May 5, 1855; and April 21, 1856, but whether it stopped at New Orleans on its way is unconfirmed. The *SS Daniel Webster* is known to have stopped at New Orleans, but its ultimate destination was San Juan de Nicaragua. The *SS Star of the West* and the *SS Texas* were also active in 1855-1856, but the former's destination cannot be determined and the latter's destination was San Juan de Nicaragua. The *SS Empire City* and the *SS Philadelphia* are both ships Emily Louise may have taken to Central America, but their itineraries and specific destinations are unknown.

The three possible destinations on the Atlantic side of the isthmus and what factors and circumstances may have influenced Emily Louise's travel decisions are discussed below.

Chagres, the Chagres River, and Gorgona

Uncertainties were abundant at Chagres. Reefs and sandbars at the mouth of the Chagres River prevented deep-hulled ships from entering the river, requiring them to anchor offshore. Particularly at low tide, the debarking passengers were forced to rely on native men in canoes called bungos to shuttle them from the moored ship to the town of Chagres.[86]

Even after arriving safely in the town, the traveler's lot was by no means secure. Chagres was a boomtown, with brothels and bars aplenty, but far fewer accommodations for the discriminating traveler with a small child in search of a hotel.[87]

Between Chagres and the ship on the west coast awaiting its human cargo lay seventy miles of jungle, with all manner of snakes, insects, and dangers. As one author put it, "[The Panama Route] was widely known for high prices, bad food, a chaotic and ineffective government, and such often fatal diseases as malaria and cholera."[88]

---

[85] "The Ships List," accessed June 3, 2014, http://www.theshipslist.com/ships/descriptions/panamafellt.html.

[86] "The Isthmian Crossing," accessed August 9, 2016, http://www.bruceruiz.net/PanamaHistory/isthmus_crossing.htm.

[87] Sarah Marum Brooks, *Across the Isthmus to California in '52* (San Francisco, 1894), cited in Glenda Riley, "Women on the Panama Trail to California, 1849–1869," *Pacific Historical Review* 55, no. 4 (1986): 538.

[88] Riley, "Women on the Panama Trail," 537.

Once on his or her way, the typical traveler, over a period of about three days, ascended the winding Chagres River, again in a bungo, approximately fifty miles to the town of Gorgona, where the river became too shallow to navigate by boat. From there, travelers covered the remaining twenty-one miles to Panama City (the western terminus of the Chagres trail) afoot or on horses or mules.[89] Steerage-class travelers were relegated to walking, while full-fare travelers rode—usually on the backs of mules.[90]

Eventually, efficiency spawned by numerous trips across the isthmus came into play, and by 1854, the trip from Chagres to Panama City took twelve hours; the opposite journey, from Panama City to Chagres, took a mere seven hours.[91] Due to the tropical climate, danger from diseases, such as cholera and malaria, and insects and poisonous snakes was ever present in the jungle between Chagres and Panama City.

If the journey up the Chagres River and then overland in the midst of the Central American jungle sounds less than inviting today, it likely had the same effect upon Emily Louise in the 1850s. She would have been reluctant to risk her own health and that of her child by crossing the Isthmus through the jungle, and it is not unlikely that her decision to remove to California was solidified by the availability of the speed, comfort, and safety a trans-isthmus railroad provided by early 1855.[92]

From Aspinwall across the Isthmus via Rail

Crossing the Isthmus via Aspinwall instead of Chagres presented an entirely different set of considerations and circumstances, thanks to the Panama Railway, which began passenger service to Panama City on the Pacific side on January 28, 1855.[93] Suddenly, the uncertainty, discomfort, and danger inherent in the journey through the jungle were replaced by the comfort and speed of a passenger train capable of covering the 47.6 miles in five or six hours as opposed to several days.

---

[89] H. W. Brands, *The Age of Gold: The California Gold Rush and the New American Dream* (New York: Anchor, 2002), 80-81.

[90] Riley, "Women on the Panama Trail," 538.

[91] Ibid.

[92] This presumes that Emily Louise traveled through Panama. As discussed elsewhere, she may have traveled across Nicaragua, which, for various reasons, was less dangerous. As an example, because the Nicaraguan Route was in a higher latitude and therefore less tropical, its travelers would have been less susceptible to tropical disease, insects, and snakes.

[93] Advertisements in 1853 were already touting a railway across the isthmus that would not be finished until January, 1855.

All things considered, it almost seems self-evident that Emily Louise made her way across the Isthmus by rail, presuming, of course, that she made the journey in 1855 or later. Nevertheless, in addition to the other options available, it is also possible that she traveled across Nicaragua.[94]

The Nicaraguan Route[95]

The point of debarkation of the Nicaraguan Route on the Atlantic side was San Juan de Nicaragua. The route across the Isthmus to Realejo on the Pacific side was entirely over Nicaragua.[96] In the late 1840s, this route had attracted the attention of Cornelius Vanderbilt, who secured the rights from Nicaragua in 1849 to establish it in the name of the Accessory Transit Company.[97] Vanderbilt inaugurated the route with the sailing of the *Prometheus* on December 26, 1850, from New York City.[98]

The Nicaraguan Route had several advantages over the Panamanian, but mainly it was shorter. The distance from New York to San Francisco via Panama is 5,245 miles, while via Nicaragua it is only 4,871 miles. From New Orleans to San Francisco by way of Panama is 4,676 miles, but it is only 4,151 miles over the Nicaraguan Route,[99] 525 miles less.[100] Even though the distance from Atlantic to Pacific over Nicaragua is 174 miles, compared with 55 miles over Panama, all but 18 miles on the Nicaraguan Route was over water (up the San Juan River on the Atlantic side and then over Lake Nicaragua), compared with a significantly longer land journey

---

[94] Somewhere in the back of my mind, I seem to remember my uncle Edwin Fenimore's telling me that his grandmother and father had crossed the Isthmus of Panama over Nicaragua, as opposed to Panama, but I am unsure if he actually made that statement to me or if it is a false recollection on my part.

[95] The designation "Nicaraguan Route" is a more precise identification of a route that also crossed the Isthmus of Panama and was, arguably, part of the Panama Route in a more general sense.

[96] Neither the French Biography nor the Johnson Biography names a specific location where Emily Louise landed in Central America on her way to California, so I see no reason to exclude Nicaragua as a possible route to California, particularly in view of some marked advantages over the Panama Route that will be discussed below.

[97] J. H. Kemble, *The Panama Route 1848–1869* (New York: Library Editions, 1970), 59.

[98] Ibid., 60.

[99] Ibid., 58.

[100] A difference of 525 miles may seem a small consideration to the 21st-century traveler capable of covering that distance in seven or eight hours by car or an hour by air. In a time when that distance was typically measured in weeks and months, it was without doubt a major consideration.

over Panama. Also, because the Nicaraguan route was in a higher latitude, it was cooler and not as conducive to tropical fevers.[101]

Emily Louise Travels in Anonymity

There is no known evidence that establishes when Emily Louise went to California. In the absence of a ship's manifest or some other confirmation, it is impossible to determine exactly the date of her departure. It is not likely that she left immediately after the disappearance of her husband, which, according to the French Biography, occurred when Grandpa Guyon was "but an infant."

To be consistent with the language that Edwin was an infant when his father disappeared, it is probable that John Guyon disappeared during 1854 or, at the latest, during the first half of 1855. During 1854, the baby's age ranged from two months to fourteen months, which certainly qualified him as an infant, but the further we venture into 1855, the more he would have been in transition from infancy to childhood.[102] By mid-1855, he would have been twenty months old, which likely qualified him as a toddler.

The French Biography states that Emily Louise made the trip to California in 1855, when her child was two and a half years old. That statement is clearly inaccurate, given his corroborated birthdate. Grandpa Guyon would have been two and a half years old in April of *1856*, and not in 1855, but it is not obvious whether his age or the year is incorrect in the French Biography. There is no reason to presume the age is correct and the year is wrong, except for the fact that the Johnson Biography states that Emily Louise and Grandpa Guyon made the trip in 1856, even though it also inaccurately adds that she made it "with her second husband."

In a publication called *The Idaho Odd Fellow*, dated January, 1908, an article about Dr. Guyon relates that "his parents went to Sacramento, Cal., by way of the Isthmus, in 1855." Despite the article's incorrect statement that "his parents" went to Sacramento, the reference to 1855 as the year is difficult to ignore.

---

[101] Kemble, *Panama Route*, 58–59.

[102] Another issue, already raised above in a slightly different context, was Emily Louise's emotional state. We can only speculate about the level and duration of stress and anxiety that must have filled Emily Louise's days and nights after the disappearance of her husband. Common sense tells us that it would have taken months, at least, to find some kind of closure, if she could find it at all. It is for that reason, along with her child's age, that I believe it *unlikely* that Emily Louise traveled to California in 1854.

In an attempt to reconcile and harmonize the known facts and circumstances, I reason that the most probable time period Emily Louise journeyed to San Francisco is sometime during 1856, when her son was between two years and two months and three years and two months old. I reiterate that it remains possible that the trip to California occurred as early as 1855.[103]

The choice of 1856 gives most importance to the French Biography statement that Grandpa Guyon was two and a half years old at the time of the journey, even if the *year* mentioned along with his age is incorrect. I reason that his age is more likely to be remembered correctly than the year. Because Grandpa Guyon was born late in the year in 1853, mental arithmetic could easily yield the wrong result by adding two to the date 1853, and forgetting that the extra half-year would push the correct answer into 1856.

Between 1848 and 1869, a total of 110 different steamers operated on the Atlantic and Pacific sides of the Panama Route.[104] Without knowing at least the year of Emily Louise's trip to San Francisco, it is impossible to determine which ships she traveled on. However, it *is* possible to narrow the possibilities by point of origin and other factors. If she traveled in 1855, forty-one of the steamers can be ignored; if she went in 1856, all but two can be eliminated.[105]

The Golden Gate and The Golden Age

Of the hundreds of vessels that arrived in San Francisco from various ports all over the world from 1849 through 1869, only fifteen are recorded to have arrived in 1856, and of those, thirteen can be easily excluded from consideration by point of origin, leaving just two possibilities: the steamer *Golden Gate*, which arrived on February 14, 1856, from Panama[106] and the steamer *Golden Age*, which arrived on October 14, 1856, thirteen days after leaving Panama.[107] If Emily Louise made the trip on the *Golden Gate*,

---

[103] Because Grandpa Guyon's father, John Guyon, disappeared when Grandpa Guyon was "but an infant" according to the French Biography, that unfortunate event in all likelihood occurred during 1854, when Grandpa Guyon was two to fourteen months old.

[104] Kemble, *Panama Route*, 117.

[105] Attempts to identify steamers between New Orleans and the Atlantic side of Central America have yielded no information at all, probably because of two factors: (1) the ships' passenger and cargo manifests were typically completed at point of origin, usually New York, and (2) Emily Louise probably was a steerage passenger, which ensured she would not be identified individually.

[106] Louis J. Rasmussen, San *Francisco Ship Passenger Lists* (Baltimore: Genealogical Publishing, 1978), 1:80.

[107] Ibid., 1:65.

Edwin would have been approximately twenty-seven months of age. If on the *Golden Age*, he would have been almost three years old.

The captain of the *Golden Gate* was A. V. H. Leroy, who left the following comments in the ship's log concerning the passage:

> Left Panama for San Francisco on January 30th at 3:00 PM. No sickness on board during the entire passage. Arrived Acapulco, Mexico at 9:00AM on February 5th, received supplies and departed at 3:00PM. Arrived San Diego, California on February 12th at 7:30AM. Took on board a supply of coal and sailed at 3:00PM for San Francisco. From Point Aguilla northward there was thick and foggy weather. Arrived in San Francisco on February 14th at 10:30AM.[108]

As cargo the *Golden Gate* carried "U.S. Mail and 606 packages of unidentified freight."[109] Also arriving in San Francisco on the ship were approximately 153 named passengers "and 508 unidentified in steerage."[110] The *Golden Gate* was a large ship of 2,282 tons.[111]

The *Golden Age* was almost exactly the same size, 2,280 tons.[112] It carried 196 named passengers "and 40 unidentified in 2nd Cabin and 428 unidentified in steerage."[113] The history of its passage was written in the ship's log:

> 13 days from Panama. Left Panama on October 1st at 11:00PM. Passed the ship "Sonora" at 9:00PM on October 2nd, 264 miles from Panama. Arrived at Acapulco, Mexico on October 7th at 8:00 AM and left there at 1:00PM. Arrived off the heads of San Francisco at 7:00AM on October 14th. During the passage had little or no sickness on board and no deaths.[114]

---

[108] Ibid., 1:80–81.
[109] Ibid.
[110] Ibid., 1:80-82.
[111] Ibid., 1:xiii.
[112] Ibid.
[113] Ibid., 1:65.
[114] Ibid., 1:64.

In addition to its human cargo, the *Golden Age* carried "U.S. Mail, 703 packages unidentified merchandise and 1 box of gold coin."[115]

If we presume that either the *Golden Gate* or the *Golden Age* was the actual ship on which Emily Louise traveled, we must logically conclude that Emily Louise did not cross the Isthmus of Panama over Nicaragua. Both ships' logs indicate their point of departure as Panama and only one stop at Acapulco, Mexico, and not Realjo, Nicaragua, the Pacific terminus of the Nicaragua Route. The logs of both ships do not indicate that any passengers were taken on after the voyages were under way from Panama.

Children on the Panama Route

It is even more difficult to confirm Edwin's shipboard presence than his mother's during the journey from New Orleans to San Francisco. Children were on board both the *Golden Gate* and the *Golden Age*, but none is identified by name or age. Even among the adult passengers who are identified by name, their children were anonymous, and there was no differentiation between children in steerage and those in more comfortable accommodations. The *Golden Gate* carried forty children along with four passengers designated as "boy" and six "infants."[116] The *Golden Age* lists thirty-two children, two boys, and three infants.[117] Luckily there was no sickness to speak of on either vessel during the journey.

Fare Wars

Because of my inability to pinpoint the timing of the voyage and the exact ship, it is impossible to determine the actual cost to Emily Louise. Due to fierce competition among carriers, mingled with government subsidies and other forces, the fares changed often. Nevertheless, there is enough information in the historical record to determine what was probably paid by Emily Louise and her fellow travelers.

The following discussion is limited to fares from 1852 to 1857, which includes the time period of Emily Louise's journey, even if we do not know its exact dates. Most of the fares discussed are for a through trip from New York to San Francisco unless otherwise stated. Emily Louise's fare would have been less on the Atlantic side of the journey because she would have boarded the ship at New Orleans.

---

115 Ibid.
116 Ibid., 1:80–82.
117 Ibid., 1:64–65.

In early 1852, the New York and San Francisco Steamship Line offered a through trip for $315 first cabin, $255 second cabin, and $200 steerage.[118] By January, 1853, via the mail lines, the through trip cost $305 first cabin, $200 second cabin, and $85 steerage. On those same lines, the fares from Panama to San Francisco only for second cabin and steerage were $145 and $50, respectively.

Later in 1853, bitter rivalry between the Pacific Mail Steamship Company and the Accessory Transit Company (also known as the Nicaragua Transit Company and the Nicaragua Steamship Company) established reduced fares on the mail steamers of first cabin $100 (down from $300), second cabin $75, and steerage $50 (down from $150).[119]

By October 1853, the rate war was over, and first cabin fares climbed to $220 and $250 on the mail steamers and to $300 on the Nicaragua Transit steamer *Pacific*. Second-class and steerage fares of $150 and $100 on the mail steamers were increased on the *Pacific* by $25 to $175 and $125, respectively.[120]

Cornelius Vanderbilt had been nudged out of control of the Accessory Transit Company in late 1853. Shortly thereafter he, along with Edward Mills, organized the Independent Line, which offered through rates in February 1854, of $150 and $75 steerage. By June 1854, first cabin was reduced to $100, second cabin to $80, and steerage to $35.

Vanderbilt's rates forced the mail lines and the Nicaragua Transit line to lower their own fares to be competitive. As a result, March, 1854, found upper-deck staterooms on the *Golden Gate* and *George Law* to be $200, main cabin rooms at $150, second cabin $125, and steerage $45, although these fares were from Panama to San Francisco only.[121] At the same time, fares offered by Nicaragua Transit were $200–$225 first cabin, $175 second cabin, and $60 steerage. By June, 1854, the rates of the mail lines were increased to $255 first cabin, $130 second cabin, and $75 steerage.

Two years later, in June 1856, the rates via Nicaragua had dropped to $175 first cabin, $125 second cabin, and $90 steerage, and as the year wore on, they were reduced even further. By November 1856, the Nicaragua steamers offered first-class cabins at $125 and $150, second cabins at $120, and steerage at $50.

Via the mail lines the steerage fares were the same, but first cabin accommodations cost $250 and second cabin $125.[122] A year later, during

[118] Kemble, *Panama Route*, 64.
[119] Ibid., 67.
[120] Ibid., 69.
[121] Ibid., 70.
[122] Ibid., 75.

the summer of 1857, mail line rates had risen to $300 first cabin, $250 second cabin, and $150 steerage.[123] Advertisements in New Orleans newspapers during 1856 touted "lowest fares" to San Francisco, but typically did not publish specific fares, doubtless an indicator of the volatile market.

In summary, between 1852 and 1857, rates for first cabin varied from a low of $150 to a high of $315. Second cabin rates were as low as $80 in 1854 to as high as $250 in 1856. Steerage rates were as low as $35 in 1854 and as high as $150 in 1857.

Financial Considerations and Relative Values

The cost of travel from New Orleans to San Francisco was not unimportant to Emily Louise and anyone who may have made the journey with her. In Emily Louise's case, after the disappearance of her husband and his income, it is likely that she found herself in dire financial straits, although she had relatives in New Orleans who could have helped her if she needed it, and probably did. The fares, ranging from below $100 to several hundreds of dollars, may seem small compared with today's costs of travel, but comparing them dollar for dollar would be misleading because of the dollar's buying power in the 1850s. To fully understand the cost of the trip to San Francisco we must convert 1850 dollars to present dollars.

There are many ways to calculate the relative value of money in 1856 compared with today, but they are all inexact and based on a multitude of variables that produce little more than educated guesses. I rely on a calculation based upon the Consumer Price Index, which yields a present value of an 1856 dollar at $28.80.[124] Using this method, every increase of $25 in the fare was, to Emily Louise, an increase of at least $720 in today's dollars. A $50 increase would raise the fare at least $1,440, and a $100 increase would have been at least $2,880.

---

123 Ibid., 77.
124 See Samuel H. Williamson, "Seven Ways to Compute the Relative Value of a U.S. Dollar Amount - 1774 to Present," MeasuringWorth, accessed August 10, 2016, https://www. measuringworth.com/uscompare/. There are at least six additional ways to calculate this value; the Consumer Price Index calculates the lowest value.

Despite the cost and all other obstacles, Emily Louise successfully reached California with her son and started a new life there during the period of 1855–1858. Where they were in the meantime has not been confirmed, but the maternal grandmother Elizabeth Shattuck appears in Sacramento in the 1857 city directory: "Shattuck, Mrs. Elizabeth dw[e]l[ling] Third W[est]s[ide] bet[ween] M and N, La."[125] The "La," according to the directory, reflects "nativity, or country or State last hailing from." It is possible, and perhaps even probable, that Emily Louise and her son lived, at least temporarily, with Elizabeth Shattuck after their arrival in California.

---

[125] Irwin, *1857/58 Sacramento Directory*, 86.

Chapter 4.

PIONEERING IN OREGON
VIA
BRITISH COLUMBIA

circa 1858–1865

When a woman marries again it is because she detested her first
husband. When a man marries again, it is because he adored
his first wife. Women try their luck; men risk theirs.
— Oscar Wilde, *The Picture of Dorian Gray*

This chapter discusses the lives of Emily Louise, Edwin, and the latter's new stepfather Henry C. Smith beginning with Emily Louise's second marriage in 1858 and extending into 1865.

The Second Marriage of Emily Louise

A California marriage record confirms the following event presided over by "William H. Hill, Rector of Grace Church Sacramento":

> I certify that in Sacramento at the dates mentioned, I solemnized the following marriages, viz: . . . 1858. June 10. Henry C. Smith, of Sacramento aged 29, a native of Ohio, to Mrs. Emily L. Guyon of Sacramento aged 28, a native of Missouri, parties white.

The statement that both Emily Louise and Henry C. Smith were "of Sacramento" may suggest that both of them had resided in that city for months, if not years, prior to their marriage.

Henry Ventures to British Columbia Alone

The newlyweds spent little time in Sacramento, at least as a couple. The ink on the marriage certificate was barely dry when Henry left his new bride and stepson there and headed north to British Columbia. His and his family's experiences and adventures over the following two-year period[126] are described as follows:

> Deciding to seek his fortunes in the North, [Emily Louise's] husband left the family in Sacramento, California, and went up into British Columbia, where he secured a contract from the captain of a British ship to supply his vessel with a cargo of mast poles. He proceeded to fulfill the order, but just about the time he was ready for the delivery of the products of his labor a heavy storm set in, the ship was destroyed and the labor of a year went for naught. In the meantime his family had joined him in the North.[127]

The phrase "[d]eciding to seek his fortunes in the North" introduces an element of uncertainty into Henry's departure from Sacramento. His decision to travel north alone suggests that he had no specific objective or promised employment in British Columbia. The statement that he "secured a contract from the captain of a British ship" is evidence that he did not have an employment agreement in place when he left Sacramento, but finalized it after arriving in Canada.

Presuming the accuracy of the statements in the French Biography, Henry went to British Columbia[128] during or shortly after June 1858, and his family joined him later. Henry was alone for an unspecified period, likely three to six months, between mid-1858 and early 1859.

Henry may have gone north alone because he had no existing connections in Canada and did not want his wife and stepson to accompany him in uncertain circumstances. Perhaps the journey of Emily Louise and her son was delayed until Henry could afford to send for them, a plan that was postponed because Henry's job harvesting masts would not produce income until the masts were delivered late in 1859 at the earliest.

---

[126] The maximum time period Henry and his family could possibly have spent in Canada between his marriage on June 10, 1858, and the US Census of July 31, 1860, locating the family in Marion County, Oregon, is just over two years.

[127] French, *History of Idaho,* 1256. Mid-19th-century masts made from a single tree were known as "pole masts" and, depending on the size and type of ship to which they were affixed, varied in length from 130 to 160 feet.

[128] The province of British Columbia did not officially exist until August 1, 1858, when it also got its first governor.

No written contract between Henry and the ship's captain can be found. The captain may have paid him something on account at the beginning of the project. If not, the costs of bringing his family to British Columbia would have been paid from existing family funds.

Though the captain was unable or unwilling to pay for Henry's masts, why Henry could not have sold the harvested masts to another purchaser is not clear. According to the terse statement in the French Biography that "the labor of a year went for naught," Henry apparently got nothing from his endeavors.[129]

Was Henry in Search of Canadian Gold?

Edwin circa 1858

There is another reason why Henry may have gone to British Columbia. A significant gold rush occurred there on the Thompson and Fraser Rivers, beginning with the arrival in Victoria on Sunday, April 25, 1858, of 450 prospectors on the *Commodore*, a wooden side-wheel American steamer. These hardy adventurers appeared "just as the townspeople were returning homeward from church."[130]

The gold strike attracted men (and women) from everywhere, including a large number of San Franciscans.[131] The population of the small town of Victoria, the only ocean port providing access to the inland gold fields, increased virtually overnight from 300 to approximately 30,000.[132]

If Henry moved his family to Victoria immediately after his marriage on June 10, 1858, he would have had

---

[129] From a legal perspective, it may also be worth noting that an event such as an unforeseeable storm that intervenes and makes it impossible for one party to a contract to perform may excuse that party from performance under the doctrine of "force majeure" as an act of God.

[130] City of Victoria, "History," accessed August 10, 2016, http://www.victoria.ca/EN/main/cynnybuty/about/history.html.

[131] Mark Forsythe and Greg Dickson, *The Trail of 1858: British Columbia's Gold Rush Past* (Canada: Harbour Publishing, 2008), 38.

[132] City of Victoria, "History."

difficulty finding reasonable accommodations because of the burgeoning population drawn there by the lure of gold. A rough-and-tumble mining area away from civilization would have been not only uncomfortable, but also dangerous. An innocent bystander could easily find himself a victim of an unruly antagonist in an environment ruled by drinking, carousing, and fighting over women or gold. Despite the dangers and inconveniences, Henry's family joined him in British Columbia in late 1858 or early 1859. Against the backdrop of the gold rush, Henry's spending a year harvesting ship masts takes on somewhat of an apocryphal cast, although it is both possible and feasible. The account of the loss of the ship at the end of the year may also seem unlikely. However, the waters around Vancouver Island are known as the "Graveyard of the Pacific"[133] due to the large number of shipwrecks in the area, supporting the account that Henry's employer's ship was lost there in a storm.

It may be more than coincidental that the gold rush began a mere six and a half weeks before Henry and Emily Louise were married, and Henry may have already been in British Columbia before the gold rush was two months old. It is difficult to conclude that Henry's decision to go to Canada was not influenced by the promise of golden wealth; in fact, that may have been the reason he went to Canada in the first place. But it does not necessarily mean that he stayed there because of it.

All in all, particularly in view of the fact that the mast-harvesting story has a faint ring of truth, perhaps the French Biography's account of the Canadian venture should be given the benefit of the doubt.

Poorer But Wiser, the Travelers Return to Oregon

The French Biography states: "After this disaster (i.e., the loss of a year's work harvesting masts), the family returned to Sacramento, but shortly afterward removed to Portland, Oregon, which was then a mere village."[134]

There are no known connections to Portland that explain the Smiths' relocation to that city. Regardless of their reasons for alighting there, the family did not remain in Portland proper for long.[135] The United States Census confirms that on July 31, 1860, Henry, Emily Louise, and Edwin

---

[133] Ibid.

[134] The description of Portland as a "mere village" is not entirely inconsistent with Guyon family oral history that Edwin could "count all the buildings in Portland on his fingers" upon his arrival there.

[135] It may well be that the family considered itself to be located in Portland, although that perception was not technically accurate.

were living in South Salem, Marion County, Oregon, less than fifty miles from Portland. Henry's "Profession, Occupation, or Trade" is listed as "Harness Maker." Emily Louise's occupation is blank, as is Grandpa Guyon's, although a check mark explains that "E F," six years old, had "Attended School Within The Year."[136]

The French Biography also states that after the family's return to Oregon, Grandpa Guyon "attended school to the age of twelve" in Portland. Grandpa was seven years old in the fall of 1860, which accords with the French Biography that he attended first through sixth grades in Portland from 1860 to 1865. The Johnson Biography is less detailed, but it avers that Grandpa Guyon "was educated in the public schools of California and Oregon" from approximately 1860 to 1865.[137]

The Arrival in Pilot Rock

Other than the indication in the 1860 census that Henry was a harness maker in Marion County, Oregon, it is unknown what he and Emily Louise did to make a living in the Portland area during the five years between 1860 and 1865. Whatever it was, it was not permanent. The family left Portland around 1865 and, according to the French Biography, Henry "bought some Indian cattle and began ranching at Pilot Rock, Oregon" and "Edwin was taken there to assist in farm work."[138]

Why Pilot Rock was chosen for Henry's cattle operation is unstated in the French Biography, as is the length of time the family pursued farm work.[139] Neither is there any known account of the family's circumstances, except for a letter written by Grandpa Guyon later in life that describes a colorful chapter in his life as a preteen.

---

136 Schedule 1, United States Census of 1860, South Salem, Marion County, Oregon, p. 392.

137 Later in life, Grandpa Guyon confirmed his attendance at the public schools of Portland in a certain "Application for Membership in the Volunteer Medical Service Corps" dated September 3, 1918, but did not state that he had ever attended school in California. However, the fact that the family returned from British Columbia to Sacramento before moving to Oregon may be an indicator that Grandpa Guyon attended school in Sacramento for a short time before the move to Portland.

138 The move to Pilot Rock was clearly a serious one that required the involvement of the whole family to make it successful. That Edwin was only twelve years old and expected to work on the family ranch might raise eyebrows today, or even trigger the involvement of the Department of Social Services, but the harsh reality in the 1860s in Oregon was that everyone in the family was expected to work, and work hard.

139 Because the French Biography is clear that Henry's operation in Pilot Rock was a cattle-ranching venture, it seems likely that Edwin's role was primarily one of ranching, and not farming, although there could easily be overlaps in his duties.

A one-page typewritten missive from Grandpa Guyon to an unknown recipient describes an experience in his twelfth year that allows a glimpse into his world in Pilot Rock in the mid-1860s. The document is undated and is missing the first page, which may have contained the date and addressee. The page marked "2" begins "[t]he old man and his wife were very kind people and sent the way farer [sic] on his way rejoicing." The balance of the page records Grandpa Guyon's personal recollections:

> On the next day July the 5th [1865] we started on our way for Granite.[140] We had to leave the wagon we used on our way from Umatilla and travel on horse back as there was no wagon road from Alta to Granite Creek at that time.
>
> We camped that night at bases [sic] springs on the top of the Blue Mountains.
>
> The next day July the 6th, we reached Ensign's ranch. He kept travelers and we spent a very pleasant night there. This ranch was first called Daly's ranch, Then Ensign's. Then Starky's. The next morning we continued our journey and reached the next station which was called Sheep Ranch. It was conducted by a man named Jack Morton. He was quite a musician and entertained us with his violin until bedtime.
>
> We were now in the midst of wild nature, in the depths of solitude and surrounded by the silence of an impenetrable forest untouched by the haunts of men.
>
> The next day July the 8th, we resumed our journey and arrived at our journey's end. This spot was known as Skedaddle Hill. This hill came by its name from the following cause. About 1862 a gulch which heads into this hill was taken up by three men and was worked quite

---

[140] The present Granite City is about one and a half miles upstream from the original Granite City as it existed prior to 1867 and as referred to by Grandpa Guyon. The original city, called Granite Creek Mines, was settled by miners who discovered gold along Granite Creek on July 4, 1862. See "Granite, Oregon," Wikipedia, accessed August 10, 2016, https://en.wikipedia.org/wiki/-Granite,_Oregon. The town of Granite continued to exist as the fourth smallest incorporated city by population (pop. 38) in Oregon as of 2010.

steadily for a time and all at once these men disappeared and no one knew just when they left or where they went and it was ever afterward dubbed Skedaddle Gulch and from this the hill adjacent was named Skedaddle Hill. My step father, H. C. Smith took up a claim there and his partners also did the same and dug a ditch seven miles long in order to get water on their ground. My step father being named Smith and there being so many Smiths in that region that the miners there, in order to know which Smith was meant in their conversations they gave each Smith a nick name. So there was Peg Leg Smith, Cayuse Smith, Limpy Smith, Skedaddle Smith and a few more which I can't call to mind. This name [Skedaddle Smith] followed my step father the balance of his life.

We resided at Skedaddle hill until November the 14th, 1865 and we then came back to Birch Creek for the winter. We had but three horses to convey us and

1864 Campaign Ribbon found in Edwin's effects

there was four of us in the posey.[141] Mr. Nelson who lived on Butter Creek was a miner at Granite and was coming to his ranch at the above named place stopped at our cabin

---

[141] This is a likely misspelling of "posse" as a tongue-in-cheek description of the little band.

and stayed all night and persuaded us to go with him. My mother had a horse of her own and Mr. Nelson, my step father and my self rode turn about on our only riding horse, the other horse carried our bedding. You can imagine that we did not ride enough to hurt.

We soon found a place to winter which was on the farm of Henry Bowman.

My mother and I never went back to the mines and my step father soon disposed of his claim to Winn Johnson & Ike Clough in 1866 and invested what money he had in cattle and with my help he became, in a few years, independent.

Gold had been discovered in the Blue Mountains in 1861,[142] and it is altogether possible that this venture at Skedaddle Gulch in 1865 was a natural follow-up to the earlier event.

The Seven-Mile Ditch

The sheer length of the miners' ditch attests that the task was daunting, even if the miners had tools other than picks and shovels to rely on. That the miners had to leave the wagon they brought from Umatilla near Granite seems to have limited their equipment options to whatever they could pack on a horse or mule, unless their predecessors had lugged heavier equipment to the site and abandoned it there. The ditch was probably shallow, perhaps shored up by rocks, packed earth, and tree branches.

The Skedaddle Hill claims were undoubtedly gold claims mined by the placer method, which explains the need for the ditch. Water brought by the seven-mile-long channel would wash the dirt and gravel down a sluice to separate the heavier gold from the lighter earth and rocks, trapping the gold behind riffles in the bottom of the sluice-box.

The newly named Skedaddle Smith and his family were at the mining claims in the Blue Mountains for about four months, from July 8 to November 14, 1865, during which time Grandpa Guyon celebrated his twelfth birthday on November 7. Whether gold was found is debatable,

---

142 Eastern Oregon Visitor's Association, "Eastern Oregon Ghost Towns," accessed August 10, 2016, http://www.visiteasternoregon.com/entry/eastern-oregon-ghost-towns/.

but the fact that Skedaddle sold his claims a year later at least indicates that they had at least a perceived value. It also suggests that after the Blue Mountains mining experience, he was satisfied to be a cattle rancher, at least for the time being.

The Legacy of Skedaddle Smith

Henry Smith's nickname "Skedaddle" is decidedly unusual, but its almost haphazard bestowal upon one of many Smiths seems too artless or common to account for such a colorful and memorable name. It is easy to understand why, once given, the name stuck permanently.

Skedaddle Smith continues to generate interest and inspire researchers into the romance of Oregon's past. A contemporary reference to perhaps the very mining adventure described by Grandpa Guyon states that the town of Granite sprang up in 1862 after the discovery of gold in Bull Run and that "for 80 years, boisterous Granite produced gold and some legendary characters like Skedaddle Smith."[143]

The reference to Skedaddle Smith as legendary seems consistent with his nickname, although details concerning him are scarce. On the surface, it is likely that he was at least somewhat unusual in his dress or actions, and it would not be surprising if people around him thought him eccentric in one way or another. His willingness to take risks, evidenced by the daring journey to British Columbia in 1858 and his gold-seeking quest in the Blue Mountains in 1865, suggests an ardent adventurer with real pioneer spirit who might fly off to one interesting exploit or another without hesitation. Yet his willingness to be tied down to harness-making, cattle ranching, and family life during the in-between times demonstrate a warmer, softer, unprecarious side.[144]

J. L. Sharon, a former resident of Pilot Rock who knew Skedaddle Smith personally, described him many years later as "a good man but rather peculiar as a citizen."[145] The statement that he was a "good man" can

---

[143] Oregon Department of Transportation, "The Elkhorn Drive Scenic Byway," accessed August 10, 2016, https://tripcheck.com/Pages/SBelkhornDr.asp#.

[144] Despite suggestions of eccentricity or perhaps non-conformism, by all accounts Henry was a nurturing and caring stepfather to Edwin and a loving husband to Emily Louise. Emily Louise's intricately carved headstone in the Pilot Rock cemetery, weathered and broken after almost 140 years, testifies that she was dearly loved by the two most important men in her life.

[145] J. L. Sharon, letter to the editor, *East Oregonian* (Pendleton, OR), June 29, 1948. Mr. Sharon was a former resident of Pilot Rock who boarded with Grandpa Guyon, Maggie, and Maud in the mid-1880s. This letter was in response to a request for information initiated by my father relating to Effie's application for a pension, discussed in detail in Appendix VI below.

mean both anything and nothing, but being "peculiar" may suggest an independent character who was probably not overly anxious to join groups or make friends, although he does not appear to have been reclusive or antisocial.

Whether Skedaddle Smith achieved legendary status because of his nickname, his colorful personality, his peculiarities, or some other reason, there can be no doubt that the lives of his family and the population at large were enriched and enhanced by this charismatic character history remembers.

Cattle Ranching Proves Temporary

Very little is known about the Smith family after Skedaddle sold his gold claims in 1866 and began cattle ranching. Grandpa Guyon's statement that "in a few years" Henry became independent with his help suggests that their collective efforts were successful. How long this endeavor actually continued is not known, although there appears to be no reason to doubt that it lasted at least for the "few years" reported by Grandpa. At some point circa 1869–1870, however, there was a significant change in Henry's direction.

The Smith Family's Focus Changes

The United States census dated June 10, 1870, although not entirely legible, provides information about the "Inhabitants in Pendleton to Willow Creek Branch," or words to that effect. The Post Office appears to be "Cayuse," although that is likewise difficult to read. The head of household was Jacob Frazier, originally from Ohio, age forty-nine, male, white, whose occupation was listed as "Stock Raiser." His real estate was valued at $2,000 and personal property at $5,500.

Also identified as living in the home was Henry Smith, age forty-two, male, white, occupation "Gold Miner." Born in Kentucky, he owned no real property, but had personal property valued at $100. Also included was Louise(a) E. Smith, age forty-two, female, white, occupation "Keeping House." No real or personal property values were listed for her. Her place of birth was Missouri. The last person in the household was "Smith, Edwin F.," age sixteen, male, white, occupation "Farm Laborer." His place of birth was Louisiana.

The relationship between Jacob Frazier and Henry and his family is not entirely spelled out in the census record, but it is likely that the Smith family lived with Mr. Frazier and provided him services in the form of labor in return for board and room. The Smiths also may have been paid wages, but there is no known evidence to support that possibility. Emily Louise was probably obliged to keep house and cook meals for her family and Mr. Frazier, and in return both Henry and Grandpa Guyon likely did whatever work was necessary to promote Mr. Frazier's stock-raising enterprise.

If Henry bought cattle and started ranching in about 1866 in Pilot Rock as asserted in Grandpa's letter quoted above, then the obvious question is what happened to the cattle and the idea of ranching between 1866 and 1870 when he is described as a gold miner but working for a cattle rancher? The most plausible answer to that question seems to be that Henry either voluntarily changed his mind midstream or was unsuccessful in cattle ranching, putting him in a position where he was forced to work for someone else. The latter possibility seems inconsistent with Edwin's account that Henry became independent at cattle ranching within a few years. It may be that Skedaddle's self-described occupation of gold miner in the 1870 census was his passion, while stock raising was his reality, either working independently or otherwise. Born in the early 1820s, Henry was about fifty years old in 1870, and it is not difficult to imagine that he was stretched to the limit between his urge to find the proverbial mother lode and the pressing need to support his family.

Chapter 5.

COWBOYS, PERPLEXING SECRETS, AND SURPRISES

circa 1865–1878

The only secret people keep is immortality.
— Emily Dickinson

This chapter begins to focus more directly on Grandpa Guyon, beginning in his early teens into his mid-twenties, and discusses his experience as a cowboy, the death of Emily Louise and the unforeseeable revelation that he was not the biological offspring of Henry Smith, his life in general in Pendleton and Pilot Rock, and the exciting experience he had as a volunteer in the Bannock Indian War of 1878.

Grandpa Guyon's Life as a Cowboy

After the Skedaddle Gulch gold mining enterprise, little written evidence survives to confirm events or experiences in Grandpa Guyon's life from about 1865, when the Smith family returned to Pilot Rock, to the late 1870s. He likely continued to live with his mother and Henry in the Pilot Rock/Pendleton area, and worked alongside Henry, wherever that took him. According to the French Biography, his practical knowledge expanded significantly during this period:

> He knows well what cowboy life meant according to the order of the old West, and the remuda, the round-up, the chuck-wagon, branding, roping and cutting-out are all terms that are familiar to him from his own experience.

Knowing the meaning of cowboy life suggests more than a passing acquaintance, and it is for that reason I have included the iconic Saddles in the title of this biography. Grandpa Guyon was a cowboy in the most authentic sense of the term during the 1870s in Oregon, and perhaps even earlier, but never the romanticized cowboy manufactured by Hollywood. The realities of cowboy life Edwin experienced included hard work, little pay, long hours, little rest, dangerous working conditions, and food that was never in danger of being described as a gastronomic delight.

It was during this same period that Edwin reached the age of majority, and in the process acquired the necessary knowledge and experience in ranching and cowboying. Branding, roping, rounding up, and cutting out cattle were not abstract concepts to him. He knew by the age of eighteen in late 1871, if not before, that they were his keys to survival and employability, and it was important for him to be adept at all of them.

Grandpa Guyon had to be an expert horseman, which he would have learned from Henry and others around him—and by riding a horse practically every day of his life. The ability to control an animal weighing a half-ton or more with a personality and mind of its own was a necessary skill that was not learned best in the abstract. He had to know how to rope and subdue cattle for branding and neutering, all of which were dangerous and required a high degree of practical knowledge and experience.

There is no suggestion in either the French Biography or the Johnson Biography that Edwin ever went on any legendary cattle drive like his counterparts in the movies. Most likely, his activities were limited to the environs of Pendleton and Pilot Rock, but the fact that his experience as a cowboy in Oregon in the 1870s was included in the French Biography suggests that it was an important part of his personal experience and development.

Religious Persuasions

Probably during the 1860s and 1870s, Grandpa Guyon developed a knowledge of and appreciation for things spiritual under the watchful eyes of his parents. The fact that he was an only child was an advantage in that he could command the full attention of both his parents; the big disadvantage was that he likely *had* the full attention of both his parents.

I envision him attending church regularly, if not entirely cheerfully, with Emily Louise and Henry or, if no church was available, studying the Bible under their tutelage and direction. His Bible-based advice, including quotations, to his daughter Maud later in life suggests that he had more than a passing familiarity with the Good Book.

The year 1876 marked a religious milestone in his life. In that year, at the age of twenty-three, he had a spiritual experience he described to Maud more than fifty years later:[146]

---

[146] E. F. Guyon to Maud Brown, 16 September 1927.

I had the New Birth as mentioned in the New Testament when I was 23 years old, and I know I am saved as I have the Witness within myself. Just ask and pray for it and you will get the same positive evidence as I did. I was born of the Spirit.[147]

According to the French Biography, Dr. Guyon was a conscientious member of the Methodist Episcopal Church. The Johnson Biography reports that he "was brought up in the Methodist Faith." His personal religious leanings were certainly conservative, yet he was tolerant of opposing religious views and is not known to have attempted to impose his own upon others. His religious beliefs may be summed up in his later advice to his daughter Maud in 1927: "No religion will save you, God alone through Jesus Christ can save and you will know when this is done if you seek it."[148]

Good Shepherds

Ranching and cowboying were not Grandpa Guyon's only activities in the 1870s, according to the *East Oregonian*, Saturday, June 23, 1877:

CHAMPION SHEARERS – Ed. F. Smith, Jake and John Arrasmith claim that they will take the belt so generously accorded to Jerry Despain for sheep shearing; each of them has sheared 110 in a day, and a poor day for shearing at that.

In a day when electric shearers were entirely unknown, the shearing of 110 sheep in a single day sounds like a meaningful achievement.[149] Whatever the level of the accomplishment, Grandpa Guyon was no stranger to hard work. Whether he or Jake and John Arrasmith actually won the contest for shearing the most sheep is apparently lost to history.

---

[147] E. F. Guyon to Maud Brown, 8 December 1927.

[148] Ibid.

[149] Pendleton eventually became an important railhead for the shipping of wool from growers in the region, but the sheep-shearing in 1877 predated the present woolen mill in Pendleton, which was not established until 1908. The present mill structure was originally built in 1893 as a wool scouring plant, then converted to a woolen mill in 1895 to make blankets and robes for Native Americans. Both the 1893 and 1895 enterprises failed, from which the present milling operation sprang.

Self-Determination

The move to Pilot Rock circa 1865 necessarily interrupted Edwin's formal education in the Portland area, but did not bring learning to a halt. Education was always important to him, and it is no overstatement to say he had an unquenchable thirst for knowledge that accompanied him his entire life. It is likely that he took every opportunity that came his way to attend schools as he grew up. Where formal educational opportunities were limited by a scarcity of schools, teachers, or the competing need to work to make a living, he educated himself through reading and self-study. The few books that remain of his personal library indicate that his interests included such subjects as algebra, steam engine technology, the works of Edward Bulwer-Lytton (1803–1873), and Shakespeare. During his lifetime, his personal library doubtless contained many other books on other diverse subjects. None of his books was meant to be ornamental.

The Quest for Higher Education

As we have seen, Edwin was no stranger to hard physical labor, and certainly recognized its necessity and value, but he also had an intellectual side that hungered for development. According to the French Biography, his studious nature impelled him to attend and graduate from Walla Walla College near Walla Walla, Washington, in 1875 with the degree of Bachelor of Arts.[150] However, according to the Walla Walla College published history, "the college opened on December 7, 1892, with 80 students and nine faculty."[151] That fact appears to foreclose any possibility that Grandpa Guyon even attended that institution, much less graduated from it, since he had already finished medical school by that time.

The Johnson Biography states that Edwin graduated not from Walla Walla College, but from Whitman College, which was also located in Walla Walla and which was established in 1859.[152] That statement is also technically inaccurate because Whitman College did not graduate its first class until 1886.[153]

---

[150] French, *History of Idaho*, 1256.
[151] Walla Walla University, accessed May 12, 2011. http://www.wallawalla.edu/about-wwu/an-introduction/history/
[152] G. Thomas Edwards, *The Triumph of Tradition: The Emergence of Whitman College 1859-1924* (Walla Walla, WA: Whitman College, 1992), 6.
[153] Ibid., 65.

The school Edwin actually attended was Whitman Seminary,[154] the predecessor of Whitman College. The institution was established by the Reverend Cushing Eels in 1859 with the passage of the Whitman Seminary charter by the Washington territorial legislature.[155] Contrary to the Johnson Biography, he attended for only two years and did not receive a degree.[156] Courses he took and his educational objectives are entirely unknown, although it is safe to assume that Edwin was serious about learning in general—as much as and as quickly as possible.

The Untimely Death of Emily Louise

The French Biography, speaking of the "cowboy life" in Oregon in the late 1860s and 1870s, states, "[Edwin's] life, for the most part, passed in this manner until about twenty-five years of age, when his mother died at Pilot Rock, Oregon."

Emily Louise died on March 2, 1878, of unknown causes, likely of a lingering nature, before she was forty-nine years of age. The loss to Edwin was great, and the sadness he felt at her passing was an emotional burden likely surpassed only by her deathbed disclosure that his father was not Henry Smith as he had been told.

Family Secrets Revealed

Shortly before the end of her life, Emily Louise revealed to Grandpa Guyon for the first time that his biological father was John Guyon and not Henry C. Smith. We can safely assume that at a minimum Emily Louise also told him about John Guyon's Huguenot ancestry, and she most likely told him that John Guyon was born in New Jersey, along with the other information to be found in the French Biography and the Johnson Biography. Emily Louise may have also divulged the time and place of her marriage to John Guyon, but if she did, those facts were not passed down in the Guyon family oral history. She certainly told Grandpa Guyon what she knew about John Guyon's disappearance in New Orleans. She probably explained to him why she had kept this information from him for twenty years, and why she had changed her mind and elected to tell him about it on her deathbed. None of Emily Louise's statements to her son about John Guyon and his

---

154 The word *seminary* at the time did not necessarily emphasize theology or suggest preparation for the ministry; rather, it was more akin to the word *academy*.

155 Edwards, *Triumph of Tradition*, 6.

156 Application for Membership in the Volunteer Medical Service Corps, 3 September 1918.

ancestry, insofar as is presently known, was ever personally recorded by Edwin, although the information in the French Biography and the Johnson Biography almost certainly had to have come from Grandpa Guyon's own recollections.

The magnitude and importance of Emily Louise's revelation can hardly be overstated from a genealogical perspective. Grandpa Guyon's descendants would likely know absolutely nothing of their connection to John Guyon or even the Guyon family, had Emily Louise not told my grandfather about him. Even though the specifics of the connection remain undiscovered, knowing it exists at all opens a world of possibilities in the genealogical sense and invites a continuation in the search of the Guyon line.

Possible Reasons behind Emily Louise's Deception

Endless speculation is the lot of he or she who studies Emily Louise's motives for concealing Grandpa Guyon's paternal genealogy from him and

Edwin circa 1880s

then for electing to tell him about it at the end of her life. What was so horrible or scandalous about her marriage and relationship with John Guyon that she felt compelled to conceal it from her only child for more than twenty years?

In an effort to rationalize the known facts with possibilities and probabilities, I favor the idea that Emily Louise did not know what happened to her husband beyond the fact of his disappearance. This is consistent with the oral history of the Guyon family, but does not necessarily exclude other possibilities.

From Emily Louise's perspective, John Guyon disappeared from her life and the life of her child, leaving them abandoned. Whether John Guyon *intentionally* abandoned his family is another question that may never be answered. Regardless of what actually happened, the belief that she and Grandpa Guyon were intentionally abandoned may have compelled Emily Louise to pretend John Guyon never existed, at least for the following two decades.

Emily Louise's Resolve Softens

Twenty years after her husband's disappearance, Emily Louise had a change of heart. Her initial apparently irrevocable decision to forget about John Guyon and completely erase him from her life and the life of her only child became revocable. Likely this change was triggered by the knowledge of her impending death and her need to unburden herself from the weight of her deception, and was punctuated by her unselfish desire for her only child to know the identity of his biological father, regardless of the circumstances of the latter's disappearance.

The information Emily Louise related to her son was the truth as she knew or believed it to be. One simply does not keep a secret for twenty years and then divulge a lie *in extremis* in place of the secret. The fact that in our legal system dying declarations are exceptions to the hearsay rule (which would otherwise exclude such statements as evidence in legal proceedings) reflects the overall societal view that voluntary declarations made with the knowledge of impending death are likely to be true and can reasonably be relied upon.

Emotional and Psychological Turmoil

The effect Emily Louise's deathbed confession had on her son is not known, but we can reasonably surmise that it was a shock of major proportions to be told about his biological father for the first time at the age of twenty-four and to learn that this very important information had been kept from him by those closest to him.

Suddenly, Grandpa Guyon's father became his stepfather; he had a new family tree to consider; and his surname was not Smith. That he adopted the Guyon name and used it for the rest of his life is some indication that he got over the surprise and shock of it and that he believed his mother's statements at the end of her life to be true.

Edwin Becomes a Cattle Rancher in His Own Right

Prior to the death of Emily Louise, Grandpa Guyon had worked for or with his stepfather, but after she passed on, he saw an opportunity to operate his own cattle ranching operation. According to the French Biography, in the late 1870s Grandpa Guyon

> bought a few cattle, going in debt for most of them, and
> took up ranching independently, following it for a short

time and succeeding so well that at the end of his first year he was practically free from debt.[157]

Despite his success as an independent cattle rancher, Grandpa Guyon would eventually decide to follow his internal compass in a different direction that would ultimately lead him to his life as a physician and surgeon.

A Supposed Indian Uprising

In the meantime, on July 3, 1878, Grandpa Guyon became a witness to an apparent, but falsely reported, Indian uprising that spilled over into the Pendleton area along with the fear, anxiety, and confusion it generated. The series of events surrounding the alleged uprising directly involved Edwin, who at the time lived near Pilot Rock, approximately sixteen miles south of Pendleton. In an undated, typewritten letter, reproduced here without any changes in punctuation, spelling, or capitalization, Grandpa Guyon describes the scene:

> On the third day of July 1878 about noon is a day I shall never forget and one which was fraught with much fear and deep concern. It was on the occasion of a party of our boys in and around Pilot Rock and up and down Birch creek numbering about 30 who had gone out toward Camas Pararie to scout and to locate the indians we heard were there and out on their way to the head waters of Birch Creek, among whom is Doug Baily the Lawyer, Jim Willemore, Charlie Finch, Charlie Clark. I have forgotten the balance, but they were the boys in the vicinity. I think they started on their scouting trip early on the morning of the 3rd. of July and they met with no signs of indians until they were near Camas Pararie and could look down through the timber on the valley. The indians had a scout

---

[157] To what extent Henry, Emily Louise, and Grandpa Guyon were successful cattle-raisers in the economic sense prior to 1878 is unknown. The fact that Grandpa Guyon started his own cattle operation after 1878 may indicate that his experience with his stepfather was positive and his move toward independence was the next step in the family's initial plans. It also could mean that he was unhappy with the way Henry had run his operation, and felt he could do better. Whatever the reason, there is no apparent evidence of conflict with Henry, and the fact that he and Henry shared living space after Emily Louise's death suggests they remained on good terms.

out on the mountain and the boys run on to him and they caught him and shot him and the indians were racing along down the valley to get in ahead of our boys and they had to run in a line to get ahead of the indians which they succeeded in doing and the indians got in behind them and chased them closely shooting as they run. Charley Finch's horse gave out and he hid in the brush until night and then walked in home. Another one of the men secreted himself along the road and the indians found him and killed him. I forget his name. They sent word to all the people along the two branches of Birch creek by runner and in a short time here they came on horse back and in buggies and in wagons helter skelter toward Pendleton. The roads were dirty and you could not see your horse. At that time Mrs. Madison Jones and two younger sons and Maggie and Erma were stopping at our house having been scared by rumors of approaching Indians and having a case of Diphtheria in the family they could not secure shelter in a family having small children we invited them to stay with us. My mother died in March and my step father and I we were batching and we took them and it was just when every body was frightened and were fleeing toward Pendleton and we hitched up our team to our ludlow wagon[158] and put the family all in and away we went to Pendleton. I was up against it as we could not expose the people to diphtheria and I did not know where to go for accommodations. Finally I saw the Sherif and he let me move in a room over the old jail where we were isolated properly. I will never forget that ride to Pendleton on the 3rd. of July 1878. It was a hot day and dusty and the road was crowded with wagons. Buggies and horsemen and they were in a hurry and the noise and yells they made was enough to increase our fears of the proximity of the Indians and we drove our team as fast as we could. We made the trip in safety and we were thankful, but we were still uneasy as it was rumered that the Indians were headed for Pendleton and we were very ill at ease. Guards were thrown out and I was in the

---

158 The Ludlow spring wagon was a short-tongued wagon with springs between the axles and frame, invented and patented by Otto H. Hesse and manufactured in Leavenworth, Kansas.

gang and fully expected the Indians to show up any minute. I was glad that Major Throgmorten with a company of soldiers and arriving about midnight and finding out our location the Major detailed a good strong guard to help us if anything occurred. But nothing happened. I was glad.

After arriving in Pendleton, Grandpa Guyon volunteered for military service. His statement that he was "in the gang" of guards confirms his direct involvement in an organization he later identified as Captain Emmett Wheeler's Oregon Volunteers. He was twenty-four years old and single and likely wished to do whatever he could to ensure his own personal safety and that of the populace. Affidavits filed in support of his pension application many years later establish that he "was mustered for guard and picket duty" and rendered services which "consisted of guard and scout duty actively . . . over a period of 6 weeks to 2 months."[159]

The Bannock War

The events Grandpa Guyon described in his letter provide a very small window into an armed conflict between Indians and whites that is known to history variously as the Bannock War, the Bannock Indian War of 1878, or the Bannock Campaign.[160]

The causes behind the Bannock War are many and varied, as well as beyond the scope of this biography, although the spark that ignited it was the departure of a large number of Bannock Indians from the Fort Hall Reservation in Idaho, heading toward the Oregon border.[161] The Indians' intermediate objective was to increase their numbers by collecting volunteers from other Indian tribes along the way in hopes that with superior numbers they could successfully wage war against the whites at a later time.

During June, 1878, the Bannock chief Buffalo Horn led this band of approximately 200 Indians into an area near the Snake River close to the border of Idaho and Oregon, where the Indians attacked and wounded two white cattle drivers, who both escaped alive to tell the tale. Shortly thereafter, the Indians killed a settler between Big Camas Prairie and the Snake River. In response to these attacks, General O. O. Howard sent

---

[159] Affidavit of J. T. Arrasmith and Maggie M. Finch, October 8, 1931.
[160] For purposes of this biography, I will refer to it as the Bannock War.
[161] Technically speaking, Idaho was a territory in 1878, having been organized in 1863, and did not become a state until 1890. Oregon gained statehood in 1859.

74

troops into the area from Vancouver, Walla Walla, Lapwai, and other points, and engaged the hostile Indians in several battles, one of which resulted in the death of Buffalo Horn.

After Buffalo Horn's death, the Pah Ute chief Egan took command of the Indians, who by then numbered about 500 warriors and 1,500 women and children. [162] Under Chief Egan, the Bannocks moved west into Oregon, and then north, hoping to join with other Indians in the region, including the Umatilla Indians on the reservation near Pendleton, although the latter in reality had no intention of fighting against the whites.

During this chain of events, a false rumor spread in the Pendleton–Pilot Rock area that the Umatilla Indians were fighting with the Bannocks against the whites at John Day River. It was apparently this rumor that triggered the rush to Pendleton described in Grandpa Guyon's letter. The flight to safety was much more widespread than the immediate area of Pendleton. Panic-stricken refugees from outlying areas crowded into Heppner, Umatilla, Wallula, Weston, Milton, and Walla Walla in the same fashion as Pendleton. [163]

The "boys in and around Pilot Rock" described in Grandpa Guyon's letter were recruits of a volunteer company organized at Pilot Rock under the command of Captain Emmett Wilson on or about July 2, 1878. [164] This volunteer company was on its way to John Day River to engage the hostiles it believed to be there when it came upon the scout mentioned in Grandpa's letter. [165]

The size of the Indian band is described in history as "large," but with no specific number. It was clearly much larger than the group of thirty volunteers, which compelled their retreat, almost exactly as described by Grandpa Guyon. [166] This incident spurred the organization of a second company of volunteers under Captain Sperry, which left Pendleton on the 6th of July.

---

[162] These events in Idaho Territory coincided with attempts by a medicine man named Smohalla and known as the "Dreamer" to unite the Pah Ute, Bannock, Snake, Umatilla, Cayuse, Walla Walla, Warm Springs, Yakima, Colville, Columbia, Spokane, and Pend d'Oreille tribes and wage war against the whites. They were to be aided by thousands of resurrected warriors.

[163] Oregon Genealogy, "War with the Snake, Bannock and Paiute, Umatilla County, Oregon," accessed August 14, 2016, http://www.oregongenealogy.com/umatilla/indianwar.htm.

[164] Ibid.

[165] Ibid.

[166] In fact, one wonders whether historians had access to Grandpa Guyon's letter as an historical source, as opposed to the other way around.

In the meantime, the Major Throckmorton identified by Grandpa Guyon arrived in Pendleton from Walla Walla and was joined the next day by troops from Lapwai, amounting to 150 men in all.[167]

In addition to the forces brought to bear by the military detachments, groups of volunteers, which could easily have included Edwin, were sent to drive roving bands of Indians from the Blue Mountains and to perform whatever other services may have been necessary to quell the uprising. Eventually, the perpetrators of the incident and their followers were either subdued or disbanded, and life in the area returned to relative normalcy.

Despite the passage of roughly 140 years, Grandpa's depiction of the events surrounding the chaotic dash to Pendleton and the aftermath of the Bannock War still evokes interest, in part because he described it as a witness and participant. His words demonstrate the uncertainty of life in Oregon in pioneer times. They may also remind us that the issues of land ownership and occupation rights underlying the conflict between Indians and white settlers were so fundamentally important to them both that lives were regularly lost on both sides of the equation.

The arrival of Major Throckmorton[168] and his soldiers is not entirely reminiscent of Hollywood depictions of the US cavalry's timely rescue of scores of beleaguered would-be victims of Indian attacks, as the bugler sounded the charge with a precision hardly possible on a galloping horse. The soldiers' arrival "around midnight" in Pendleton was without such fanfare, but their presence was no less gratifying to those whose safety hung in the balance, or at least seemed to.

The events described by Grandpa occurred barely two years after the defeat of General Custer on the Little Big Horn River in Montana in June, 1876. The recency of that event may help explain the anxiety and fear he described, engendered by the belief that Indians were on the warpath. It may also provide an explanation for the proximity of the soldiers who arrived in Pendleton around midnight on July 3, 1878, to protect the civilian population. The fact they were close enough to arrive so quickly may be coincidental, but it may also indicate that they were already close by as part of an overall military plan of readiness.

The narrative contains a number of additional facts important to my present examination of Grandpa Guyon's life. The first is the mention of Charley Finch, who was one of the group of thirty locals who went in search of the Indians. Almost fifty years later, Congress passed a law that

---

[167] Oregon Genealogy, "War with the Snake, Bannock and Paiute."
[168] The name is misspelled in Dr. Guyon's quotation above.

authorized pensions to individuals who had participated in Indian conflicts, and Charley Finch and his wife Maggie, among others, supplied affidavits in support of Grandpa Guyon's application. Unfortunately, despite the efforts of these eye-witnesses and other information, the petition was denied.

The mention of Maggie Jones also has significance in Grandpa Guyon's life; she and Edwin were married just one year and three days later. The couple probably knew each other prior to July 3, 1878, but whether they were "promised," engaged, or merely friends at the time of the Indian scare is unknown.

Other than the recollections of Grandpa Guyon and the sworn statements of witnesses who were present, there is no known record, public or private, that confirms Grandpa Guyon's membership in Captain Emmett Wheeler's Oregon Volunteers or his service in the Bannock War. The lack of official records would cause him and his family a good deal of frustration later on.

Chapter 6.

LIFE IN PILOT ROCK
AND
THE CALL TO MEDICINE

circa 1879–1891

Medicine is the most distinguished of all the arts,
but through the ignorance of those who practice it,
and those who casually judge such practitioners,
it is now of all the arts by far the least esteemed.
— Hippocrates, *Law*

The period from 1879 to 1891 discussed in this chapter was an elemental, causal, and preparatory period in the life of Grandpa Guyon; the seeds of marriage, family, and various vocations planted in Oregon's fertile soil bloomed collectively into his eventual embrace of the practice of medicine as his life's work.

Marriage and Family

On July 6, 1879, Edwin and Margaret Matilda Jones, known as Maggie, married in Pilot Rock. Maggie was the daughter of local stockman Madison Jones. The marriage was announced in an article in the *East Oregonian* on July 19, 1879:

> GUYON-JONES – At the residence of the bride's father on Birch Creek, July 6th, by Rev. R. J. Rhodes, Ed. F. Guyon (Smith) to Miss Maggie Jones. Cake received.

Below the announcement, the following appears:

> May your honey moon [sic] be perpetual and peace and prosperity attend you throughout the journey of life.

Aside from the importance of the occasion of his marriage, the announcement publicly identified Edwin by his Guyon surname, possibly for the first time.[169]

Two children were born to Edwin and Maggie: Maud, who arrived on March 27, 1880, in Pilot Rock, and Lafayette Madison, who appeared ten years later in Pendleton on June 4, 1890.[170] Much later in his life, Dr. Guyon expressed a very sweet and poignant recollection of Maud's birth in a letter to her:

Edwin's and Maggie's wedding photograph – 1879

You were my first baby and when old Doctor Simpson brought you in to the world and I saw you for the first time I was so overcome with joy that as I went out that night on an errand up to Johnny Sylvester's store just above the old town of Alta to get some cotton and bandages I just danced all the way up there like a crazy man, so happy I was beside myself. It was about two o'clock or later in the morning and it was about a mile and a quarter I had to go, but I made record time and was back much sooner than they expected. I just burned up the road in my haste. To think I was a father was a new experience, and one new to me and I wouldn't have changed places with any King or Potentate of the World. I thought you were the only baby in the World and I haven't changed my mind even to this day.[171]

---

[169] By the time of his marriage to Maggie, he had known the identity of his biological father for less than eighteen months.
[170] French, *History of Idaho*, 1256.
[171] E. F. Guyon to Maud Brown, 2 May 1927.

Jack of All Trades

During his youth Edwin had been imbued with the idea that he could do anything or be anyone he wanted to be, and he was in no way shy of undertaking new challenges. This accounts, at least in part, for the numerous occupations he dabbled in before he settled on medicine. He was unable to accept as his lot in life a calling that did not sufficiently challenge him.

In 1878, he was a schoolteacher in the Pilot Rock-Pendleton area. Little is known about this endeavor, including its duration, although an article published later on states that "[Edwin] followed school teaching for a number of years."[172] Schooled in Portland in the 1860s, Grandpa Guyon was a logical candidate for a teaching position at a time when formal education beyond eighth grade was unusual. It is likely that he approached the position with characteristic fervor. It is probable that he taught several grades and subjects at the same time in the iconic one-room schoolhouse so familiar to students of American history.

The Village Smithy

The United States Census of 1880 reports Grandpa Guyon's family in mid-June located at Alta, Umatilla County, Oregon. "Smith, Edwin F.," age twenty-six, is listed as the head of the family. His wife, Margaret, age nineteen, is also identified by the surname "Smith." Maud, their two-month-old child, is identified as "Smith, Mary," age 2/12. The census confirms that Edwin was born in "Lou," that his father was born in "N.J.," and his mother in "Mo." Grandpa's stated occupation is "Blacksmith."

Also identified in the 1880 census in the Guyon household are Thomas Blew, age twenty and single, described as a "servant," and Henry C. Smith, widowed and identified as Edwin's stepfather.

The identification of Thomas Blew as a servant seems mildly comical, and must be a characterization by the census-taker as opposed to a description provided by Grandpa Guyon. Because Thomas Blew's occupation is also listed as blacksmith, it may be that the younger man was employed as an apprentice or helper to Grandpa.[173] It is also possible, of course, that the positions were reversed or that the two were co-equals.

---

[172] *Idaho Odd Fellow* 13, no. 6 (1908, January).
[173] Legally speaking, "master-servant" is still used to describe certain employment relationships, although many consider the designation to be somewhat archaic.

How long Grandpa Guyon followed the trade of blacksmith, and what training or experience he possessed, are both uncertain. Guyon family lore is that as a result of his experience as a blacksmith, in later life he was unusually rugged and possessed uncommon physical strength.

Storekeeper and Postmaster at Pilot Rock

After blacksmithing, Grandpa Guyon followed a number of other occupations. In April 1883, he managed a branch store in Pilot Rock of Alexander and Frazier, which was purchased in that year by J. H. Sharon and Sons.[174] How long he followed that occupation is unknown, but on May 5, 1886, he was appointed postmaster at Pilot Rock,[175] a position he held for several years.

Neither a Borrower Nor a Lender Be

On December 27, 1887, Edwin signed a promissory note in the face amount of $327.77 at 8 percent interest in favor of S. H. Johnson Co. The note was cosigned by Edwin's father-in-law Madison Jones and Jacob Treurer (sp?). The note was marked "paid" on March 27, 1889. There is nothing on the note itself that indicates the borrowed funds were earmarked for a particular purpose. In all probability, the money was used to finance a business venture that included the cosigners.

The Politician

Grandpa Guyon exhibited an interest in local politics during the 1880s, beginning a trend that he would follow intermittently for the balance of his life. On March 24, 1888, a newspaper article identifies Ed. F. Guyon among those registering at the Bowman House in Pendleton, doubtless to attend the Democratic Party convention, then in full swing.[176] In the same newspaper issue he, along with M. L. Weston, was "spoken of for assessor," although in this circumstance he was identified as "Ed. F. Smith." On the same day, he received twenty-nine votes on the first ballot and "was therefore declared the nominee." His nomination was also

---

[174] J. L. Sharon, letter to the editor, *East Oregonian* (Pendleton, OR), June 29, 1948.

[175] Certificate of Appointment, 28 May 1886, by William F. Vilas (Vol. I, No. 7).

[176] *East Oregonian*, March 24, 1888, accessed August 14, 2016, http://oregonnews. uoregon.edu/lccn/sn88086023/1888-03-24/ed-1/seq-4/.

reported in the *Oregon Scout*, Union, Union County, Oregon, on March 30, 1888. The outcome of the election is unknown.

Debt Collectors

Shortly after the convention, on April 17, 1888, "Ed. F. Guyon and Dr. Wm Parkinson" (Grandpa Guyon's boyhood friend from the 1860s) jointly purchased from C. C. Powers fifteen "book a/c's," which appear to be accounts receivable. Not all the amounts of the accounts are entirely legible, but it appears that Grandpa Guyon and Dr. Parkinson paid $93.57 for accounts with a face value of $98.07, a discount of $4.50. The $93.57 represented an investment equal to at least $2,300.00 today, depending on how the difference in the present value of money compared with 1888 is calculated. The outcome of this effort at collecting money is unknown.

Indian Agent in Pendleton

In approximately May, 1889, Grandpa Guyon accepted the position of United States Indian Agent, Umatilla Agency, in Pendleton. Despite what his intentions may have been when he accepted the appointment, it lasted only about three months before the direction of his life changed drastically.

The first known written indication of his new plans is an August 23, 1889, letter of recommendation from Lee Moorhouse, another agent at the Umatilla Agency, for Grandpa Guyon, stating that the latter was leaving his job of his own free will to study medicine in the East.[177] "East" meant Ohio and the Medical Department of the University of Cincinnati.

Whether his decision to attend medical school was made on the spur of the moment or had been considered for months or years is not known with certainty. It seems somewhat incongruent that Grandpa Guyon would accept the position as Indian agent in Pendleton and then leave after occupying it for only three months. That alone may be an indicator that the decision was not the product of months of agonizing reflection over what to do with his life.

Grandpa Guyon may have applied for the government position well in advance and may have been surprised when he was hired. When offered the job, he may have felt obligated to accept it (or may even had agreed contractually to take it if offered as part of his application), even if he knew he would not hold it for long. When he resigned the position, the die was

---

[177] Lee Moorhouse, US Indian Agent, United States Indian Service, Umatilla Agency, Pendleton, Oregon, to "Whom It May Concern," 23 August 1889.

cast, and this family's life was to change dramatically because of his decision to attend medical school.[178]

The Promise of the Practice of Medicine

Guyon family oral history is silent concerning exactly *why* Grandpa Guyon made the decision to attend medical school. The French Biography suggests that it was because he was "of a studious nature and intent on

securing a good education" and adds that he had "decided to follow medicine as his life pursuit" without giving a specific reason. The Johnson Biography makes no statement on the subject other than that he graduated in 1891 "from the medical department of the University of Cincinnati."

Grandpa Guyon was very versatile and internally driven. His dalliances with a variety of occupations before he decided to attend medical school might be characterized as irresponsible by some, but his relentless quest for something better was merely the embodiment of his personal drive. It is likely that he found his pre-medical

Edwin circa 1880

school occupations less satisfying after a relatively short time and eventually decided to pursue something more intellectually challenging and stimulating as his life's work.

He was constantly engaged, not only in his occupation *du jour*, but also in extracurricular activities like running for political offices and maintaining membership in the Odd Fellows organization. He was in "full court press" mode most of his life. Whatever forces impelled him forward, they seem not to have dissipated, or even diminished, at least until he was physically unable to continue due to age-related infirmities.

---

[178] Dr. Parkinson, who was Grandpa Guyon's partner in the purchase of accounts receivable discussed above, may have influenced Grandpa Guyon's decision to attend medical school, despite Grandpa Guyon's age. As a practicing physician, Dr. Parkinson was in a unique position to convince Grandpa Guyon of the advantages of a medical education and license, as well as the application process itself.

Cincinnati Separation: The Piper Must Be Paid

The decision to study medicine was a monumental one for Edwin and his family. He was thirty-six years old in November of 1889, a time when most men were firmly installed in a profession or line of work that they would follow until retirement or the end of their lives, whichever came first. In view of the life expectancy of thirty-eight years[179] for white males in 1853, the year of Grandpa Guyon's birth, such an enterprise may appear in retrospect to have been not only ill-advised, but outright frivolous.

Edwin's daughter Maud was only nine years old in 1889, with friends and family connections in Oregon she was reluctant to leave. Margaret, only nineteen when she and Edwin married in 1879, was now twenty-nine and had those same connections to Oregon. On the other hand, Edwin's move to Cincinnati was not to be permanent, and he must have felt that the sacrifice was justified. There was every indication that after medical school his opportunities to better his own life and that of his family would increase many-fold.

Keepsakes and Tokens

On August 19, 1889, Grandpa Guyon shipped some of his belongings to Cincinnati. The date is known with certainty because of the loss in transit of "irreplaceable keepsakes and tokens" described in a claim he submitted to the railroad company the following year.[180]

The irreplaceable keepsakes and tokens were promptly characterized by the railroad as "sundries" and "HH Gds" (household goods) having a value of $320.90.[181] Edwin's anticipated stay in Cincinnati would be only two years, but the fact that he took his irreplaceable property with him instead of leaving it with Maggie seems moderately inconsistent with the idea that he intended to return home to Oregon after medical school, although that is exactly what he did.

Unaccompanied in Cincinnati?

In all likelihood, Grandpa Guyon was in Cincinnati alone, although it seems safe to say that many of his descendants have always presumed that

---

179 "Ninety Years' Progress in Life Expectancy," *Journal of Heredity* 31, no. 1 (1940): 18, accessed August 14, 2016, http://jhered.oxfordjournals.org/content/31/1/18.full.pdf.
180 E. F. Guyon to J. E. Ingersoll, Claims Agent for Or. and No. Company, 24 May 1890.
181 J. E. Ingersoll to E. F. Guyon, 11 August 1890; railroad claim form 959, 11 August 1890.

his family accompanied him. Maggie's parents lived in the Pilot Rock-Pendleton area, where she may have lived with their daughter Maud during Grandpa Guyon's absence. This would have completely avoided uprooting Maud from her friends and her schooling, and at the same time would have allowed Grandpa Guyon a level of freedom in Cincinnati for study and related activities that would have been impossible with his family there.

Exactly when Edwin left Oregon for Cincinnati is unknown, but it was after August 19, when he shipped his valuables, and before September 28, when he began attending classes. During that period, Maggie became pregnant, which further complicated matters. She could have remained in Oregon during her entire pregnancy, or she could have gone through at least part of it in Cincinnati, and then traveled back to Pendleton to give birth to her second child.

Grandpa Guyon's anticipated absence was for two years, but the rigors of that period were expected to be a serious challenge, both intellectually and emotionally. The price to be paid for the flexibility to study medicine was isolation from his family, although the effects of that separation were certainly minimized by correspondence. Whether there were also personal visits is unknown.

It seems safe to assume that it was a financial sacrifice to incur the expense of medical school and travel to Ohio and that there was little extra money. The French Biography affirms that Grandpa Guyon was self-supporting, which seems consistent with his work ethic.

18th and 19th-Century Medical Education

By 1889, when Grandpa matriculated at the University of Cincinnati, medical education in America had within the previous century undergone unprecedented changes in theory, accessibility, and public perception, to name but a few, although vestiges of the remote and recent past remained. To more fully understand and appreciate Dr. Guyon's place in and contribution to the medical profession as a whole, I offer the following brief review of medical education and practice in the 18th and 19th centuries.

Heroic Medicine, an Ancient Tradition

The period from colonial times forward until approximately 1850 is known as the Age of Heroic Medicine, a European tradition that contemplated treatments with immediate effect. Practices included the aggressive use of venesection (bloodletting), the use of calomel to induce intestinal purging, prescribing tartar emetic to cause vomiting, the use of diaphoretics to cause profuse sweating, and causing blistering, all as ways to rid the human body of impurities. Bloodletting in the 1760s and 1770s was generally reserved for cases of pleurisy and rheumatism; however, its popularity increased over the next half-century and by 1810 the practice was so widespread that virtually every malady called for massive venesection, often to the point of the patient's unconsciousness.[182]

Heroic medicine can be better understood against the backdrop of medieval medicine, which inherited its knowledge from antiquity and then bequeathed it to its more modern heirs. The belief that the visible world consisted of earth, air, water, and fire had a parallel belief that the human body had four humors (fluids): black bile, blood, phlegm, and yellow bile. Ideally, the four humors were in balance; sickness was the result of imbalance of one or more of the humors. The removal of blood from the body was believed to restore balance. Mercifully, the practice is extinct, but only since the mid-19th century.

Preceptors and Apprentices

Prior to 1700, the practice of medicine was considered to be a trade, like blacksmithing, coopering, or printing. Those wishing to become physicians first became apprentices to their masters, also called preceptors, for terms of five to seven years.[183] Ideally, the apprentice would learn the doctor trade by observing his master with patients and "reading medicine" from medical books in his master's library.

All too often, the system broke down. Preceptors and their apprentices were in contractual, non-standardized relationships, unsupervised by any authority outside the parties themselves. The transmission of vital medical information and experience from preceptor to apprentice ebbed and flowed at the pleasure of, and subject to the whims and idiosyncrasies of, both the preceptor and his apprentice. Inevitably, the apprentice either blossomed or wilted as the direct result of the dedication, or lack thereof, of his master as well as his own.

Because the preceptor-physician was in all likelihood himself a product of the apprenticeship system, he may have had meager knowledge to impart at best. He may have had a very limited library, if he had one at all, to supplement his inadequacies. In such situations, the apprentice could—and

---

[182] Benjamin Rush, *Medical Inquiries and Observations*, 3rd ed. (Philadelphia: 1809), quoted in Martin Kaufman, *American Medical Education: The Formative Years, 1765-1910* (Westport, CT: Greenwood Press, 1978), 57.

[183] Kaufman, *American Medical Education*, 7.

often did—become little more than his master's body servant, charged with caring for his master's horse, sweeping out his office, and collecting his fees.

Some modicum of experience and knowledge would inevitably pass from the preceptor to the apprentice, but each succeeding apprentice would in all probability never recover all the knowledge of his preceptor, no matter how limited to begin with. The inadequacies of the players in the drama would increase as they were perpetuated from one generation of physicians to the next.

Exceptional Preceptors and Exceptional Apprentices

Despite its obvious failings, the apprenticeship system in all fairness could and did produce very positive results, particularly where the physician-preceptor was educated in a European institution, possessed a meaningful medical library, and had more than a passing interest in raising the standards of the practice of medicine.[184]

The apprenticeship of Benjamin Rush, a signatory to the Declaration of Independence, merits special attention. Rush began his medical education in February, 1761, under the tutelage of John Redman, whose medical practice was the most extensive of any physician in Philadelphia. Redman at any one time never had more than two apprentices,[185] which ensured that he could keep his charges constantly engaged in the process of learning the theory and practice of medicine. In the case of Rush, during his apprenticeship of more than five years, he was absent from his work only eleven days.[186] Rush was an avid student who reported:

> I read in the intervals of business and at late and early hours all the books in medicine that were put into my hands by my master or that I could borrow from other students of medicine in the city. I studied Dr. Boerhaave's lectures upon physiology and pathology with the closest attention, and abridged a considerable part of Van Swieten's commentaries upon his practical aphorisms. I kept a common place book in which I recorded everything that I

[184] Ibid.
[185] Kaufman, *American Medical Education*, 9.
[186] Ibid.

thought curious or valuable in my reading and in my master's practice.[187]

Those trained at the hands of a less dedicated preceptor often sought to supplement their apprenticeships by attending European universities. Before 1750, the University of Leyden (also spelled Leiden) was popular with American students, in no small part because of access to the great medical clinician Herman Boerhaave. After 1750, the University of Edinburgh, with its famous faculty members William Cullen and Alexander Monro, became much more popular with American students. Benjamin Rush himself studied medicine at Edinburgh in 1766–1768, presumably to supplement his five-year apprenticeship with John Redman.[188] Prior to 1776 only 41 American students had attended Edinburgh; by 1812, no less than 139 had graduated.[189]

The number of those whose medical training approximated that of Benjamin Rush[190] under the preceptorship of John Redman and who supplemented their apprenticeship experience by attending European universities was dismally small. Of the more than 3,000 physicians practicing medicine in America between 1607 and 1776, less than 400 were products of medical schools.[191] The grim reality was that the great majority of America's physicians in the mid-18th century were products of the apprenticeship system.

A Dangerous Minority of 18th-Century Physicians

Due to a number of factors, not the least of which was a lack of systematic regulation or control over the practice of medicine, there was in 18th century America a group of individuals who, for one reason or another, had simply decided, without education or training, to become practicing physicians. In the latter group, one such physician was described by Dr. Alexander Hamilton in 1744:

> [The man] had been a shoemaker in town and was a notable fellow at his trade, but happening two years agoe

---

187 Quoted in Kaufman, *American Medical Education*, 9.
188 "Heroic Medicine," Wikipedia, accessed August 14, 2016, http://en.wikipedia.org/wiki/Heroic_medicine.
189 Kaufman, *American Medical Education*, 9.
190 As an aside, it is interesting to note that Benjamin Rush was a strong advocate of heroic medicine, including venesection.
191 Kaufman, *American Medical Education*, 10.

to cure an old woman of a pestilent mortall disease, he thereby acquired the character of a physitian, was applied to from all quarters, and finding the practice of physick a more profitable business than cobling, he laid aside his awls and leather, got himself some gallipots,[192] and instead of cobling of soals, fell to cobling of human bodies.[193]

Such at-will transformations from other vocations into physicians may not have been atypical, if colonial newspapers can be trusted. The *Independent Reflector*, a New York City journal, printed in 1753 that these pretenders were "licensed assassins," "pests of society," and "human butchers" and called for vengeance upon them.[194] In 1766 the *New-York Mercury*, in an article reporting abuses of so-called physicians, alleged that they stole £20,000 from "the purses of the Publick, under the specious pretense of acting the physician, [which was] an enormous sum to murder mankind."[195]

A letter to the editor of the *Boston Gazette*, also in 1766, and a 1785 letter to the editor of the *Maryland Journal and Baltimore Advertiser* both expressed dismay at the lack of qualifications of those plying the medical trade, blaming the situation on a lack of medical education and a lack of regulation. Both inadequacies, the letters urged, could be remedied by a medical license law that would allow a group of competent physicians to examine those wishing to join their ranks.[196]

America Attracts European Physicians

By 1700, colonial America had transformed itself from a collection of immigrants primarily concerned with survival to a prosperous society that offered financial and other opportunities and incentives to European-educated physicians.[197] As a result, such physicians began to collect in the colonies. One study of physicians who had settled in Virginia in the 18th century revealed that twenty-three came from Scotland, eleven from England, four from France, two from Switzerland, one from Portugal, one

---

192 A small, usually ceramic, vessel used for ointments and other medicaments.
193 Kaufman, *American Medical Education*, 11.
194 Ibid.
195 Ibid.
196 Ibid., 13.
197 Ibid., 8.

from Germany, and one from Italy.[198] Many other physicians with roots in Europe came to other American colonies.

Among transplanted Europeans were physicians destined to become the most eminent members of the colonial medical profession, simply because they were the only university-educated physicians in America. John Kearsley settled in Pennsylvania and became the preceptor of some of Philadelphia's most prominent physicians, including William Shippen and John Bard, whose sons were instrumental in the founding of American's first two medical schools. Kearsley was also the preceptor of John Redman, who in turn became preceptor to John Morgan, Benjamin Rush, and Caspar Wistar, all of whom became notable physicians in their own right and were professors in the first medical school in America.

American Medical Schools Appear

In the mid-1700s, there were no medical schools in America. Any aspiring physician who refused to accept anything less than a medical school diploma was forced to obtain it in Europe's recognized centers of medical learning, although those conditions would soon change. The first medical college in what was to become the United States opened its doors on November 14, 1765, as a branch of the College of Philadelphia, later the University of Philadelphia.[199] The second, King's College Medical School, opened in New York City on November 2, 1767,[200] and the third, Harvard Medical School, was established on November 22, 1782.[201] Dartmouth College was the fourth in 1797, followed by the fifth, Transylvania University in Kentucky, in 1800.[202]

Regulation of the Profession

The medical profession was barely regulated at all until well into the 19th century. There were attempts by well-meaning, learned, and skilled physicians to raise the competency bar in early years, but they were not overly successful. A medical society was founded in Boston as early as 1835 and others in Connecticut and New Jersey in 1766.[203]

---

[198] Ibid.
[199] Ibid., 20.
[200] Ibid., 23.
[201] Ibid., 25.
[202] Ibid., 27.
[203] Ibid., 12.

The first law regulating the practice of medicine in America was passed in 1760.[204] Even though it was effective only in New York City, its preamble suggests a significant level of recognition and understanding of the problem of medical incompetency in general, and it was one of the first public attempts to define the problem and take action to correct it legislatively:

> Whereas many ignorant and unskillful persons in Physic and Surgery, in order to gain a subsistence, do take upon themselves to administer physic, and to practice surgery, in the city of New York, to the endangering the lives and limbs of their patients, and many poor and ignorant people inhabiting the said city, who have been persuaded to become their patients, have been great sufferers thereby; – for preventing such abuses in the future.[205]

The law itself required physicians admitted to practice to first undergo an examination by His Majesty's Council and physicians named to assist them, and provided the pattern for a similar law passed in New Jersey in 1772.[206]

It was not until the 1870s and 1880s that state licensing laws began to be passed, but even then the laws were generally inadequate. Lack of uniformity allowed unqualified practitioners to move from a regulated state to a non-regulated one or to one whose requirements were less stringent. Some states created multiple medical boards, allowing practitioners to be disqualified by one and qualified by another. Generally, such laws licensed every medical school graduate, regardless of competence.[207]

There were at least two reasons why medical license legislation was so painfully slow in developing. First was the proliferation of American medical schools. There were 90 medical schools in the United States in 1880, most of them inferior.[208] Ten years later, there were 116, and by 1900 there were 151.[209] Six short years later, there were 161.[210] The

---

[204] Ibid., 13.
[205] Ibid.
[206] Ibid.
[207] Ibid., 121.
[208] Ibid., 120.
[209] Ibid.
[210] Ibid.

inevitable results of this growth were increased competition among medical schools for students, the decline of entry and retention standards to attract them, and diminished graduation requirements,[211] all of which created a natural resistance to regulations that might disqualify eventual practitioners in large numbers.

Second was the harsh reality that physicians, particularly those starting in practice and in rural areas, had a difficult time making a living by practicing medicine.[212] Inability to support oneself in and of itself contributed to a decline of the profession in the public eye. It was easier to respect a farmer who provided for his family by tilling the soil than a physician who tilled the soil as a sideline because his profession would not support him.[213] Legislation imposing additional licensing requirements was perceived as making a difficult economic situation even worse.

The Medical Student

Edwin's attendance at the Medical Department of the University of Cincinnati began on September 28, 1889,[214] as a member of the junior

class. The date coincides generally with the proliferation of new medical schools in America from about 1880 to 1900, although the medical school at the University of Cincinnati itself was founded in 1819. It is not known if the competition among medical schools to attract students was a factor in Grandpa Guyon's decision to attend. His attendance at a long-established medical school suggests it was not.

Little is known of Edwin's sojourn in Cincinnati. There is no known correspondence that might reveal his circumstances, and his writings from later life provide no insights into his experiences. We learn from a city directory of the period that "Guyon Edward F. medical student" lived at the address of 508 West Seventh

Edwin circa 1890

---

211 Ibid.
212 Ibid., 63.
213 Ibid.
214 The French Biography statement that he began his medical education in 1879 is in error.

Street in Cincinnati in 1890.[215] No other persons with the last name of Guyon are identified as living with him at that address, or anywhere else in Cincinnati, suggesting that he was without his family, at least in 1890. The city directories for Cincinnati by the same publisher for 1889 and 1891 do not identify him. Neither does the United States Census of 1890 provide any information concerning Grandpa Guyon in Cincinnati or Maggie in Oregon.[216]

A diverse collection of people living at the West Seventh Street address in 1890, including an engineer, two widows, a machinist, a clerk, a wood engraver, and a teacher of elocution, suggests that the address was a tenement or apartment building, or a residence converted into apartments. The boardinghouse accommodations provided in 1890 disappeared in the intervening years. The area of 508 Seventh Street in modern Cincinnati contains only streets and freeways.

Medical School, First Semester

The Winter Session of the Medical Department began in September, 1889, and extended through March 1, 1890. A publicized notice advised the students that

> Clinical Instruction will be given in the Cincinnati Hospital and in the Dispensary of the College, where the student will have abundant opportunity of familiarizing himself with the various phenomena of disease and perfecting himself in the use of instruments necessary in medical investigation. . . . Practical Instruction in Anatomy, Physiology, and Chemistry will be given in Laboratories fitted up for the purpose, under the direction of thoroughly competent teachers.[217]

---

[215] *Williams' Cincinnati Directory* (Cincinnati, OH: Cincinnati Directory Office, 1890), 504.
[216] The original population schedules of the 1890 census were badly damaged by a fire in the Department of Commerce in 1921, leaving less than 1 percent of the schedules extant, consisting of 6,160 names. Although the surviving records included residents of Hamilton County, Ohio, in which Cincinnati is located, those records do not reflect any information concerning Grandpa Guyon.
[217] *Cincinnati Lancet-Clinic* 18 (1889, Jan-June): 660.

An impressive array of faculty members, lecturers, and demonstrators was on hand to present the actual lectures for the Winter Session.[218] The Spring Session of 1890 was advertised to begin April 1 and continue for six weeks.[219] During that period, the students were notified that

> Two lectures will be delivered each day by members of the Faculty and Lecturers. In addition to topics usually considered will be Hygiene, Bacteriology, and New Remedies. . . . The numerous Clinics and the College will be conducted throughout the session, and the Dissecting Rooms and laboratories will be open. . . . In accordance with the established custom of this College, students will receive bedside instruction from members of the Faculty connected with Cincinnati, St. Mary's and the Children's Hospitals. Clinical lectures and demonstrations in Morbid Anatomy will be given daily at the Cincinnati Hospital.

The faculty, lecturers, and demonstrators for the Spring Session of 1890 and the courses they taught were identical to those advertised during the Winter Session of 1889. This suggests that the students had a choice when to take any specific course. The fact that the Winter Session of 1889–1890 was six *months* long, compared with the Spring Session of 1890 at six

---

[218] **Faculty**: John A. Murphy, A.M., M.D., Emeritus Professor of Principles and Practice of Medicine; Wm. H. Taylor, M.D., Dean, Professor of Obstetrics and Clinical Midwifery; J. C. Mackenzie, M.D., Secretary and Treasurer, Professor of Principles and Practice of Medicine and Clinical Medicine; Byron Stanton. M.D., Professor of Diseases of Women and Children; Dan. Millikin, M.D., Professor of Materia Medics and Therapeutics; N. P. Dandridge, A.M., M.D., Registrar, Professor of Practice of Surgery and Clinical Surgery; Joseph Eichberg, M.D., Professor of Physiology and Hygiene, and Clinical Medicine; F. W. Langdon, M.D., Professor of Anatomy; E. W. Walker, M.D., Professor of Principles and Surgery and General Pathology; Robert Sattler, M.D., Professor of Ophthalmology, Aural Surgery and Clinical Ophthalmology; Karl Langenbeck, Professor of Chemistry and Toxicology, and Medical Jurisprudence; and Charles E. Caldwell, M.D., Adjunct Professor of Anatomy and Clinical Surgery. **Lecturers and Demonstrators**: Eric. E. Sattler, M.D., Clinical Lecturer on Diseases of the Throat; A. Thompson, M.D., Clinical Lecturer on Diseases of the Throat; K. B. Sayres, M.D., Demonstrator of Anatomy; F. O. Marsh, M.D., Demonstrator of Histology; C. R. Holmes, M.D., Clinical Lecturer on Diseases of the Eye and Ear; O. P. Holt, M.D., Demonstrator of Pathological Histology; J. C. Oliver, M.D., Clinical Lecturer on Diseases of Children; R. B. Hall, M.D., Clinical Lecturer on Gynecology; B. M. Ricketts, M.D., Clinical Lecturer on Plastic Surgery; Geo. H. Goode, M.D., Clinical Assistant in Ophthalmology and Otology; W. L. Mussey, M.D., Assistant Demonstrator of Anatomy and Clinical Lectures on Dermatology; and Karl Langenbeck, Demonstrator of Chemistry.
[219] *Cincinnati Lancet-Clinic* 24, no. 26 (1890, January 28): xii.

weeks long, must have been an important consideration to both professors and students.

With the exception of the course in clinical gynecology discussed below, it is not known what courses Grandpa Guyon attended in medical school. A few of his surviving personal papers from that era provide some small indication of his life as a student. Three very small pieces of paper, all in his handwriting (the largest is approximately 8" x 1 5/8" and the two others roughly 1 5/8" x 3")[220] appear to be study outlines and cover subjects like intestinal parasites and diseases of the mouth. Why these notes were kept by Dr. Guyon after medical school is unknown.

In Grandpa's personal effects after his death was a small book entitled *Chemical Experiments for Medical Students*.[221] The book's preface states as one of its objects "the practical teaching of the general principles of inorganic chemistry, toxicology, and physiological chemistry to medical students." Along with many of Grandpa Guyon's notes in the margins and on blank pages, there were several loose pages of notes on separate pieces of paper. The book also bears the handwritten inscription "E. F. Guyon, Med. College of Ohio, Sept 15th, 1889," indicating the book was either a textbook or supplement to a course or courses he took during his first term as a medical student.

Medical School Graduation

Thursday, March 5, 1891, marked the newly minted Dr. Guyon's graduation from medical school as one of a class of ninety-four students from many different locations and walks of life. According to the local newspaper,

> The [graduation] exercises will open with music, followed by prayer by Rev. R. A. Gibson and a few remarks by W. W. Seely, the Dean. Hon. Aaron F. Perry, President of the Board of Trustees, will deliver an address and award the diplomas. Gems from Flotow's "Martha" will follow, when the prizes will be awarded. A cornet solo will then be rendered by Herman Hellstedt, jr., followed by the

---

[220] The writing in these notes is remarkably small. One would think they were written with a nib the size of a human hair. Although they can be easily seen through a jeweler's loupe, one is hard-pressed to discern them with the naked eye.

[221] W. S. Christopher, *Chemical Experiments for Medical Students* (Cincinnati, OH: Robert Clarke, 1888).

valedictory address by Prof. James T. Whittaker. The conclusion will be a charivari of collect songs. The Cincinnati Grand Orchestra will furnish the music.[222]

The next day, March 6, 1891, the same paper recounted the proceedings previewed on March 5, and then described what to the audience was one of the most interesting features of the evening. This was the

ANNOUNCEMENT OF THE PRIZES,
Which was made by Prof. James G. Hyndman, Secretary of the Faculty. These were as follows:

. . .

Prof. Reamy's prize for best examination in clinical gynecology, gold medal, awarded to Dr. Edwin F. Guyon, Pendleton, Oregon.[223]

The silver-dollar-size gold medallion, preserved in Dr. Guyon's personal effects, is engraved with the following:

On the obverse: Awarded to Edwin F. Guyon by Prof. Thad A. Reamy, March 5th, 1891.
On the reverse: Medical College of Ohio, Best paper in final examination, clinical gynecology.

The Inimitable Professor Reamy

Thaddeus Ashbury Reamy, MD, LLD (1829–1907), was a professor of obstetrics, gynecology, and pediatrics at the Medical College of Ohio, Cincinnati, beginning in 1871. Recognized as a pioneer in obstetrics, in 1874 he established, in Cincinnati, the first women's hospital west of the Allegheny Mountains, later absorbed by Bethesda Hospital. In 1881, he was elected president of the Academy of Medicine of Cincinnati. As a result of his efforts, the first combined residency of obstetrics and gynecology was established in Cincinnati, as well as the first obstetric clinic in the United States.[224]

---

222 *Cincinnati Enquirer*, March 5, 1891, p. 4.
223 *Cincinnati Enquirer*, March 6, 1891, p. 4.
224 University of Cincinnati Libraries, accessed June 20, 2015. http://www.libraries.uc.edu/list/

Proficiencies of the New Dr. Guyon

It has been rumored in the Guyon family that Edwin was a brilliant medical student who graduated second in his class. I have been unable to verify his actual class standing, although his performance under Professor Reamy is at least one indicator that he was an excellent student. Certainly, Dr. Guyon had an extraordinary writing ability that factored into winning Professor Reamy's gold medal. That demonstrated writing ability became more important as time went on.

By the early 20th century Dr. Guyon had acquired and learned to use a Royal typewriter for much of his professional, fraternal, and personal correspondence, but he intermittently wrote in cursive. Regardless of the mode he used, his style was always clear and concise. In the case of his handwritten missives and other documents, his exceptionally attractive penmanship was a bonus to the reader.

To attempt to come to some overall conclusion about the extent and quality of Dr. Guyon's medical education based on dates of attendance, courses followed, or the name and reputation of his school—or even Doc's performance as a medical student—would be largely speculative. Medical school was merely the gateway to his career as a physician and surgeon. As we shall see in the following chapters, in his medical practice Dr. Guyon was esteemed among his colleagues and the public at large and valued and admired by his patients. He worked toward, supported, and served on medical societies to ensure that only competent physicians were allowed to practice medicine. He crafted legislation designed to establish minimum standards for medical licensure. Reportedly, he acquired and maintained a significant personal medical library, which allowed him to continue his medical education perpetually. Such facts and others, established over a period of more than forty years after his graduation, are surely a better measure of the man than any experience he may have had in medical school.

Postgraduate Medical Education

The French Biography also states that Dr. Guyon "took a year of postgraduate work at the same institution." It was not uncommon for 19th-century medical schools to offer, in addition to the standard curriculum of classroom lectures on the theory of various subjects, courses of a clinical

---

history/archives.html.

or practical nature. The practical classes were not, as a rule, mandatory, but many students took advantage of them so as to acquire the highest degree of practical knowledge possible. It is highly probable that Dr. Guyon attended postgraduate courses while in Cincinnati as the French Biography states, and it is no less likely that those courses included surgery, a subject seemingly impossible to learn in the abstract. Dr. Guyon performed surgeries on various occasions in his medical practice, and it seems highly unlikely that he learned surgery by practicing on patients.

Edwin circa 1890

Guyon family oral tradition holds that Dr. Guyon performed surgery only as a last resort, a reluctance based upon his overall philosophy that the least invasive treatment would usually produce the best outcome, and not upon any inability on his part to operate on patients when necessary. His business records consistently reflect operations performed during the course of his long professional life in Montpelier; the fact they do not appear often is supportive of his reluctance to expose the patient to greater risk where other, less dangerous, alternatives were available.

Part III

—

Scalpels

Chapter 7.

THE FLEDGLING PHYSICIAN TAKES FLIGHT

circa 1892–1900

Tout passe, tout casse, tout lasse.
— French proverb[225]

This chapter discusses Dr. Guyon's medical practice and career beginning in Pendleton in early 1892; his eventual migration to Montpelier, Idaho, for health reasons; and his activities there until the beginning of the 20th century.

Dr. Guyon's Medical Practice Opens in Oregon

On January 1, 1892, approximately ten months after Dr. Guyon's graduation from medical school, Pendleton's local newspaper, the *East Oregonian*, carried the following advertisement:

E.F.GUYON, M.D. OVER GOULD & Wurzweiler's drug store.

From the outset, Dr. Guyon's medical practice appears to have been as diversified as his life prior to medical school. On February 27, 1893, he was appointed as the examining surgeon for the Department of the Interior in Pendleton[226] upon the recommendation of Senator J. N. Dolph.[227] That appointment likely supplemented, but did not interfere with, his private practice.

---

[225] "Everything passes, everything perishes, everything palls." (Approximate pronunciation: "too pass, too cass, too lass.") A more literal translation is "everything passes, everything breaks, everything wearies," but this would interfere with the alliteration the translator clearly tried to preserve. A simpler but decidedly less literary and poetic version is "everything is in a state of entropy."

[226] Department of the Interior, Bureau of Pensions, to E. F. Guyon, 27 February 1893.

[227] Andrew Davidson, Acting Commissioner of Department of the Interior, Bureau of Pensions, to U. S. Senator J. N. Dolph, 15 February 1893.

The *Dalles Daily Chronicle* reported on June 16, 1893, that Hank C. Vaughan underwent an operation to save his life, done "with care and skill by Dr. McKenzie, assisted by Drs. Smith and Guyon, of this city."[228] Less than a month later, the same newspaper reported a serious railroad accident involving Captain N. B. Humphrey, who slipped under a train while it was preparing to stop at the station and was dragged about fifty feet. According to the account, "he was brought to Pendleton and Dr. C. J. Smith, assisted by Drs. Guyon, Martin Pelkington and Vincent, amputated the injured limb about four inches above the ankle."[229]

Later that same year, on December 11, 1893, Dr. Guyon was appointed for a temporary period of six months as physician at the Fort Hall Agency near Pocatello, Idaho, at an annual salary of $1,200.[230] How much time was required of him at the Fort Hall Agency is unknown. The distance from Pendleton to Pocatello exceeds 350 miles, and it seems unusual that Dr. Guyon would have accepted such a position—unless he was planning a move further east.

From Pendleton to Montpelier

Within the next three years, Dr. Guyon made the decision to relocate to southeast Idaho. According to the French Biography, he wrapped up his Oregon business on February 28, 1896, to begin his new practice in Montpelier.[231] Why he moved there is explained in the Johnson Biography:

> Dr. Guyon began the practice of medicine in Pendleton City, Oregon, in 1891,[232]and continued it there successfully for five years, when his health began to fail and he sought a higher altitude and a dryer atmosphere at Montpelier. The colder climate agreed with him, and he regained his health, and by the time he had done so he had built up a large and

---

228 *Dalles (OR) Daily Chronicle*, June 16, 1893. Dr. C. J. Smith and Dr. Guyon were associated in the practice of medicine in Pendleton during virtually the entire four years Dr. Guyon spent there, according to a report in the *East Oregonian*, October 23, 1909, p. 8.

229 *Dalles (OR) Daily Chronicle*, July 7, 1893.

230 Department of the Interior, Office of Indian Affairs, to E. F. Guyon, 11 December 1893.

231 French, *History of Idaho*, 1256.

232 This may be additional support for the notion that Dr. Guyon started his medical practice soon after graduation from medical school and may weigh against the idea that he did postgraduate work, although of course the actual date he started his practice in Oregon is not provided by this statement.

rapidly growing practice, in which he has been successful professionally as well as financially.

The statements in the Johnson Biography ring true. It seems unlikely that Dr. Guyon would have moved his family and his medical practice for any reason less important than his health. He had already invested four to five years in Pendleton that had reportedly produced professional and financial rewards. The Pilot Rock and Pendleton area was his home and he was well known, facts which likely account for his professional and financial success and the promise of a bright future there.

By the mid-1890s Dr. Guyon's reputation had already spread far and wide from Pendleton. During his transition to his new home in Montpelier, he visited his old friend Dr. Parkinson in Logan, Utah, where he was described in the local paper as "one of the best known physicians in the west."[233]

Dr. Guyon Anticipates a Bright Future in Montpelier

On March 7, 1896, the *Montpelier Examiner* reported:

> Dr. E. F. Guyon, of Pendleton, Oregon, was looking over our city this week with a view of locating. The doctor is secretary of the Oregon Medical association and is known all over the Webfoot state. For several months past he has been unable to attend to his practice owing to ill health, and his trip here is for a twofold purpose, seeking health and a location. He has been looking up Montpelier's possibilities, and is astonished that so large and rich a county is back of so small a town. No doubt he will locate here permanently.[234]

Dr. Guyon's positive outlook in general was also mentioned:

> [Dr. Guyon] believes like many of his fellow citizens that Idaho has the brightest future of any state of the Union. He bases this belief on the facts that there are vast mineral deposits here yet undeveloped; thousands of acres of arid land of phenomenal fertility when water is provided; a wealth of the most beautiful scenery to be found in the

---

[233] "Local News," *Utah Journal* (Logan), February 29, 1896.
[234] "Additional Local," *Montpelier (ID) Examiner*, March 7, 1896, p. 4.

world; and those amenities of climate that made it the most healthful spot to be found anywhere.[235]

A week later the following article appeared in the same newspaper:

> Dr. E. F. Guyon has concluded to locate with us. He comes well recommended, and no doubt will build up a good practice here. The Doctor can be found at Riter Bros. Drug Store. See his card in another column.[236]

Dr. Guyon's business card, printed in the newspaper along with those of other professionals, announced him as a Physician and Surgeon. The newspaper on the same page revealed his location in "a handsome office in the Riter Bros. Drug Co. Block."[237]

A New Doctor in Montpelier

Doc Guyon, as he was to be known, commenced his medical practice in Montpelier on March 3, 1896,[238] at the age of forty-two. The city of Montpelier itself was only thirty-two years old at the time, having been settled by Mormon pioneers in 1864.

Exactly why Dr. Guyon chose to relocate specifically in Montpelier as opposed to other places with similar health benefits is debatable, but Montpelier offered conditions that may well have been irresistible to him from the standpoint of his health.

Always the largest community in Bear Lake County, Montpelier is located in the Bear Lake Valley at an altitude of 5,942 feet above sea level. The air is thin, dry, and clear, and the cool nights during the summer are near perfect for sleeping. The area is described as semi-arid in the grand scope of climates. Natives joke that there are only two seasons: summer and winter. Anyone who has lived through a winter or two in Montpelier will scratch his or her head at the prospect that someone might want to move to Montpelier for the climate.

Fierce blizzards known as "Bear Lakers" are not uncommon historically, and most longtime residents remember extended periods of

---

[235] *Montpelier (ID) Examiner*, March 7, 1896, p. 4.
[236] "Local Happenings," *Montpelier (ID) Examiner*, March 14, 1896, p. 1.
[237] "Professional Cards," *Montpelier (ID) Examiner*, March 14, 1896, p. 4; "Additional Local," *Montpelier (ID) Examiner*, March 28, 1896, p. 4.
[238] French, *History of Idaho*, 1256.

time when temperatures dipped to twenty degrees below zero or even lower after dark and did not get significantly higher even during the days.

But those are winters. Summers in Montpelier are generally very agreeable. Even on an unusually hot day, a person can escape the heat of the burning sun by simply finding shade. As nice as summers are, many people who have experienced both seasons will admit that it is a close question whether it is worth it to brave the winters to be able to experience them.

Mormons and Gentiles

Health benefits aside, Montpelier was arguably an unusual choice for Dr. Guyon for other reasons. Originally called Clover Creek by its Mormon founders and for a short time later on called Belmont,[239] the city was later

named Montpelier by Brigham Young himself, reportedly because the area reminded him of his native state of Vermont.

The challenges of a Methodist "gentile"[240] living and raising a family in a Mormon community can be daunting. In Dr. Guyon's era, perhaps the biggest issue to test non-Mormons was tolerance of polygamy. The Mormon Church eschewed the practice publicly in 1890, just six years before Dr. Guyon's arrival in Montpelier, but there were vestiges of it lingering when he arrived. Adherents to the principle of polygamy who had already established multiple families could hardly be expected

Dr. Guyon circa 1890

to abandon these relationships or the children produced by them because of a statement over the pulpit or the stroke of a pen in Salt Lake City, headquarters of the Mormon Church. The level of Dr. Guyon's knowledge of the doctrinal underpinnings of plural marriage or of its residual effects after 1890 is unknown. In all probability he educated himself and became at least conversant with both. Dr. Guyon did not publicly voice any known

---

[239] Jens P. Wilde, *Treasured Tidbits of Time: An Informal History of Bear Lake Valley* (Providence, UT: Watkins and Sons, 1977), 1:34.

[240] The term *gentile* was a convenient way for members of the Mormon Church to differentiate members from non-members. The popularity of the word has diminished over time. Although some may argue differently, the word was probably never meant to be a term of derision.

intolerance for Mormon beliefs or practices, with which he probably disagreed.[241] On one occasion he actively aided at least one person to avoid arrest by federal marshals for the practice,[242] but more about that later.

A likely close second to polygamy on the list of peculiar Mormon beliefs encountered by Doc Guyon was the Word of Wisdom, a revelation that enjoined members of the church from using "strong drink, tobacco, and hot drinks." The proscription included tobacco in all its forms, coffee, tea, and alcoholic beverages. In a time when the use of alcohol, tobacco, tea, and coffee was almost universal among the general populace, the influence of this tenet must have been at least inconvenient and annoying, if not maddeningly frustrating.

Doc Guyon's office and home were on the 2nd floor of this building in Montpelier at the intersection of 4th and Washington Streets

Mormons generally expected their gentile neighbors to live and let live when it came to the practice of polygamy, but they were largely unwilling to compromise on alcohol, tobacco, tea, and coffee, which they considered to be vices. To protect themselves and their children from temptations to use these proscribed substances, the Mormons' typical response was to make them unavailable to everyone, regardless of religious affiliation. Montpelier was no exception. For a time prior to 1891, the town had a fence dividing "uptown" Mormons from "downtown" gentiles. This fence stretched north-south along Eighth Street, with a gate on Main Street that could be closed and locked at night.[243] There were no saloons or other questionable establishments uptown, with only one possible exception.[244] Such dens of iniquity were relegated to downtown. The fence

---

241 The French Biography describes Dr. Guyon as "a man of enlarged sympathies" and "broad and liberal" in his religious views, which may account for his ability to tolerate, if not embrace, Mormon beliefs and practices.

242 E. F. Guyon to Maud Brown, 9 March 1925.

243 "Montpelier, Idaho Virtual Travel," UntraveledRoad, accessed August 15, 2016, http://idaho.untraveledroad.com/BearLake/Montpelier.htm.

244 A. McKay Rich, *The History of Montpelier, Idaho from 1864 to 1925* (Montpelier, ID: Bear Lake Publishing, 2003), 59.

was designed to prevent uptowners from mingling nocturnally with downtowners and their vices.

Doc Guyon smoked cigarettes until he gave up the habit in October, 1919.[245] There is no known credible evidence that he habitually used alcohol, at least to excess, but he certainly drank coffee. His non-Mormon in-laws, colleagues, and friends, unburdened by the inconvenience of the Word of Wisdom, perhaps tipped a bottle of spirits now and then.

It is unlikely that Dr. Guyon's feelings concerning Mormon idiosyncrasies occupied a prominent position in his decision to come to Montpelier and remain. Between the founding of Montpelier in 1864 and his arrival there thirty-two years later, the railroad had come to town in 1882, bringing with it numerous workers and their families, all of whom were potential patients. Most of these immigrants to Montpelier were gentiles and probably had never even heard of the Mormon Church, much less wanted to be influenced by its beliefs.

It is highly probable that by Dr. Guyon's arrival in Montpelier in early 1896, gentiles were in the majority by at least two to one. Montpelier's population in 1870 was a mere 120 souls, certainly mostly Mormons. By 1890 its population had increased almost tenfold to 1,174. The increase in population over those two decades was likely due primarily to gentiles who came to Montpelier to work on the railroad after 1882.

This curious mixture of Mormons and non-Mormons over time created a unique blend of relationships and beliefs that were initially separate. Inevitably, Mormons married into non-Mormon families, as is the case with my father, Doc Guyon's son Wendell, and my mother LaJune Mourtsen, whose Mormon roots were as deep as it was possible to grow.[246]

Beliefs on both sides of the religious equation waxed and waned according to the strengths and convictions of their adherents, and the tension created by these relationships and alliances is one of the most charming aspects of Montpelier even today. Neither was the phenomenon in the Guyon family limited to Montpelier, as the marriage of Doc Guyon's oldest son Edwin Fenimore to Norma Cluff, a Mormon girl from the Driggs-Victor area of Idaho, attests. After 150 years, strands of

---

245 E. F. Guyon to Maud Brown, 8 April 1921.
246 LaJune Mourtsen's great-grandparents Samuel Allen Wilcox and Martha Parker Wilcox were converted to Mormonism in Upper Canada (the predecessor of modern Ontario) and traveled 1,500 miles by wagon to join the Mormons gathering in Commerce, Illinois before its name was changed to Nauvoo. One of their many children, Phebe Rozeltha, married John Henry Berrey, whose daughter Martha Elizabeth married Danish immigrant Peter Christian Mourtsen, LaJune's father.

Mormonism and "non-Mormonism" in Montpelier and the Guyon family remain woven together, all distinct in their own ways.

The Oregon Short Line Railway

An important consideration for Doc Guyon was the accessibility of the outside world from Montpelier. His active involvement in a variety of professional and fraternal activities required extensive travel; isolation was not a viable option. Travel from Montpelier was made possible by the Oregon Short Line Railway ("OSL"), which arrived in Montpelier on August 5, 1882,[247] about fourteen years prior to Dr. Guyon's arrival. The OSL stretched from Granger, Wyoming, where the main line of the Union Pacific was accessible, to Huntington, Oregon, and was envisioned to provide railroad service to all of Idaho. Along the way west, the OSL also provided access to the Union Pacific main line at McCammon, Idaho.

In its railroad heyday, in addition to a yard office and depot to accommodate travelers waiting to board, Montpelier sported a roundhouse that contained a turntable capable of handling steam locomotives, along with fifteen locomotive stalls and an adjacent machine shop with all the facilities and tools necessary to dismantle, repair, and service the locomotives. During the period from 1905 through the 1930s, more than six hundred locomotives *per month* were repaired and serviced in Montpelier's railroad facilities.[248] Montpelier was also the location where train crews coming east from Pocatello would "lay over" before returning to Pocatello on a westbound train, while crews from Montpelier would take an eastbound train to Green River, Wyoming, and then return to Montpelier to await their next trip.

The arrival of the railroad and its positives and negatives must have been bittersweet for the Mormon inhabitants of Montpelier, who likely were as suspicious of the arriving gentiles as the gentiles were of them. The presence of the railroad and its employees undeniably boosted the local economy, which was theretofore almost entirely agrarian. However, the railroad brought with it a parade of elements that the Mormons would rather avoid, even at the cost of losing the economic benefits. To them, an increase in the number of gentiles meant a likely increase in the use of alcohol and tobacco, followed by more saloons, gambling, and the like, to

---

[247] J. P. Wilde's local history gives the date as July 24, 1882.
[248] http://www.rootsweb.ancestry.com/**idbearl/shortline.htm

say nothing of a rise in the relatively low crime rate. Like it or not, however, the railroad was in Montpelier to stay.

Qui Se Ressemble, S'Assemble[249]

Doc Guyon initially came to Montpelier alone. The arrival of his family approximately a month later, on April 10, 1896, was reported in the *Montpelier Examiner*:

> Mrs. Guyon and family arrived from Pendleton, Oregon yesterday and Doc. is therefore happy. They will live in the new Webster house on Washington avenue. Montpelier people will welcome them to their new home, feeling sure they will not regret the step taken.[250]

"Mrs. Guyon and family" was composed of Maggie, who was thirty-six years old in 1896; Maud, who had turned sixteen on March 27; and Fay, who would be six on June 4.

The Montpelier Weather Station

Shortly after his arrival, the industrious Dr. Guyon established a weather signal station, by which the weather forecast originating in Portland, Oregon, was broadcast to Montpelier and the surrounding area via signal flags. The local paper described the enterprise:

> A Weather Station. Through the efforts of Dr. Guyon, Montpelier will shortly be made a weather signal station. A flag pole sixty feet high will be put on Riter Bros. Drug store for the flag signals, and every morning a forecast of the weather for 48 hours will be received from Portland, Oregon, and the same will be given to the people by means of flags displayed from this flagstaff. They will be indicated as follows: White, clear weather; blue, rain or snow; white and blue, local rain or snow; white with black center, cold wave. There will also be other flags which will describe the direction of winds, etc. this station will be of great benefit to

---

249 French proverb: "Birds of a feather flock together."
250 "Additional Local," *Montpelier (ID) Examiner*, April 11, 1896, p. 4.

the farmers during the harvest season, and the signals can be seen all over the valley. Dr. Guyon will be in charge.[251]

Printed versions of the weather signal flags were also published in the Montpelier Examiner consistently through the Fall of 1897, but thereafter the idea seems to have lost traction with the public and eventually was abandoned.

A Little Bank Robbery in Montpelier

Slightly more than five months after Dr. Guyon's arrival in Montpelier and four months after the arrival of his wife and children, an event occurred that forever enshrined Montpelier's place in the colorful and romanticized history of the Old West and likely caused a great deal of anxiety and excitement locally.

On Thursday, August 13, 1896, three heavily armed men later identified as George "Butch" Cassidy, Bob Meeks, and Elza Lay entered the city on horseback and quietly rode down Washington Street to the Montpelier Bank. The trio dismounted and strode up to the front door, where Mr. Gray, the bank's cashier, and another man were talking. One of the three drew a six-shooter and persuaded Gray and the other man to go into the bank. Once inside, the two men were ordered to stand facing a wall with their hands up, the same fate that awaited two more men who happened to be passing the bank a few minutes later.

One of the brigands went behind the counter, collected all the money in sight, and then demanded that Bud McIntosh, the assistant cashier, divulge the location of the bank's greenbacks. McIntosh refused and the robber struck him over the eye with his six-shooter. The robbers then ransacked the bank vault, put the contents in a sack, mounted their horses, and left with about $5,000 of the bank's money.[252]

Attempts to apprehend the malefactors proved futile, and they made a clean getaway. Eventually, Bob Meeks was apprehended, charged, tried, and convicted of the crime in the Bear Lake County courthouse in Paris, Idaho. The loot was never recovered. Neither Butch Cassidy nor Elza Lay was ever prosecuted for the crime.[253]

---

[251] "A Weather Station," *Montpelier (ID) Examiner*, November 13, 1896, p. 1.
[252] "Daring Robbery!," *Montpelier (ID) Examiner*, August 15, 1896, p. 1 and August 22, 1896, p. 4.
[253] A. N. McIntosh, one of the tellers, attributed the incident to the bad luck generated by the number thirteen: the event occurred on the thirteenth day of the month, after the thirteenth deposit of the day of $13, at 3:13 in the afternoon.

Dr. Guyon attended the trial of Meeks, which was probably an uncomfortable reminder that Montpelier was not as safe as it pretended to be. There could have been multiple murders during the fray, given the assailants' drawn revolvers and the apparent willingness and ability to use them. Despite the drama and potential for danger, Dr. Guyon made no known adjustments to his plans to remain in Montpelier.

Steadfastness in Montpelier

Some citizens of Montpelier remained unconvinced of Doc Guyon's resolve to stay permanently. Murmurings of his supposed plans to locate elsewhere compelled him to generate a public statement of his intentions near mid-1897:

> Certain parties in Montpelier have circulated the report that I am going to leave here. I wish to inform my friends that such reports are *base fabrications*, and that I am *here to stay*. [signed] E. F. Guyon [italics in original][254]

Doc made good on his vow until mid-1900, when he was presented with an unanticipated opportunity he couldn't refuse. He and his family moved to Diamondville, Wyoming, where Doc was assistant surgeon for the Diamond Coal Company for about three years. During his stay, he studied tuberculosis and other tubercular diseases and gained experience in treating the diseases. Eventually, Doc would return to Montpelier permanently.

Travel via the Oregon Short Line

In 1897, Dr. Guyon accepted the position of assistant surgeon for the OSL, a position he would hold until 1903. Whatever the time requirements of the position were, he seems to have had sufficient time to devote to his private medical practice, which, by all accounts, was thriving. He also continued to maintain his friendship with Dr. Parkinson of Logan, Utah, who had visited him in Montpelier the previous August. In addition to a visit the previous February, Dr. Guyon visited Dr. Parkinson in Logan on March 16, 1897, and June 8, 1897.[255]

---

254 *Montpelier (ID) Examiner*, May 5, 1897, p. 2.
255 *Utah Journal* (Logan), August 18, 1896; February 22, 1896; June 8, 1897.

Present-day travelers between Montpelier and Logan, Utah, take to the road with little concern about the seventy-six miles between the two (via present-day Highway 89), but the situation in 1897 was significantly different. There were no automobiles to drive in 1897 and no paved highways. Road travel choices were limited to coach, buggy, or horseback, all uncomfortable and slow. The journey took several days one-way, depending on whether the route went through Logan Canyon or through Franklin and Preston, Idaho, via Emigration Canyon.

Luckily, there was a faster and more comfortable alternative. In 1897 the denizens of Montpelier could either take the OSL eastbound train for Granger, Wyoming, 116 miles distant, or the OSL westbound train for McCammon, Idaho, about sixty-four miles from Montpelier. Both locations allowed access to the main line of the Union Pacific Railroad for travel to and from Salt Lake City, Ogden, Logan, and other points on the Union Pacific line.

Dr. Guyon always traveled by rail whenever possible. His attendance at IOOF and medical-related events in various locations in Idaho, and particularly those outside the state, would have been virtually impossible but for the speed, comfort, and convenience of the railroads.

Author and Critic of Medical Legislation

From the start, Dr. Guyon exhibited an almost inexhaustible supply of energy and personal drive. The ill health that had brought him to Montpelier in the first place had lost its grip, and he was ready to take on additional challenges. He somehow found the time to become involved in the legislative machinery of the State of Idaho, which in 1896 considered the passage of a law to regulate the practice of medicine and surgery.

Dr. Guyon objected to the passage of the law in the form of a pamphlet[256] which explained that he, individually, had no objection to its passage; however, he believed it would be defeated in the legislature because it was discriminatory:

> The proposed law is in some respects unjust and discriminating and I am confident that for this reason it will array the majority of the legal practitioners of the State

---

[256] "Objections to the Proposed Medical Law for the State of Idaho. Also a few suggestions on same."

114

against it, and thus defeat the measure when it comes up for consideration at the next session of the legislature.

Dr. Guyon's efforts were reported in the *Montpelier Examiner*:

> Dr. Guyon recently issued a little pamphlet entitled "objections to the proposed medical law for Idaho," and has sent a copy to nearly all the physicians in the state. It has caused quite a discussion on the subject and may have the effect of getting a good law passed at the next legislature. Dr. Guyon and another physician are the fathers of the Oregon medical law, and therefore he knows what the state needs.[257]

His labors, which bore fruit, would likely have been anonymous if not for the gracious intervention of J. C. Rich, an Idaho state senator from Montpelier, whose published letter to the editor of *The Medical Sentinel*,[258] a medical journal, gave Dr. Guyon his due:

> Dear Sir: – Having noticed an editorial in the April ninth of the Medical Sentinel praising several of the physicians of Boise and other places who were instrumental in aiding the passage of the present medical law of Idaho, I failed to notice any mention of the physician who was the author of this measure, and knowing the history of this bill more thoroughly than any one else I feel it my duty, out of justice to him, to inform you that Dr. E. F. Guyon of Montpelier, Idaho, is the person who formulated this measure, and I am still in possession of the "original draft" in his own hand writing. He handed this bill to me on the eve of my departure for the capitol[sic], and requested me to introduce the same provided it met with the approval of the senate. Finding two other medical bills up for consideration, and finding that the joint judiciary committee would not accept either, I handed them the bill given me by Dr. Guyon. The judiciary committees of both houses endorsed this bill at once with but few changes and

---

257 *Montpelier (ID) Examiner*, August 27, 1896.
258 J. C. Rich, letter to the editor, *Medical Sentinel* 5 (1897): 345.

introduced it as "the joint judiciary committee's compromise medical bill."

Dr. Guyon is certainly deserving the honor of being the father of this "Bill," and I want him to have it. I do not wish to take away any of the praise and honor due other physicians for the noble part they took in this matter, but I wish the name of Dr. Guyon added to the list. His appointment on the Board of Medical Examiners by the governor is no doubt a just recognition of the part he took in giving to Idaho the medical act now in force. I wish to add further without egotism, that if anyone is entitled to more praise than myself for engineering the bill through the senate I would like him to arise and explain, and would also say that no one assisted me more than Senator J. W. Turner, of Cottonwood, and while I am not seeking praises or notoriety, I simply desire that the facts only are presented and this communication to you is wholly for the purpose of giving you the plain truth, and I hope you will give this letter space in the columns of your journal. J. C. RICH, State Senator.

Doc's efforts to see the passage of his version of Idaho's medical law were only a small part of his lifelong commitment to ensure minimum standards of education, expertise, and experience among physicians admitted to practice medicine in Idaho. Shortly after his arrival in Montpelier, he was appointed by Idaho Governor Steunenberg to a two-year term on the Idaho State Medical Board, newly organized in 1897 to require all medical practitioners in Idaho to be licensed. [259] The appointment may have been in part a result of his paper on "Peculiar Forms of Continued Fever," read before the Idaho State Medical Society in the fall of 1896 by Doc's colleague Dr. C. A. Hoover.[260]

Local and Statewide Medical Affiliations and Activities

Dr. Guyon also became active in the Idaho State Medical Society, which had only existed since 1892. In the fall of 1897, he became a member

[259] "State Medical Board," Idaho Statesman (Boise), May 9, 1897.
[260] Idaho Statesman (Boise), September 18, 1896.

of the Transportation and Censure committees of that body,[261] and the following year became an elected officer. As reported in the *Journal of the American Medical Association*:

> The sixth annual meeting of the [Idaho State Medical] Society was held in Moscow [Idaho], September 6 and 7. The following officers were elected for the ensuing year: President, C. W. Shaff, Lewiston; vice-president, E. F. Guyon, Montpelier; secretary, Edward E. Maxey, Caldwell. The next annual meeting will be held at Lewiston, Sept. 5 and 6, 1899.[262]

In the meantime, Dr. Guyon and the Bear Lake County Commissioners organized themselves into a "Board of Public Health" in an attempt to respond to contagious and infection diseases that might appear.[263] Still later Doc Guyon, along with Dr. C. A. Hoover, was appointed by the Montpelier Mayor James Redman to establish quarantine regulations in Montpelier to combat an outbreak of scarlet fever.[264]

A Dedicated Odd Fellow

Throughout his professional life Dr. Guyon was an active member of the Independent Order of Odd Fellows ("IOOF" or "Odd Fellows"), a fraternal organization originally founded in the British Isles, of which the American version was organized on April 26, 1819, in Baltimore, Maryland. Also known as the Three Link Fraternity because of its symbol of three interlocking links in white, blue, and red, the IOOF was, and presumably continues to be, an altruistic and charitable organization dedicated to the elevation of mankind and the betterment of society at large whose members are expected to "visit the sick, relieve the distressed, bury the dead and educate the orphan."[265]

The teaching of the principles and truths espoused by the fraternity is accomplished through ceremonies and symbols, and one's progress is marked by passage from level to level, called "Degrees," which are pre-

---

261 "Local News," *Montpelier (ID) Examiner*, September 22, 1897, p. 3.
262 *Journal of the American Medical Association* 31, no. 13 (1898, September 24): 741–42.
263 "Editorial Squibbs," *Montpelier (ID) Examiner*, December 29, 1897, p. 9.
264 "Mayor's Proclamation," *Montpelier (ID) Examiner*, May 18, 1899, p. 1.
265 "Independent Order of Odd Fellows," Wikipedia, accessed August 15, 2016, http://en.wikipedia.org/wiki/Independent_Order_of_Odd_Fellows.

sented largely through drama and allegory and are conferred by the local lodge attended.[266]

In 1895, Dr. Guyon joined the Odd Fellows' Eureka Lodge No. 32 in Pendleton, Oregon. Shortly thereafter, he joined the Encampment branch and then transferred to the Montpelier Encampment branch of Enterprise Lodge No. 18 "by card"; after arriving in Montpelier in 1896, Dr. Guyon "passed the chairs in both branches of the Order."[267]

The best known record of Dr. Guyon's substantial history of involvement in the IOOF is an undated list of positions he held, partly typewritten and partly in his handwriting, with some corrections by interlineation of typed words. The document, which has "Suggested form of CARD for Bro. Guyon" typewritten in red at the top, also bears the handwritten word "Important" in large letters slightly below. Following are the official positions held, along with several of the tongue-in-cheek variety:

> Member Enterprise Lodge #18
> Member Montpelier Encampment #11
> Member Hope Rebekah Lodge #20
> Member Canton Columbia #3
> Member Kremlin Ufa, I.O.M.
> Member P.G.M. & P.G.P. Assn.
> Member Grand Lodge of Idaho
> Member Grand Encampment of Idaho
> Member Department Council
> Past Grand
> Past Grand Patriarch
> Past Grand Representative
> Past D.D.G.M.
> D.D.G.P.
> Secretary Enterprise Lodge #18
> Secy, Trustees of Enterprise Lodge #18
> Financial Secretary Enterprise Lodge #18
> Scribe Montpelier Encampment #11
> Financial Scribe Montpelier Encampment #11
> Past Chief Patriarch
> Asst Surgeon General P.M.
> Examining Physician Enterprise Lodge No. 18

---

[266] Ibid.
[267] *Idaho Odd Fellow* 13, no. 6 (1908, January).

Captain Degree Main Enterprise Lodge No. 18
Captain Degree Main Montpelier Enc. No. 11
Representative Enterprise Lodge No. 18 without pay
Representative Montpelier Enc. No. 11 Paid
Prospective Janitor's Asst.
General Prosecutor of the Moss backs of Drs. No. 18
Water boy to the story tellers club of E. Lodge No. 18
Delegate, by special appointment of the Grand Master,
    from the Grand Lodge of Idaho to the League to
    Enforce Peace, in Philadelphia, May 16, 17, 1918
Prevaricator-General of the District (Designated by
    himself)
Good Fellow, and Good Odd Fellow
Asst. Surgeon General, with the rank of MAJOR

Dr. Guyon also held the position of Grand Junior Warden in 1908,[268] although that position is not on the list. Dr. Guyon's IOOF sessions and encampments in which he is known to have actively participated over the years number thirty-five and are listed in Appendix III. The sessions and encampments were identified from ribbons and medals issued for each individual event, but there may well be others.

It is difficult to overstate Doc Guyon's time commitment to the IOOF or his dedication to its principles and objectives of promoting personal and social development, among others. The IOOF's vision of a universal fraternity was entirely consistent with his world view. The IOOF had included women as Rebeckahs since 1851, the first American fraternal organization to do so.[269]

The composite reproduced below, graciously supplied to the author courtesy of venerable Montpelier historian Max Lauridsen, dates from about 1897 to 1898 and presumably includes all members of the lodge in Montpelier at that time, most of whom are identified by number as follows: (1) Thomas Lauridsen, (2) Duncan McLennan, (3) James Redman, (4) G. C. Patten, (5) Fred C. Hansen, (6) Unknown, (7) Henry Douglas, (8) Unknown, (9) Unknown, (10) Jake Rohner, (11) Stephen Staley, (12) Sam McCart, (13) J. E. Winchell, (14) Henry H. Hoff, (15) Charles H. Hammond, (16) Unknown, (17) Charles Hoff, (18) Unknown, (19) Samuel

---

[268] Ibid.
[269] Independent Order of Odd Fellows, accessed January 27, 2017, https://en.wikipedia.org/wiki/Independent_Order_of_Odd_Fellows#2.

L. Lewis, (20) Thomas L. Glenn, (21) ? Freeman, (22) ? Jensen, (23) E. F. Guyon, (24) Alex Beckman.

Chapter 8.

AN IMPORTANT INTERLUDE IN DIAMONDVILLE

circa 1900–1903

There is nothing permanent except change.
— Heraclites

The relatively short period between 1900 and 1903 was a time of opportunity for Dr. Guyon, who moved to Diamondville, Wyoming, to accept the position of assistant surgeon at a coal mining company. This opportunity provided him the prodigious expertise in the diagnosis and treatment of tuberculosis that would vault him into national and international prominence.

The Removal to Diamondville

By 1900 Doc Guyon had built up and maintained a sprawling, thriving, and financially remunerative practice in Montpelier that included, but was not limited to, Star Valley, Wyoming, fifty miles and three to seven days distant one-way; Cokeville, Wyoming, thirty miles away in another direction; and the furthest reaches of Bear Lake County.[270] He also held the position of assistant surgeon with the Oregon Short Line Railroad.[271] Seemingly suddenly, he made the decision to accept the position of assistant surgeon at the Diamond Coal Company in Diamondville, Wyoming, a position he would hold for roughly three years.[272] The event was reported on the front page of the Montpelier paper in the following article borrowed from the *Diamondville News:*

---

[270] Although his ledgers did not consistently identify patients by location, Dr. Guyon noted patients from as close by as Bennington, Ovid, Fish Haven, Dingle, Raymond, Georgetown, Bloomington, Paris, St. Charles, Laketown, and Sharon, and as far away as Nicholas, Idaho; Thayne, Wyoming; Rigby, Idaho; Springville, Utah; Pocatello, Idaho; and Cokeville, Wyoming. This is not to suggest that Dr. Guyon spent all of this time traveling to treat people. In fact, his ledgers suggest that his practice was dominated by visits to his office by his patients, which often resulted in prescriptions, but which may have led to other treatments and services that required him to travel to the patients.
[271] French, *History of Idaho,* 1256.
[272] Ibid.

Dr. E. F. Guyon, of Montpelier, Idaho, a medical man of more than ordinary ability will locate in Diamondville, as assistant to Dr. Gamble. The Doctor stands very high in the profession, and will be a valuable addition to the medical fraternity of Wyo. He is a graduate of the Ohio Medical College, of Cincinnati. Is an active member of the Idaho Medical Exchange Board and author of several important contributions to medical literature. The people of Diamondville are to be congratulated that so able and noted a medical man is to locate among them soon. His family will not be here for the present. --
Diamondville News.[273]

The *Montpelier Examiner* then continued its own article about Doc's change in location:

The above will come as a surprise to Dr. Guyon's many friends in this city.

Dr. Guyon has been in Montpelier for about three[274] years, and during that time has acquired a large practice and made many friends. He is a gentlemen in every particular, and ranks with the most able men in the country as a physician and surgeon. His removal from this city will be cause for keen regret, and besides is a distinct loss to the town. In Dr. Guyon and Dr. Hoover the people felt that they had access to the most skillful and learned physicians in the west.

The removal of either of them is like taking a link out of the everyday life of Montpelier, as neither could be easily replaced in the confidence of the people.

Sorry as we are to lose Dr. Guyon and his estimable family, we congratulate Diamondville on its good luck, as such people are acquisitions that any city may be proud of the chance to welcome.

---

[273] "Dr. Guyon Will Move," *Montpelier (ID) Examiner*, May 4, 1900.
[274] Dr. Guyon had actually been in Montpelier approximately four years by 1900.

May the Doctor meet with unbounded success in his new home, for he deserves it, is the wish of the Examiner and hosts of friends in this part of Idaho.

The glowing tone of the article confirms the esteem in which Grandpa and his family were held in Montpelier and the surrounding area after a relatively short four years. His medical credentials were probably a large part of the reason he seemed irreplaceable, and may have accounted in part for his having been woven so quickly and deeply into local society.

Reputation alone, however, does not adequately explain the phenomenon, which can only be understood in the context of his professional performance and relationships with his patients and friends. Somehow, his combination of knowledge, skill, experience, social graces, integrity, and personality dovetailed nicely with the needs and perceptions of the populace.

The taker of the 1900 United States Census must have barely caught Dr. Guyon and his family in Montpelier on June 5, 1900, when he reported that Grandpa, his wife Matilda, their daughter Maud, age twenty, and their son Lafayette, age nine, were living there in a rented home,[275] preparing for their imminent relocation to Diamondville.

Life in Diamondville

The small town of Diamondville is located about two miles south of Kemmerer.[276] It owes its existence to Harrison Church, an explorer and mountain man who discovered coal near the Hams Fork River in 1868 and, along with investors, built the town to house coal miners. The superior-grade coal resembled black diamonds, which accounts for the town's name.[277] Mine Number One, opened in the 1890s, had two workable seams of extractable coal, seven and fourteen feet in width respectively, above which was a roof of sand and soapstone, which allowed its safe removal. Another mine was opened in the 1890s in Oakley, south of Diamondville, and in 1900 the Glencoe Mine was opened about six miles south of Diamondville. The Diamond Coke and Coal Company,

---

[275] Twelfth Census of the United States, Montpelier, Bear Lake County, Idaho, June 5, 1900.
[276] Although Kemmerer obviously has two "er" syllables, only one is pronounced (i.e., "Kemmer").
[277] "Diamondville, Wyoming," Wikipedia, accessed August 15, 2016, http://en.wikipedia.org/wiki/Diamondville,_Wyoming.

controlled by the Anaconda Smelting Company, operated the mines[278] and is probably the company that employed Dr. Guyon.

There is no hint in either the French Biography or the Johnson Biography that Dr. Guyon accepted the position in Wyoming primarily because he could make more money. The suggested reason for his departure from Montpelier was that it gave him an opportunity to learn about tuberculosis and other tubercular diseases, which were doubtless rampant among miners in Diamondville, owing to the environment created by the extensive coal mining industry in that area of Wyoming. During the three years he spent in Diamondville, he developed an enviable expertise in the diagnosis and treatment of tuberculosis at a time when little was known about the disease. His activities included experiments and the acquisition of data that would make him "one of the world's best authorities on tubercular diseases."[279]

Dr. Guyon was not always a workaholic in Diamondville, as evidenced by a newspaper article reporting the July 4, 1900, celebration in Evanston, Wyoming. The festivities included "a free-for-all trot and pace," with four entries, including "Dr. E. F. Guyon's bay pacer, piloted by Robert Hocker."[280] Although not reported in the Evanston newspaper, Dr. Guyon's horse was the winning entry.[281]

Dr. Guyon and J. C. Penney

According to Guyon family lore, during his time in the Kemmerer area Dr. Guyon became the personal physician to James Cash Penney, the dry goods retailer, and remained friends with him thereafter. This relationship was confirmed by Grandpa Guyon's son Edwin Fenimore and at least two additional factors. First, J. C. Penney opened his first store in Kemmerer, Wyoming, in 1902,[282] and lived and worked there when Dr. Guyon did. Second, Penney, a native of Missouri, was forced to come west due to health problems. He originally lived in Longmont, Colorado, where he became affiliated with the founders of the Golden Rule stores.[283] In June,

---

[278] Wyoming Genealogy, "Lincoln County, Wyoming History," accessed August 15, 2016, http://wyominggenealogy.com/uinta/lincoln_county_history.htm.

[279] Wilde, *Treasured Tidbits of Time*, 1:320.

[280] *Wyoming Press* (Evanston), July 7, 1900, p. 1.

[281] "Additional Locals," *Montpelier (ID) Examiner*, July 6, 1900, p. 2.

[282] "About JCPenney," JCPenney Newsroom, accessed August 15, 2016, http://www.jcpnewsroom.com/about-history.html.

[283] "James Cash Penney," Wikipedia, accessed August 15, 2016, https://en.wikipedia.org/wiki/James_Cash_Penney.

1897, his doctor advised him that he needed a change in climate, which prompted his move to Kemmerer,[284] where he probably sought out Dr. Guyon for medical advice or treatment.

Neighboring Evanston

In Diamondville, Dr. Guyon's professional activities were not limited to that immediate area. Much of his work as reported by the local papers found him in Evanston, a larger town about fifty miles distant by horse, carriage, or wagon.

The OSL conveniently went through the Kemmerer-Diamondville area, making it possible for Doc Guyon to travel by rail via the OSL from Kemmerer to Granger, a distance of forty-two miles, and on the Union Pacific main line from Granger to Evanston, a distance of fifty-six miles. Although longer, the journey by rail was much faster and far less grueling than traveling under horsepower. Depending on train schedules, the trip by rail took hours; by other methods, days.

The Expert Witness

Despite the important part his experiences in Diamondville would play in his professional life thereafter, few details are known concerning Dr. Guyon and his family during their sojourn there. The French Biography acknowledges his stay there for three years, but makes no statements concerning his activities.

A number of newspaper articles from the period give indications of his involvement in professional activities. In the minutes of the Uinta County commissioners, Dr. Guyon's name regularly appears as a recipient of payments for professional services, such as acting as an expert witness for the county coroner and apparent assistance to the board of health, along with one article that identifies him as the "assistant mine surgeon at Diamondville" and an expert witness at "the Elam murder trial."[285]

A curious advertisement in the local paper in June, 1901, announced that "Dr. E. F. Guyon [,] Physician and Surgeon [could be contacted in his] Office at Diamond Drug Store. Night calls – room 3 at Daly Hotel." As later events would confirm, Doc's location at the local hotel and his

284 Robert W. Bruere, *J. C. Penney, the Man With a Thousand Partners* (New York: Harper & Brothers, 1931), 17-20.
285 *Wyoming Press* (Evanston), no. 31, p. 8.

availability for night calls were likely indicative of personal difficulties between Doc and his spouse.

Marital Discord and Divorce

On December 27, 1901, a Decree of Divorce was entered in the Third District Court of Uinta County, Evanston, Wyoming, in an action styled "E. F. Guyon, Plaintiff, vs. Maggie Guyon, Defendant."

The Decree of Divorce was presumably the culmination of marital difficulties that could have been brewing for years. Dr. Guyon at the time had just turned forty-eight, Maggie was about forty-two, Maud was twenty-one, and their son Fay was about eleven.

After the divorce, Grandpa Guyon maintained a close relationship with Maud throughout his life, but his relationship with Fay was perpetually strained. Fay lived with his father in Montpelier after his parents' divorce for some period, but no specific details are known. By late 1910, Fay was married with a child (or his wife was very close to having one), and he was either living with, or in close proximity to, his sister Maud in Salt Lake City.[286]

Private Practice and Politics

There is some evidence that Dr. Guyon had decided to resume private practice in Kemmerer and Evanston while still employed in Diamondville. He reportedly purchased the stock of drugs maintained there by Dr. Lovejoy, and may have had every intention of remaining there permanently.[287]

An article in the local paper in early 1902 reported that George Johnson reportedly got so drunk on whiskey "that he was no longer a sane being." While in that state, he stabbed three men during a fracas he initiated, which led to charges of "murderous assault." The three victims were "attended" by Dr. Guyon.[288] His involvement seems less likely if he was not in private practice.

In the fall of 1902, the Evanston paper identified "Dr. E. F. Guyon of Kemmerer" as the Democratic candidate for coroner in Uinta County.[289] He

---

[286] E. F. Guyon to Maud Brown, 26 December 1910.
[287] "Business Change in Kemmerer," [borrowed from the Kemmerer Camera] *Montpelier (ID) Examiner*, March 21, 1902, p.8.
[288] "A Christmas Celebration," *Wyoming Press* (Evanston), January 4, 1902, p. 1.
[289] "Democratic Convention," *Wyoming Press* (Evanston), August 9, 1902, p. 1.

got the nomination and ran against the Republican candidate, Frank E. Curtis.[290] Although he lost that election, Dr. Guyon successfully ran for a seat on the Kemmerer City Council in what was described as a "Democratic landslide."[291]

In October, 1902, another example of Dr. Guyon's private practice appeared in the Evanston newspaper in an article that reported a stray bullet hitting a man named Qualy while he innocently stood in a business office. The shot came from an individual named Graham who had been target practicing. The article reported: "Dr. Guyon dressed the wound and found the small bone of the forearm shattered, the bullet having been a 45-calibre."[292]

By the fall of 1902, Dr. Guyon had been at his job as a coal company surgeon in Diamondville for two and a half years, but restlessness is suggested by his concurrent involvement in local politics and what appears to be a private medical practice. Whatever his challenges were in Diamondville, and despite the expertise he had acquired in the diagnosis and treatment of tuberculosis, they were collectively insufficient to satisfy his urge to do more, see more, and learn more.

The Appearance of Effie Burke

Dr. Guyon's life shortly became even more complicated. An article in the Evanston newspaper reported:

> Dr. E. F. Guyon and Effie M. Burke of Kemmerer were granted a marriage license by County Clerk Brown last Saturday. The groom is candidate for coroner on the democratic ticket. Accept our best wishes.[293]

Effie M. Burke was destined to be the mother of Dr. Guyon's three younger sons: Edwin Fenimore, my father Wendell Shattuck, and Royal Chatterton.

In some ways the marriage of Effie and Doc Guyon seems improbable. Born in 1874, Effie was twenty-eight years old in 1902, twenty-one years Dr. Guyon's junior. Physically, Effie was a shade under six feet tall and very slender, even willowy. She appeared almost fragile, although she was

290 "Certificate of Nominations," *Wyoming Press* (Evanston), November 1, 1902, p. 8.
291 "Municipal Elections in Wyoming Towns," *Wyoming Press* (Evanston), August 23, 1902, p. 5.
292 "Shooting at Fossil," *Wyoming Press* (Evanston), October 25, 1902, p. 8.
293 *Wyoming Press* (Evanston), September 20, 1902, p. 1.

anything but. Effie was fair-skinned with reddish blonde hair. Her weight was a closely guarded secret, but was definitely not a large number.[294]

Dr. Guyon was only 5'8" in height and weighed 140 pounds, but what he may have lacked in size he made up for in other ways. His personal magnetism and charisma were supplemented by a lean, firm physique from his years as a cattle rancher and laborer and heavily muscled arms and shoulders from his earlier life as a blacksmith. In his youth Dr. Guyon was handsome and black-haired with a dark complexion. He more than likely would have retained that complexion as he neared the age of fifty, but he was already bald or balding except for the sides and back. Judging from photographs of him, he was always clean-shaven, except for his mustache.

In other ways, the marriage seems to have been the unavoidable destiny of both. Where and how they met is a matter of conjecture. Effie was a resident of Kemmerer[295] in 1902, presumably where they met.

Effie Burke circa 1890s

However, Guyon family lore suggests otherwise, which, if true, makes their eventual union seem even more fated.

Effie's sister Sarah ("Sadie") had married Peter J. McDermott ("P. J."), who lived in Montpelier in the early 1900s. Sadie was not robust, and her health deteriorated, rendering her unable to care for her children. Effie, the re-maining single daughter and the youngest child in the Burke family, was summoned to Montpelier to help.[296] During Effie's stay in Montpelier thus engaged, she met Dr. Guyon and, apparently, they fell in love. The destiny aspect of their relationship is cemented by the fact that Dr. Guyon, who at the time was

---

[294] From my personal observations during visits in the late 1950s and early 1960s in Montpelier, Effie maintained her extremely slender appearance by refraining from eating anything whatsoever. The most I ever saw her consume was a glass of warm water, spiked with lemon juice.

[295] In Dr. Guyon's effects were several small handmade cards ("cartes de visite") bearing Effie's name and her address as Kemmerer, Wyo.

[296] Unconfirmed rumors suggest that Effie, allegedly somewhat of a social butterfly in her late 20s, may have devoted less time than expected to the task that brought her to Montpelier.

living in Kemmerer, must have been in Montpelier on professional or personal business for the meeting to have taken place.

A Reconciliation with Maggie?

Dr. Guyon and Maggie had been divorced since December 27, 1901, and some nine months later he and Effie Burke were granted a marriage license. In the meantime, a very short article appeared in the Evanston newspaper concerning proceedings on the district court docket: "Edwin F. Guyon vs. Maggie E. Guyon. To vacate decree of divorce, etc."[297]

Whether Dr. Guyon and Maggie had second thoughts about their divorce is unknown, but the reason the motion appeared on the docket is probably no more than a simple matter of internal court procedure. When a motion is filed and not pursued within a prescribed time, it is common for a court to notify the parties to "show cause" why the motion should be dismissed for failure to prosecute. This forces a resolution by requiring the parties to either pursue the motion or allow it to be dismissed. An identical report appeared in the same newspaper in August of 1903,[298] after Effie and Dr. Guyon were married, which raises the probability that the motion simply was abandoned and that no one had taken the time or made the effort to take it off the court's calendar.

A New Knot Is Tied

Dr. Guyon and Effie were married on May 18, 1903, at Paris, Bear Lake County, Idaho, by J. H. Rodgers, pastor of the First Presbyterian Church, Montpelier, Idaho. Witnesses to the wedding were Blanche L. Burke, Effie's sister-in-law, and Henry J. Burke, Effie's brother. Effie's stated residence was Montpelier, Idaho, and Dr. Guyon's was Kemmerer, Wyoming.

---

[297] *Wyoming Press* (Evanston), March 21, 1903, p. 8.

[298] "September Court Docket," *Wyoming Press* (Evanston), August 29, 1903, p. 8. Under "List of Cases to Come Up For Hearing in the Third District Court at Evanston on the 7th," it states, "Edwin F. Guyon vs. Maggie E. Guyon To vacate decree of divorce."

Chapter 9.

A REPEAT PERFORMANCE IN MONTPELIER

circa 1903–1910

To return or not to return to Montpelier?
That is the question.

This chapter discusses the newlyweds' return to Montpelier, the births of their three sons, family life, Dr. Guyon's professional reputation and status, his involvement in local theatrical productions, his personal talents, and other interests.

Equivocation

The Montpelier newspaper included the following article in its edition of August 14, 1903:

> Dr. Guyon and wife have concluded, after visiting other sections, to locate in Montpelier again. Their many friends welcome them back.

During the three months since their marriage, the couple had lived approximately two months in Kemmerer and a month in Franklin, Idaho, before returning to Montpelier.[299] A July 20, 1903, letter to Effie was addressed to nearby Preston, probably because Franklin lacked its own post office. The "visiting other sections" part of the newspaper article suggests reluctance to immediately return to Montpelier. Dr. Guyon would be fifty years old in November of 1903, which may have influenced their decision. An obvious advantage to Montpelier was that Dr. Guyon could likely reactivate the medical practice he had built up during the 1896–1900

---

[299] "Local News," *Montpelier (ID) Examiner*, July 31, 1903. Dr. Guyon's reasons for leaving the Diamondville/Kemmerer area are vague. His position as assistant surgeon at the Diamond Coal Company may not have turned out to be the promising opportunity it appeared to be in 1900 for any number of reasons, from insufficient funding of his studies of tubercular diseases to the realization that his true calling in medicine was as a practitioner and not a researcher. Whatever the reasons for his change in direction, it was significant. Whether his deteriorating relationship with Maggie was a cause of or had an effect on his decision to leave Wyoming is unclear, although common sense suggests it had a part to play, even if a minor one.

period. Another important factor was that Effie's mother was living in Montpelier. These circumstances may have generated an article in the local newspaper in August, 1903, that reported: "The Doctor has decided that Montpelier is good enough for him and he will locate here permanently."[300]

Dr. and Mrs. Guyon – 1903

Even after Doc and Effie returned to Montpelier, there is evidence of lingering doubts. In early 1904, Dr. Guyon seriously entertained an offer from the OSL that would have required his relocation in Glenn's Ferry.[301]

In all probability, the pair wanted to leave no stone unturned that might influence their tentative plans to return to Montpelier. They knew that wherever they decided to live would be where they raised their children and Doc pursued his medical career for the foreseeable future, and wanted to make the best choice possible.

The Medical Conservative

Doc Guyon's reputation in Montpelier was that he was conservative in his treatments. He believed that in most cases the body would heal itself if allowed and encouraged to do so; a minimum of interference in that process would produce the best results. He did not deviate from that philosophy in his own life.

Grandpa had a benign growth approximately the size of a doubled-up fist in the middle of his back between his shoulders. Family lore acknowledges the condition, but assigns no particular importance to it, suggesting that if the growth was noticeable, it was barely so. Several of his doctor friends offered on a number of occasions to surgically remove it,

[300] "Local News," *Montpelier (ID) Examiner*, August 21, 1903, p. 5.
[301] "Local News," *Montpelier (ID) Examiner*, March 18, 1904, p. 7.

but he always declined. I believe he applied the same standard to himself that he applied to his patients—surgery only as a last resort.

Another example of Dr. Guyon's conservative approach to the practice of medicine can be gleaned from his correspondence in 1928 to his daughter. Maud's doctor in Salt Lake City had advised her to have her tonsils surgically removed. Her father's adamant response was, "[d]on't let the doctors down there influence you to have your tonsils cut out." Instead, he told her to spray her tonsils with oil of Thuja compound for six weeks, rest a week, and then repeat, asserting, "I cure every case that comes to me, if they come in time."[302]

Grandpa Guyon often sprinkled bits of medical advice in letters to his children and grandchildren. His counsel was always thoughtful, always practical, and always conservative. Many times, he backed up his

Effie Guyon – 1903

advice with suggestions for taking various drugs and medicines, both prescription and over-the-counter. All advice was accompanied by an explanation of the reasons behind it and the anticipated recovery time.

Expertise in Tubercular Diseases

In Diamondville, Dr. Guyon had significantly increased his medical knowledge and expertise about tubercular diseases in general and tuberculosis in particular:

> [The move to Diamondville] proved to be an excellent choice for the young man. While at Diamondville he conducted experiments and gathered data that was to make him one of the world's best authorities on tubercular diseases.

---

302 E. F. Guyon to Maud Brown, 13 November 1928.

By 1905, he was well on his way to becoming an international authority on the subject. He became a member of the Board of Control of the National Association of Physicians and was elected as one of five U. S. Physicians to attend the International Convention of Physicians in Paris, France where he delivered a treatise on "Tuberculosis Developing Environments."[303]

I have been unable to independently confirm the validity of the quote above concerning Dr. Guyon's invitation to the International Convention of Physicians in 1905, which is particularly frustrating because even the treatise he is supposed to have delivered is named. If Dr. Guyon *had* gone to Paris for professional reasons, it seems likely that he would have at least mentioned it in his surviving records, but there is no such indication. Neither is there any mention of it in the French Biography, which seems unusual if Dr. Guyon had actually delivered the paper. It is not the kind of activity that generally goes unreported.

His business ledgers reflect office visits throughout the entire year of 1905. Any trip to France would have to have been sandwiched between the recorded patient visits. The months with the fewest recorded visits are March, April, May, and June 1905, but even during those months the longest periods without a recorded office visit are fourteen days in May and twelve days in June. Neither of those periods is a sufficient amount of time to allow round-trip travel to Paris. A two-way trip via ocean liner from New York to the coast of France consumed ten days in 1905,[304] without considering the time required for the round trips via rail from Idaho to New York, from the French coast to Paris, and for the convention itself.

Even more importantly, the month of June 1905 marked the birth of Effie's and Grandpa Guyon's first child, which makes it improbable that Grandpa Guyon would have left town for any reason during the weeks immediately preceding and following the birth.

History records that the Congrès International de la Tuberculose (the "Congrès"),[305] the first coordinated effort in France to study the disease, was held in Paris on October 2–7, 1905,[306] but there is no indication that

---

[303] Wilde, *Treasured Tidbits of Time*, 1:320.
[304] Jean-Paul Rodrigue, "Liner Transatlantic Crossing Times, 1833-1952 (in Days)," accessed August 15, 2016, https://people.hofstra.edu/geotrans/eng/ch3en/linertransatlantic.html.
[305] "International Congress on Tuberculosis."
[306] Selman A. Waksman, *The Conquest of Tuberculosis* (Berkeley, CA: University of California Press, 1964), 98.

Dr. Guyon attended or that he submitted a paper to be presented. It is recognized that this convention has a different name from the International Convention of Physicians where he is alleged to have delivered the paper, and convened at a different time, but the subject matter of the Congrès seems to at least raise the possibility that it and the International Convention of Physicians may be one and the same.

Because of his expertise in tubercular diseases it is certainly possible that Dr. Guyon was invited to present a scholarly paper at the Congrès, but regardless of whether he did or did not present the paper in France in 1905, his interest and experience in treating tubercular diseases continued to bring him recognition long after his experiences in Diamondville.

Music Man

Dr. Guyon was a capable and gifted musician. At a minimum, he played the violin, bass violin,[307] piano, mandolin, and guitar, and reportedly played them all rather well. Edwin Fenimore recalled that his father was self-taught in music and had the ability to pick up an instrument and become adept at playing it in a relatively short time.[308]

Whether he had perfect pitch, the ability to intuitively recognize whether a given musical note was in tune or not, is not known. Neither is it known whether his early training under Emily Louise's tutelage included music lessons, and if he had such training, what instruments he studied. It is likely that he had some training, particularly on the violin, which took place during his formative years. Violin music he possessed during his lifetime, and presumably played, suggests a proficiency beyond mere dabbling.

The Improbable Piano

In 1906, Dr. Guyon acquired an upright grand piano made in Richmond, Indiana, in 1905. He played the piano on occasion and the instrument was available for his three sons to play—when they were not playing baseball. The latter pursuit overcame whatever tendency they may have had in favor of music. None of the three boys played the piano, at least in their adult lives.

---

[307] *Montpelier (ID) Examiner,* January 19, 1900, p. 4.
[308] Edwin Fenimore Guyon, interview with author, Victor, Idaho, September 15-16, 1990.

The Guyon family's oral history posits that Dr. Guyon treated the initial owner of the piano for terminal cancer. The patient could not work and had no income. Because of the nature and progression of the disease, the only thing Dr. Guyon could reasonably do was to ease the fellow's pain until his inevitable demise. To accommodate the desperate man, Dr. Guyon agreed to take the piano as an in-kind payment.

Grandpa's records reflect his treatment of J. L. Dougherty on a daily basis from August 25, 1906, through October 27, 1906, a period of fifty-seven days, during which he recorded office visits of one to five per day. The ledger says nothing about the details of the treatment, but the timing, frequency, and number of the visits confirms the accuracy of the oral history.

On October 30, 1906, the entry "to storage and dray" for the sum of five dollars indicates that Dr. Guyon himself paid to have the piano moved to his home. His total charges for the period of his treatment of Mr. Dougherty were $223.50, which is the amount credited for the piano. In today's dollars, the $223.50 in fees traded for the piano amounts to at least $5,587.50 and could approach $12,000.00.

Poet in Secret

It is not well known outside the Guyon family, or perhaps even within, that Dr. Guyon sometimes busied himself writing poetry. I have copies of approximately a dozen poems found in his effects, but there are probably others. One titled "The Fleet" is handwritten and reflects political sentiments that can only be characterized as unabashedly patriotic, whereas the rest are more personally reflective, nostalgic, and poignant. Like his letters, most are typewritten. I include a sampling in Appendix V, without change, as reflective of a personal, sentimental, and patriotic side of my grandfather.

Collectively and individually, the poems reveal a number of things about Grandpa that I believe are important to this biography. The most obvious is that they reflect a level of intelligence, education, and sophistication that our family has always taken for granted in a general way, but may not have been able to quantify objectively.

The mechanics of the poems are not particularly complicated, but the ideas expressed touch upon and identify universal sentiments that, after all, are at least two of the objectives of the poet. Lamentation for lost youth, existential fatalism over the realities of life, and poignant heartbreak over a lost love are all universally recognized and felt. Yet the ability to embody those feelings and thoughts in the written word in a way that touches the reader requires something from the writer that transcends the mere desire to do so.

Dr. Guyon as "The Man With the Hoe" in 1904

Doc's long list of activities and accomplishments in Montpelier included acting in plays produced locally by the Montpelier Dramatic Company or its predecessors (the "Company"). In 1899 he was cast as Paul Benton in *The Burglar*, which caused the local newspaper to quip: "[Doc] always is best as a villain [and in this case] sustained his character in good shape."[309]

In 1904 he appeared in *Human Hearts* as "Fred Armsdale, whose luck was fatal." [310] His involvement with the Company would continue for more than a decade. It is not known how many plays were presented by the Company, although at its inception its objective was to present at least one per month.[311]

Near the turn of the century, the appetite in Montpelier for theatrical productions had clearly waned,[312] although that fact did not dissuade the Company from continuing its presentations.[313] Local dramatic companies in Bear Lake County's smaller towns also continued to present plays well into the 1920s and 1930s.

Dr. Guyon reportedly wrote the play called *The Man with the Hoe*, in which he played the leading role in mid-1904.[314] Later that same year, on August 26, he was named as the musical director of the Company.[315] Still later, in September 1904, the Company also presented a play called *The Parish Priest*,[316]

---

[309] *Montpelier (ID) Examiner*, December 13, 1899.

[310] *Montpelier (ID) Examiner*, March 11, 1904, p. 1.

[311] *Montpelier (ID) Examiner*, March 21, 1896, p. 4.

[312] *Montpelier (ID) Examiner*, April 16, 1899.

[313] If an organization such as the Montpelier Dramatic Club sounds out of place today, it must be remembered that in a day when television was nonexistent, silent movies were rare, and radio transmission to general audiences had yet to be born, live public entertainment was an important part of the fabric of society. Until movies and radio became available, plays may have been the *only* form of entertainment available to Montpelier residents whose tastes required something more than the mundane.

[314] *Montpelier (ID) Examiner*, March 9, 1906, p. 1. The article observed that *The Man with the Hoe* was "written by home talent and considering that it was their first efforts along the line of play-writing, the Examiner truly congratulates the authors upon their success."

[315] "New Dramatic Company," *Montpelier (ID) Examiner*, August 26, 1904, p. 1.

[316] *Montpelier (ID) Examiner*, September 23, 1904, p. 1.

in which, according to Guyon family lore, Dr. Guyon appeared, although his role is unknown.

Doc Guyon as "The Man With the Hoe" in 1906

The following year Doc Guyon appeared as "Col. Randall, with a heart as black as night" in a production called *A Vagabond's Honor* presented on March 25, 1905,[317] and less than a month later, on April 14, 1905, appeared as "Capt. Ralston, Capt. In U.S.A." in *Between Love and Duty*.[318] Within a month thereafter, he appeared as Willard Graham, "a false friend," in the Company's rendition of *Jack o'Diamond, or the Fate of a Gambler's Wife*.[319]

In early 1906, the Company again presented *The Man with the Hoe*, with Dr. Guyon again playing the lead character John Ward. The 1906 production was notably well advertised in the local newspaper, including photographs of Dr. Guyon[320] and an unidentified female character.[321]

A number of plays, including *The Banker's Partner*, *Between Love and Duty* (mentioned above), *Little Alabama*, and *Charley's Aunt*, were advertised between 1905 and 1908, but it is not entirely clear which were actually performed; it appears to have been the Company's practice to drum up interest by placing small ads in the local newspapers that a particular play was being prepared, but giving no specific date for its performance.

---

[317] *Montpelier (ID) Examiner*, March 24, 1905, p. 3. The advertisement for the presentation was encouraging: "General admission 35 cents, children 25 cents and reserved seats 50 cents. The sale of seats at Brennan & Davis' has been large and the indications are that the company will play to a packed house."

[318] *Montpelier (ID) Examiner*, April 14, 1905.

[319] *Montpelier (ID) Examiner*, May 5, 1905, p. 2.

[320] *Montpelier (ID) Examiner*, February 23, 1906, p. 5.

[321] *Montpelier (ID) Examiner*, March 2, 1906, p. 4.

On June 2, 1911, the Company notified the public that it intended to present "in the future" the play *Arizona*, billed as "a great military drama," in which Dr. Guyon was to play the part of Tony Montano. It appears that the play was never performed.

Cast of "The Honor of the Cowboy," presented on May 23, 1915. Dr. Guyon is on the far right. Others unknown.

After a four-year hiatus, on May 23, 1915, Dr. Guyon appeared in a production of *The Honor of the Cowboy*, advertised as "a beautiful western drama."[322] A surviving cast photograph immediately above this paragraph reveals that the costumes and sets were remarkably well done. It is unknown whether he appeared in or was affiliated with the Company in any play productions after that date.

Enlightenment and Sound in Montpelier

Plays presented after sundown, along with every other indoor activity, were of necessity limited to being viewed or engaged in via candlepower or kerosene lights. Electricity for general use found its first Idaho application in Ketchum in 1882,[323] but Montpelier would have to wait more than twenty years for the valuable commodity. After the incorporation of the Montpelier Electric Light Company on September 15, 1902, and the construction of a plant, power began to flow on February 18, 1903.[324]

To facilitate communication in Bear Lake County generally, a private telephone line between Montpelier and Paris may have been in existence

---

[322] *Montpelier (ID) Examiner*, March 19, 1915, p. 1.
[323] Idaho History: Idaho Historical Overview, accessed September 12, 2016, http://www.ereferencedesk.com/resources/state-history/idaho.html.
[324] Rich, *History of Montpelier*, 86-87.

since the late 1880s, but telephone service for general use did not arrive in Montpelier until 1901.[325]

It is likely that Dr. Guyon contracted for telephone service as soon as it was available, although no specific date is known. The earliest evidence of telephone service at his office, which is consistently listed as "P. O. Box 342, Riter Bros. Block," was on letterhead dated December 26, 1910, which identifies his office telephone number as "24."[326] Four years later, on February 26, 1914, his office number is listed as "97-w" with no residence number. Still later, on April 28, 1924, his office number was "305" and his residence phone "301." His office phone number apparently changed at least once again, in 1929, when he listed it as "40," although the "301" residence number seems to have remained the same through at least 1929 and likely thereafter.

Extended Family Sadness and Sorrow

In the fall of 1904, Dr. Guyon was called, along with his colleague Dr. Poynter, to set a fractured femur of his sister-in-law, Sadie McDermott, who had fallen in her kitchen.[327] Sadie was in poor health, and her death at age forty-six on February 24, 1905, exactly six months after the accident, may have been hastened by the fall.[328]

Barely a month would pass after Sadie's death before more sorrow would visit Doc Guyon's in-laws, this time occasioned by the death in Nebraska of the family's patriarch, William Burke. This event prompted Effie, Pete McDermott, and Pete's daughter, also called Sadie after her mother, to attend the funeral and deal with family affairs in Brady Island, Nebraska.[329]

At the time, Effie was just over six months pregnant with her first child, Edwin Fenimore. Effie and Doc would have been saddened that their child would never know his maternal grandfather.

The distance from Montpelier to Brady Island is about 566 miles as the crow flies, and somewhat longer via rail. Top speed for a steam locomotive in 1905 was about 54 miles per hour.[330] The average speed of

---

[325] Ibid., 85-86.

[326] He also listed a residence number in 1910, but the portion of the page with the number is torn off, making it impossible to determine.

[327] "Met With Serious Accident," *Montpelier (ID) Examiner*, September 23, 1904, p. 1.

[328] "Death of Mrs. McDermott," *Montpelier (ID) Examiner*, February 24, 1905, p. 1.

[329] "Local News," *Montpelier (ID) Examiner*, March 31, 1905, p. 5.

[330] R. W. Western, "Some Economic Considerations Affecting Railways, *Railway Times* 87 (1905): 547, accessed August 16, 2016, http://books.google.com/books?id=ng5CAQAAIAAJ

the train taken by Effie and Pete McDermott to Nebraska was significantly less, likely closer to 30–35 miles per hour. In all probability, the trip took at least fourteen hours and possibly more than eighteen hours.

New Posterity

The years 1905–1909 were personally gratifying to Dr. Guyon in ways that transcended his professional life and the life he followed in his fraternal organizations. The beginning of that period marked the starting point of his second family—all boys—which changed his life profoundly. The first, Edwin Fenimore, was born on June 24, 1905. The middle name of Fenimore is believed to have been borrowed from James Fenimore Cooper, the respected author of *Leather Stocking Tales* and other books. At least once later on, in a letter of introduction to be carried by Edwin Fenimore on a trip to California, Dr. Guyon referred to him as "Edwin Jr." Edwin Fenimore's birth prompted the following "Local News" item in the *Montpelier Examiner*:

> A little stranger arrived at the home of Dr. E. F. Guyon last Saturday and announced his intention of engaging in the practice of medicine with his dad. For the present the young man will confine his work to sampling paregoric and compelling "the old man" to do the floor walking stunt in the wee hours of the night.[331]

The second son was Wendell Shattuck, my father, who was born on May 9, 1907. Wendell's birth was heralded as follows:

> A little son, of regulation weight and lung power, arrived at the home of Dr. Guyon yesterday morning. The mother and child are doing well, but it will require careful nursing to bring the doctor out all right.[332]

Wendell's first name was reportedly borrowed from the great jurist Oliver Wendell Holmes, Jr., and his middle name was his maternal grandmother's maiden name. Wendell had shoulder-length hair

---

pg=PA547&dpg=PA547&dq=steam+locomotive+speed+1904&source=bl&ots=CqV_wBduE m&sig=Vo457OmOWwOauN.

[331] *Montpelier (ID) Examiner*, June 30, 1905.

[332] "Local News," *Montpelier (ID) Examiner*, May 10, 1907, p. 7.

throughout his childhood and well into his teens, a choice ostensibly made—and enforced—by Effie and decidedly *not* by Wendell. This decision caused the latter no end of difficulties ranging from taunts to name-calling initiated by school-age hecklers. More than a few of these incidents reportedly resulted in fisticuffs.

The "caboose" of this new family was Royal Chatterton, born on June 15, 1909. His arrival was memorialized as follows:

> Dr. and Mrs. E. F. Guyon are entertaining a little son who arrived at their home last Tuesday morning. The doctor says that he has now got three little jacks at his house.[333]

It is not known whence Royal's names derived. As a child, he was nicknamed "Buster," which metamorphosed into "Bus" later on and stuck to him tenaciously through the end of his life.

All three boys were also nicknamed "Doc" after their father among their friends and associates. When grown, all three exceeded their father's height by at least four inches and, in the case of Edwin Fenimore and Wendell, at least two or three more.

Family Life in Montpelier

In 1905, Effie and Dr. Guyon lived above the Riter Brothers Pharmacy located at the intersection of Highway 30 and Highway 89 on the northwest corner of Washington Street and Fourth Street. Edwin Fenimore was born there, but living accommodations were shortly to change. Approximately a year after Edwin Fenimore's birth, Dr. Guyon and his family moved into their own home on South Ninth Street, purchased from Sam Lewis.[334]

The new home, which the family would occupy for the next thirteen years, was located at 216 South Ninth Street, the third house from the corner of Ninth and Jefferson Streets on the east side of South Ninth Street. The home was purchased in Dr. Guyon's name alone for the sum of $665.[335] The family occupied the house continuously until June 5, 1918, when it was sold, this time by Dr. Guyon and Effie jointly, to Harriet Bird for the sum of $1,250.[336]

---

[333] "Local News," *Montpelier (ID) Examiner*, June 18, 1909, p. 5.

[334] *Montpelier (ID) Examiner*, July 20, 1906.

[335] Official Record of Deeds of Bear Lake County, Idaho, Bk. 13, p. 27.

[336] Official Record of Deeds of Bear Lake County, Idaho, Bk. 25, p. 491. The legal description of

Compared to the apartment above the Riter Brothers Drugstore, the new home must have seemed like heaven to Effie. As far as is known, this house was her first, and having her own home in which to raise her new family had to have been of no small importance to her.

The Guyon residence sported a picket fence and a board sidewalk between the house and Ninth Street. "Conveniences" included a tap in the kitchen for (cold) water and a "two holer"[337] outhouse in the back yard for bathroom needs. A small barn, also in the back, was home to the horse that pulled Dr. Guyon's buggy in the summer and his cutter (sleigh) in the winter.

The house was generously equipped with a coal-burning range on which Effie cooked meals and heated water for baths for her family, which grew in number from three to five. Both Wendell and Royal were born at the new residence.[338] Baths for the children occurred every Saturday night in a galvanized tin washtub with water heated by Effie on the coal range. The family's clothing was cleaned on a washboard and dried on a clothesline in the back yard.[339] Refrigeration depended upon blocks of ice originally sawn from a frozen Bear Lake and then purchased from the harvester. In cold weather, heat was generated by burning wood or coal in a cast-iron stove.

During the winter when traveling in his sleigh or buggy, the resolute physician wore a hat and long, heavy, yellowish sheepskin coat (with the wool inward) that extended all the way to the tops of his feet. The coat's thick collar was supplemented by a scarf around his neck, and his feet were warmed, to the extent possible, with bricks heated in the family's oven.

The parents were strict and, according to Edwin Fenimore, physically punished all three boys if and when the need arose. Edwin Fenimore reported with no hint of overstatement that his father's middle name was "discipline." The role of disciplinarian was primarily Doc's, but Effie "switched" the children "every once in a while."[340] Edwin Fenimore considered such punishment of little note when compared to an unnamed neighbor on Ninth Street, who punished his children by lashing them with a snake whip that made them cry "bloody murder." Edwin Fenimore mused

---

the parcel is Lot 14, Block 14, Ed Burgoyne's Addition to the City of Montpelier.

[337] I have always questioned the wisdom and utility of multiple-seat outhouse arrangements, given the presumed universal and unequivocal proclivity in favor of privacy during use.

[338] Edwin Fenimore Guyon, interview with author, Victor, Idaho, September 15, 1990.

[339] Ibid.

[340] Ibid.

that such treatment of one's children in today's environment would be a hanging offense.

Hooky-Bobbing Is Dangerous in More Ways Than One

One winter circa 1915, Edwin Fenimore, and perhaps his brothers, had been cautioned by their father that they were forbidden to catch free rides on passing horse-drawn sleighs (called "hooky-bobbing" later on and perhaps even then) because of the danger.[341] Overcome with a desire for fun, Edwin Fenimore and a friend or two did it anyway.

Much to Edwin Fenimore's chagrin, his father learned of the misdeed and, in Edwin Fenimore's words, he "caught hell" for it. Punishment, in addition to warnings "never [to] do it again," was a serious spanking. During this hands-on lesson, the well-meaning father's eyes welled up with tears and he became so emotional he was barely able to utter the heartfelt words "this hurts me more than it does you." By today's standards the punishment might be characterized as abusive, but apparently it had the desired effect. In addition, the enduring message to Edwin Fenimore, who related the incident more than seventy-five years later, was that his dad loved him without reservation.[342]

The three boys had a close and loving relationship with both parents, who never argued (in front of their children). Money was not plentiful, but neither was it nonexistent. All three boys were encouraged and expected to become employed as they grew up. All three worked as call boys[343] for the OSL Railroad during their teens, and at better jobs as time went on. Wendell was able to secure a night switchman's job in September, 1929, and Edwin Fenimore eventually became a brakeman.

Frugal Buster, unlike his brothers, saved his money. Later on, in 1929, because of his financial temperance he was able to purchase an "El-Royce radio machine" at a cost of $265, along with the agency (for which he paid $125) to sell to the public.[344]

---

[341] The unscheduled passengers attached themselves to the runner or some other convenient handhold, taking care to hide from the driver by assuming a squatting position while their feet glided over the snow and ice.

[342] Edwin Fenimore Guyon, interview with author, Victor, Idaho, September 15, 1990.

[343] "Call boys" were railroad employees whose tasks included notifying railroad crews from Pocatello of their assigned westbound trains.

[344] E. F. Guyon to his granddaughter Mary Brown, 27 February 1929.

Political Moves

There is no indication that Dr. Guyon, who was fifty-three years old in November of 1906, was slowing down at all. In addition to his other activities he ran, unsuccessfully, for political office. In the general election of November 6, 1906, Dr. Guyon ran as a Democrat for state senator against William L. Rich, the Republican, and Joseph C. Rich, the "citizens' nominee." Dr. Guyon received sixty-seven votes in West Montpelier, four in East Montpelier, and two in Bloomington.[345]

In 1907, Idaho Governor Steunenberg again appointed Dr. Guyon to the State Board of Medical Examiners, whose obligation it was to ensure minimum standards of competence for physicians practicing medicine in Idaho. In that capacity he was the author of yet another law regulating the practice of medicine, eventually passed by the Idaho Legislature in that year.[346]

In 1909, he ran successfully on the Democratic ticket for the post of Montpelier City Councilman from the Second Ward.[347] This election to the city council was followed by his election as president of the council.[348]

Silent Movies in Montpelier

During this same time period, between approximately 1905 and 1910, Dr. Guyon purchased and installed the first movie projector in Montpelier.[349]Grandpa Guyon thoroughly enjoyed movies, and accurately foresaw their popularity with audiences generally. The entertainment fare of the era consisted of silent films ("talkies" would not appear until the late 1920s).

The films were presented in a small theater on the south side of Main Street several doors east of the Odd Fellows building.[350] It was either in

---

[345] "A Good Vote Cast," *Montpelier (ID) Examiner*, November 9, 1906.

[346] As discussed above, Dr. Guyon was also the author of a bill designed to enforce minimum standards of competence for practicing physicians in Idaho passed by the Idaho Legislature in 1897.

[347] "Democrats Win Best Part of the Ticket," *Montpelier (ID) Examiner*, April 9, 1909, p. 1.

[348] "City Council Doings," *Montpelier (ID) Examiner*, June 18, 1909, p. 2.

[349] Edwin Fenimore Guyon, interview with author, Victor, Idaho, September 15, 1990. Also see Rich, *History of Montpelier*, 121–22: "The first moving picture show was played in Montpelier in 1901 and silent movies became a popular form of recreation. The first theater, if it can be called such, was located where the Royal Bakery now stands."

[350] The silent film era extended from about 1894 to 1929, and initially required an in-house interpreter, whose job it was to explain the players and plots of the films, usually relatively short ones, to the patrons. After films became longer, intertitles that appeared on the screen itself were used to allow viewers to read what was happening in the film.

or near the small building occupied for many years by Eddy Grosjean's barber shop. The enterprise, dubbed the "Rex Theatre," was to be managed by Dr. Guyon's son Fay. [351] Because of unresolved—or unresolvable—conflicts between Grandpa and his firstborn son, the business failed.[352]

In-House Movie Interpreters

Reminiscent of his first foray into the movie business, Grandpa kept a printed two-page document entitled "A Cow Boy's Romance, A New Moving Picture Play." It contains a synopsis of the movie, along with a list of all the characters. Research into the movie industry during its early years revealed that *A Cow Boy's Romance* was a silent cowboy movie produced in 1909, before intertitles.

The document probably accompanied the actual film reels to the theater and was to be read during the showing of the movie by the in-house interpreter to explain the plot and characters to the audience. Whether it was actually read is not known.

More Cinema

Dr. Guyon's movie interest was thwarted by the demise of the Rex Theatre, but it was not dead. On March 25, 1916, he sent to the North American Film Corporation of New York City what he called "a few suggestions" for the sequel to *The Diamond from the Sky*, a silent-era adventure motion picture released on May 3, 1915. The film starred Lottie Pickford (the sister of silent-screen actors Mary and Jack Pickford), Irving Cummings, and William Russell. The movie was a serial with English intertitles, filmed in thirty episodes (a total of nine hundred minutes), and purposely left unfinished.[353] The company solicited suggestions from the public for the film's completion and advertised it would pay $5,000 to the winner. The document prepared by Dr. Guyon was certainly an attempt to win the contest. Sadly, his proposal was not the winning submission.

Dr. Guyon owned no known interest in any movie enterprise after the Rex Theatre debacle, but continued to be fascinated with viewing movies. He often attended the old Montpelier Theater, located on the east side of

---

[351] "Local News," *Montpelier (ID) Examiner*, July 10, 1908, p. 7.
[352] Edwin Fenimore Guyon, interview with author, Victor, Idaho, September 15, 1990.
[353] "*The Diamond from the Sky*," Wikipedia, accessed August 16, 2016, https://en.wikipedia.org/wiki/The_Diamond_from_the_Sky.

South Ninth Street in Montpelier, just south of the Bear Lake Motor Company's parking lot. Edwin Fenimore recalled that his father regularly took all three of his boys to the movies, and when he encountered children who lacked the price of admission hanging around the theater, he often bought them tickets as well.

Playing Solo

Dr. Guyon's personal entertainment was supplemented by playing cards with friends at Johnny O'Connor's saloon. The popular watering hole was conveniently located at the northwest corner of Tenth and Main Streets, just a block west of his office at Ninth and Main. The card players' favorite game was "solo,"[354] which they probably played for small amounts of money. Even though this pursuit likely encouraged beer-drinking on a relatively minor scale, its overriding objective was socializing and camaraderie.

Effie certainly did not encourage this male bonding activity, but she likely tolerated it as the least of other possible evils.

A Wyoming Gold-Mining Venture

On May 13, 1910, Doc Guyon became involved in the formation of a Wyoming corporation known as the "Grays River Placer Mining Company."[355] The new organization named its principal office in Afton, Wyoming, and other branch offices in Montpelier and Salt Lake City. Only the bylaws of the corporation have survived in Grandpa's effects. Other than the venture presumably was unsuccessful, no details are known about the other principals, the amounts invested, or mining activities.

---

[354] Solo is a four-man trick-taking card game (that uses a fifty-two-card deck), based on the English card game whist, wherein one player often plays against the other three.
[355] The correct spelling is "Greys River" and refers to the fifty-five-mile-long river just east of the Idaho/Wyoming border that flows into the Snake River and the present Palisades Reservoir at the town of Alpine, Wyoming.

Chapter 10.

PERSISTENCE IN MONTPELIER

circa 1910–1918

*'Tis easy to be pleasant, when life glides on like a song;
but the man worth while is the man who will smile
when everything goes dead wrong.*
— Ella Wheeler Wilcox

The years covered in this chapter reflect achievements that distinguished Dr. Guyon in the medical profession and among his IOOF brothers, but also mark the beginning of his economic decline and the enormous pressures it brought to bear on him and his family.

The Apogee of Dr. Guyon's Professional and Fraternal Success

Dr. Guyon's star ascended to remarkable heights during the second decade of the 20th century, both professionally and in his beloved IOOF.

Main Street in Montpelier circa 1906 as it appeared looking west from 8th Street

Not only did he secure national and international prominence and renown for his medical knowledge and skill relating to the diagnosis and treatment of tubercular diseases, but he also rose in the ranks of his beloved IOOF to the lofty position of Grand Patriarch of the Idaho Encampment,[356] a position he held in 1911.[357] Doc was a regular and popular speaker at many IOOF functions, and as Grand Patriarch delivered the keynote address at the IOOF ninety-second anniversary celebration in Blackfoot on April 26, 1911.[358] At the same time he was a stalwart Odd Fellow, he managed to maintain an affiliation with the

---

356 *Idaho Odd Fellow* 13, no. 6 (1908, January).
357 *Idaho Odd Fellow* 16, no. 3 (1911, July).
358 "Odd Fellows Will Celebrate," *Idaho Statesman* (Boise), April 26, 1911.

Woodmen of the World, another fraternal organization, although little is known about his activities in the latter. Suffice it to say that his involvement in both organizations exacted significant amounts of time, although his Odd Fellowship clearly was the most demanding.

IOOF convention, location and date unknown, but likely circa 1910 – 1920
E. F. Guyon in center foreground. Others unknown .

In local society, Dr. Guyon was often asked to speak at and participate in public events of all kinds, including a "patriotic address" as part of the Fourth of July celebration in 1911.[359] Four years later he again participated in the event, this time in charge of "character features" for the Fourth of July parade.[360]

The following quotation hints at how he was able to balance his fraternal obligations and opportunities with his social and family responsibilities:

> Possessed of a mind of rare strength and symmetry, well stored with the thrifty study of years, Dr. Guyon has achieved much in his calling. He started out in life a poor boy and by reason of his own efforts, force of energy and

[359] "Big Crowd Enjoyed Montpelier's Celebration," *Montpelier (ID) Examiner*, July 7, 1911, p. 1.
[360] "Arrangements for 4th Are Progressing Nicely," *Montpelier (ID) Examiner*, June 25, 1915, p 1.

predominating will-power he has risen from an humble station in life to one of competence, distinction and eminence.[361]

Strength of mind suggests the ability of focus as well as the power of self-direction, not to mention the abilities to learn quickly, retain information, and process that information in a way that allows its comprehension and relation to other information already learned. Symmetry of mind denotes a balanced mind, with all its parts working in harmony, a capability of not only learning, but learning efficiently.

The additional statement in the French Biography that "in every aspect of his character he is broad, liberal and enlightened and closely in touch with the higher and better development of society" is not an empty accolade; rather, I believe, it is an honest and accurate description of the man Dr. Guyon had become. There does not ever appear to be a time when he was not fully engaged in trying to better his circumstances, those of his family, and society at large through one means or another.

The Benevolent Overachiever

Dr. Guyon was a classic overachiever, defined by Webster as "one who achieves success over and above the standard or expected level esp. at an early age." This description is entirely consistent with both the French and Johnson Biographies and is supported by virtually every scrap of paper that is known to have survived him. The "force of energy and predominating willpower" echoed in the French Biography were real parts of him that provided the fuel that allowed him to attain his professional, fraternal, and family objectives.

His attempts at betterment were not limited to himself and those close to him. He had somehow been imbued with the ideal in his youth that it matters what individuals do in their lives because it affects society at large. I believe it is likely attributable to Emily Louise and his conservative religious upbringing, but whatever its source, it had a great and continuing effect upon him throughout his entire life.

Doc Guyon seems to have been extraordinarily well organized. His effects include a number of papers and speeches he authored for one IOOF or medicine-related function or another, ranging from the

---

[361] French, *History of Idaho*, 1256.

investiture of a new recruit in the ranks of the IOOF to a commentary on medical legislation to a detailed report about his attendance at an IOOF-supported convention in Philadelphia. These documents, always clear, are at times eloquent and flowery, and at other times very businesslike, demonstrating a broad range of communicative ability.

An Important Appointment in Denver

Idaho Governor James H. Hawley appointed Dr. Guyon and five other Idaho physicians[362] to represent the state of Idaho at the convention of the National Association for the Study of the Prevention of Tuberculosis held in Denver, Colorado, on June 19–21 , 1911,[363] by the National Association of Physicians. Doc's expertise and interest in the diagnosis and treatment of tubercular diseases, along with the background and experience he had acquired in Diamondville during the period 1900–1903, probably contributed to his appointment to this significant honor.

A Parkinson Partnership

In the meantime, Dr. Guyon formed a partnership to practice medicine in Montpelier with Dr. G. T. Parkinson.[364] Described in the *Montpelier Examiner* as a "young man," Dr. Guyon's new partner was probably the son or nephew of his old friend William B. Parkinson. In mid-1911, Dr. Guyon's published business card read, "Drs. Guyon & Parkinson Physicians and Surgeons."[365] The business location over Riter Bros. Drug Store remained the same, but the new partners added the statement "Night or Country Calls Promptly Attended" on their joint professional card. The partnership did not last long. By September 1911, public notices of the partnership had ceased in Montpelier.

An International Conference Beckons Dr. Guyon

Approximately fifteen months after the Denver conference, Dr. Guyon, along with four other representatives from Idaho,[366] was

---

[362] William F. Howard, Pocatello; Ellis Kackley, Soda Springs; John B. Morris, Lewiston; William C. Maxey, Caldwell; Patrick J. Scallon, Coeur d'Alene; and Ralph Falk, Boise.
[363] *Northwest Medicine* 3, no. 6 (1911, May): 176.
[364] "Short Circuits," *Paris (ID) Post*, May 5, 1911, p. 8.
[365] *Montpelier (ID) Examiner*, May 26, 1911, p. 8.
[366] Dr. George E. Hyde, Rexburg; Dr. Ralph Falk, Boise; Dr. W. R. Hamilton, Weiser; and Dr. O. F. Page, Sandpoint.

appointed to attend the Fifteenth International Congress on Hygiene and Demography in Washington, DC, from September 23–28, 1912.[367] The Congress, meeting in the United States for the first time, was the preeminent research conference in the area of public health. Its importance, both nationally and internationally, is difficult to overstate. Its significance is underscored by the presence of United States President Taft,[368] serving as honorary chairman of the Congress, who delivered the opening address.[369]

Dr. Guyon Represents the IOOF at Winnipeg, Manitoba, in 1912

Later in 1912 Dr. Guyon participated in another important event that further defined his affiliation with the IOOF and his expertise in tubercular diseases. He was chosen as an international representative of the IOOF, this time to the Sovereign Grand Lodge of the Idaho IOOF, held in Winnipeg, Manitoba.

One of the purposes of this Canadian conclave was to take steps to construct a specialized hospital where members of the IOOF suffering from tuberculosis, regardless of nationality, could be treated and cared for.[370] As in 1911, Dr. Guyon's background and experience with tubercular diseases were pivotal in his appointment.

Incidentally, his Canadian visit, according to the local newspaper, required a month of his time, and allowed Effie to visit her relatives in Brady Island, Nebraska, while Dr. Guyon went on to his convention.[371]

Doc Guyon Attends a 1915 Tuberculosis Conference in Indianapolis

Three years later, the *Idaho Statesman* reported that Dr. Guyon, among others, was appointed by the governor to represent the state of Idaho at the Mississippi Valley Conference on Tuberculosis in Indianapolis, Indiana, on September 29–30 , 1915. The Boise newspaper also groused that among the appointees to the conference, no physician from Idaho's capital city was selected.[372]

---

367 French, *History of Idaho,* 1256.
368 William Howard Taft (1857–1930) was president of the United States for only one term, 1909–1913.
369 *"Transactions of the International Congress on Hygiene and Demography, Vol. I."* Washington: Government Printing Office 1913.
370 French, *History of Idaho,* 1256.
371 *Montpelier (ID) Examiner,* October 4, 1912, p. 1.
372 *Idaho Statesman* (Boise), June 19, 1915. The heading for the article is "Boise Doctors Are Ignored

The objective of the Mississippi Valley Conference was the dissemination of knowledge, expertise, and information on various subjects relating to public health. The anticipated result was to increase public awareness and thereby to decrease the negative effects of various diseases and conditions on the public at large.

The Price of Prominence

Dr. Guyon's travel to and from the conferences, and the conferences themselves, took him away from his medical practice for extended periods, not to mention the day-to-day time drain these fraternal and professional commitments added to his already frenetic schedule. The International Congress in Washington, DC, in 1911 probably consumed at least two weeks of his time; the Mississippi Valley Conference was likely the same; and the Winnipeg conference required an entire month.

The conferences no doubt added to Dr. Guyon's professional status and charisma, but whether they were valuable monetarily is debatable. Most likely, he was reimbursed only for costs of travel and lodging.

Dr. Guyon's attendance at national and international functions did not seem to deter him from other, more local, professional activities, even though by now he was progressing age-wise into his sixties. The organization of the Bear Lake Medical Society in late 1916, with Dr. Guyon as president, is consistent with his propensities to better the medical profession in general.[373] It also suggests that at age sixty-three in late 1916, he had no inclination to contemplate retirement or even to slow down his professional activities.

Financial Successes and Failures

The world at large consistently perceived Dr. Guyon as a financial success. The French Biography trumpets that "he was very successful from the start" after he opened his medical practice in Pendleton in 1892. The Johnson Biography acknowledges he "had built up a large and rapidly growing practice [in Montpelier], in which he has been successful professionally as well as financially." His opportunity to go to Diamondville in 1900 was described as "lucrative."[374] There is nothing in the public record to suggest that Dr. Guyon was anything other than a

---

by Governor."
[373] *Northwest Medicine* 16, no. 8 (1917, August): 252.
[374] Wilde, *Treasured Tidbits of Time*, 1:319.

financial success. The truth is that he struggled financially at times during his professional life and was near penniless when he died in 1934, largely due to his inability to collect a very large amount of accumulated, but unpaid, fees.[375]

The calculation of fees earned and fees unpaid comes from three separate patient ledgers kept by Dr. Guyon during his lifetime, each of which contains a history of his medical practice during a specific period of time. Collectively, the three ledgers cover less than one-half of Dr. Guyon's career. The earliest of the three records transactions in approximately 1903 through 1905; the second from approximately 1905 through 1911; and the third from approximately 1917 through 1923.[376]

The time periods covered by the three ledgers are necessarily approximate because they often overlap. Under the double-entry accounting system Dr. Guyon consistently used, the entry of a particular patient might contain a notation like "balance n.l. 130," and show a balance owed of $50 on the right side of the ledger. The meaning is that the $50 was owed, but was carried to another entry for the same patient in another ledger on page 130 ("n.l." means new ledger, but it could as easily have the notation "o.l.," meaning old ledger, depending where the notation was made). If the ledger referred to is one of the missing ledgers, there is no way to determine whether that $50 was ever actually paid. Likewise, it is impossible to determine how many patients he saw and the amount of fees he billed during the periods when no ledger exists.

It is my personal belief, consistent with public perception, that Grandpa was financially prosperous during many parts of his professional life, but not consistently so. Whatever times of financial prosperity he had seem to have been followed by periods of relative famine. It is impossible to pinpoint them with any degree of accuracy from known records. He complained to Maud of being poor as early as 1915,[377] but it is impossible

---

[375] Readers, and particularly relatives, may wonder why I would include a discussion of such a touchy subject. After all, does it not tarnish the otherwise pristine image of Dr. Guyon? My answer is that the reasons behind his financial distresses only serve to emphasize the qualities that made him the remarkable person he was, and whether he had money and wealth to go along with those qualities is quite beside the point. The public at large may tend to measure success in life by bank account balances, but Dr. Guyon is a good example of what is truly important, despite bank balances. Perhaps most importantly, I believe his portrait would be unfinished without it.

[376] Dr. Guyon continued to treat patients well into his seventies, even though his level of activity diminished as his age advanced, and likely discontinued seeing patients sometime during early to mid-1933. The entirety of his medical practice stretched from early 1892 into 1933, a period of approximately forty-one years. The three surviving ledgers cover only about fourteen of those years. This leaves about 65 percent of his professional life undocumented.

[377] E. F. Guyon to Maud Brown, August 3, 1915.

to discern what circumstances prompted the statement, or even whether it was an earnest assessment of his condition or merely an offhand comment.

The period of 1915–1920 in all probability started to bring to bear irresistible forces that had only lingered in the background until then— forces with consequences that he had been able to ignore or keep at bay for years, hoping that his accumulated unpaid fees would eventually be paid. As long as the payment of his ongoing fees met and exceeded his present needs, he could disregard the ever-increasing mountain of debt owed to him.

Eventually, the accumulation of unpaid fees inevitably began to take its toll. Once ongoing needs exceeded current collections, the difference created an urgent requirement that could only be satisfied by collecting what was already owed. If he had had a cushion of cash to default to beginning in 1915, he would not have been devastated financially to the degree he was by the particularly meager year of 1918 (discussed in more detail below), his advancing age, or periods of illness or downturns in the economy in general or his medical practice in particular.

The Nature of Dr. Guyon's Medical Practice

The most common service provided by Dr. Guyon is identified in the ledgers by the ubiquitous notation "Rx," which doubtless means "prescription." The second most common notation is "visit," which is either written in its entirety or appears as a capital V. Both are often used together, such as "1 visit [or V] & Rx." Seldom did he exceed the two-inch space available to describe his service, and he used ditto marks wherever he could. Most of the entries in the three ledgers were for visits and prescriptions, although sprinkled throughout are varying designations, including "operation," "confinement," and "service." For convenience in the following discussion, all charges are referred to as "fees."

Dr. Guyon's fees for office visits and prescriptions varied, depending on the complexity and seriousness of the problem, time spent and other factors. Through 1923 he consistently charged two dollars for an office visit, two dollars for a vaccination, and one dollar for a prescription. Where two office visits occurred on the same day, he often discounted his fee to $3.50 for both. Other services, such as "operation [$50.00 or $80.00]," "anesthesia [$5.00]," "confinement [$15.00]," "treat fracture [$15.00]," "to treat whiskey [$100.00]," "After Treat[ment $100.00]," and "glasses [$10.00]," carried higher, and varying, fees.

He is known to have traveled, by buggy or sleigh, as far away as Star Valley, Wyoming, located fifty miles from Montpelier over the Crow Creek Road, to care for patients. Depending on weather and road conditions, which varied greatly due to the fact that the road was never paved, these trips to Star Valley took from three to seven days one way.

On the way to Star Valley, he spent the first or second night at the Halfway House midway along the Crow Creek Road, which, after 1912, offered a large barn capable of housing thirty-two teams and their drivers, provided overnight accommodations for people and animals, and catered to freighters and other travelers. He probably carried his trusty Iver Johnson .38 caliber top-break revolver[378] for protection.

The Conundrum of Unpaid Fees

Guyon family oral history asserts that Dr. Guyon was owed the staggering amount of at least $50,000 in fees at the time of his death. The basis for the $50,000 figure is unknown, but it is seriously understated, at least in today's dollars. From Dr. Guyon's existing patient ledgers it can be established that he collected slightly less than 60 percent of fees billed, and the roughly 40 percent he did not collect had a present value of at least $1.5 million and as much as $1.8 million or even more. Why he was unable to collect the unpaid 40 percent of his fees is partly the stuff of speculation and partly an exercise in accounting, but the inquiry leads to some important considerations about Dr. Guyon the physician and Dr. Guyon the human being that profoundly affect his overall portraiture.

It is a commonly held belief that members of the so-called "learned professions," that is to say doctors, lawyers, and dentists, tend to be poor businessmen. It has been rumored in the Guyon family that Dr. Guyon was no exception to the rule, and that he found himself in penury at the end of his life because of it. One thing is certain: the ever-increasing burden of uncollected fees, coupled with his inability to practice medicine consistently due to illness and economic conditions beyond his control, resulted in serious financial misfortune toward the end of his life.

Un Tiens Vaut Mieux que Deux Tu l'Auras[379]

A favorite criticism within the Guyon family is that Dr. Guyon often went on calls to treat patients, particularly to far-off Star Valley, and

---

[378] Royal C. Guyon to Wendell S. Guyon, 24 April 1956.
[379] French proverb: "A bird in the hand is worth two in the bush."

returned without anything to show for his efforts save chickens, eggs, or some other form of barter. The implication, of course, is that he would have returned with full payment in money for his services had he not been such a poor businessman.

Dr. Guyon's acceptance of barter in place of currency is confirmed generally in his ledgers, although not by location. During the 1903–1905 period he took as payment for services on various occasions meat, milk, cheese, printing services, a light bill payment, merchandise, meals, strawberries, raspberries, butter, potatoes, wood, flour, and even a stove. During the period 1905–1911, he accepted as payment a horse and colt, eggs, chicken, milk, vegetables, meat, furniture, shingles, barbering, labor, fish, ice, sawdust (presumably to preserve the ice), carpet, a rug, coal, a lawn mower, blankets, a bookcase, a pistol, loads of gravel, a tent, and a piano. The ledger of in-kind transactions for the period 1917–1923 included milk, labor and materials, a camp cot, chickens and eggs, butter, buttermilk, Christmas cards, vegetables, kindling, meat, potatoes, flour, onions, and pork. All three ledgers also reflect credits for "merchandise" not specifically described.

His practice of bartering for his services might be subject—in the business sense—to criticism by an idealistic accountant with little experience in real-world transactions, but over the years from 1903 to 1923 for which records exist, in-kind trades accounted for less than nine percent of Dr. Guyon's total income, and there is no known reason to assume that the missing ledgers would have reflected anything significantly different.

It may well be that it was not a question of whether Dr. Guyon would get money for his services, but whether he would get *anything at all* if he refused to accept trades. I do not believe criticism leveled against Dr. Guyon for trading services is justified, at least as it pertains to necessary and consumable items he would have to buy in any case, and perhaps for everything he bartered for, on the theory that it was always better to get something rather than nothing for his services.

Sympathy and Collecting Money Mingle Imperfectly

If Dr. Guyon's financial difficulties were not due to his acceptance of commodities in lieu of cash, they must have been the result of other determinants. Likely the most obvious of these was identified by his son Edwin Fenimore, who summed up the situation quickly, simply, and succinctly: his father was simply "too soft-hearted" when it came to the collection of his fees. In other words, according to his son, Dr. Guyon lacked the hardened heart—the "business" heart or the will—to ruthlessly

158

insist that he be paid for his services, despite the circumstances of the patient and all other considerations.[380] That initial terse description was soon followed by other adjectives such as "too good-hearted, and too kind-hearted."

Synonymous with the adjectives posited by Edwin Fenimore is "sympathetic," which also seems to describe Dr. Guyon with a high degree of accuracy: "given to, marked by, or arising from sympathy, compassion, friendliness, and sensitivity to others' emotions." These propensities speak volumes and explain a great deal about Dr. Guyon's lack of money toward the end of his life. His statement that "it seems like I never could make money and it seems that my children are the same way"[381] suggests that whatever the problem was, he viewed it as an intergenerational one, either learned or inherited by his progeny. Whatever the causes behind it, his conclusion was "It was not intended for me to have money."[382]

It is tempting to endlessly speculate about the psychological and philosophical aspects inherent in billing professional fees (i.e., earning money) but failing to collect it. In view of the fact that I am neither psychologist nor philosopher, such an analysis would be little more than homespun prattle that would add nothing to the true image of Dr. Guyon. Rather, I offer several additional possible reasons that may explain the phenomenon.

Wealth Is Inapposite to Higher Purposes

Several statements about Dr. Guyon in the French Biography are pertinent:

> He is well known as one of the ablest physicians of eastern Idaho.   * * *   In every aspect of his character he is broad, liberal and enlightened and closely in touch with the higher and better development of society.   * * *   He is a man of enlarged sympathies . . ..

---

[380] An example given me by Edwin Fenimore to explain his comment that his father was too soft-hearted was that a certain physician in southeast Idaho (who will remain nameless) made the collection of his fees paramount to *all* other considerations, or at least appeared to. If the patient lacked the required money, the doctor would take his horse, and by extension, his crops, his wagon, and his house, if necessary. No consideration whatsoever would justify the non-payment of the doctor's fees.

[381] E. F. Guyon to Maud Brown, 11 December 1930.

[382] Ibid.

These compliments describe a person who could easily look upon making money as an unfortunate but sometimes necessary digression on the road to some loftier goal. His calling in life was to be the best physician he could—not the richest one.

That is not to say he was not motivated by money at all, or that he did not appreciate its necessity, or that he did not want to possess it; however, the acquisition and accumulation of money was not first on his personal or professional list of priorities.

Nowhere in the French Biography or the Johnson Biography is it suggested that Dr. Guyon became a physician primarily to make money. Rather, the consistent message is that he wanted to matter and he wanted to make a difference in the world, both of which he did in the only way he knew.

The profit motive and the professional ideal or objective are often at odds in the professions; in fact, at times they are mutually inconsistent, in part because they are governed by different rules. In business, the proverbial "bottom line" is paramount; in the professions, the welfare of the patient or client is supreme.[383]

In the Shadow of the Plaited Serpents[384]

In addition to being an overachiever, my grandfather was an idealist, and I believe his unflinching idealism was also an important factor that in part explains his financial problems near the end of his life. Simply put, he was unwilling to compromise his principles as he saw them to make money. Webster reminds us that such a person is guided by his ideals, and especially a person who places ideals, whether achievable or not, above practical considerations.

The source of at least some of Dr. Guyon's ideals is the Hippocratic Oath, an ancient, binding covenant dating from the fifth century BC, by which fledgling physicians have been bound from time immemorial as part of the rite of passage from student to doctor. Probably first crafted by

---

[383] In larger professional organizations, uncollectible fees and costs, which at times are exorbitant to begin with, are very reluctantly "written off" and absorbed by the system, which continues to operate, although on a slightly less profitable margin, which will later be adjusted to cover the loss. Not so in a one-man office like Dr. Guyon's, where there was no "system" into which uncollected fees could be absorbed other than his office ledgers. He could not compensate for anticipated uncollectible fees because his fees had to be competitive in his limited market and he had to decide on a daily — and perhaps hourly — basis whether his financial concerns were to trump the demands and needs of patients whose need was far greater than their ability to pay.

[384] This refers to the caduceus, a symbol of the medical profession, composed of a staff with two entwined snakes and two wings at the top.

160

Hippocrates or one of his students, the oath has undergone a number of transformations in the intervening centuries, but in general it requires new physicians to swear to uphold certain standards relating to the healing arts.

The oath requires the practitioner, among many other things, to "use treatment to help the sick according to [his] ability and judgment." Nowhere in the oath is it suggested that treatment may be withheld for any reason. Payment for services is not even mentioned, almost as if the issue is too petty or common even to be considered along with the high ideals expressed in the oath.

Dr. Guyon's idealism did not force him into financial ruin, but neither did it hamper his descent. He felt morally and professionally compelled to treat patients who could not pay, and naïvely believed that their scruples would eventually prevail and they would complete their obligations to him. As a gatekeeper between the afflicted and a cure, Dr. Guyon was unable to say no to those in need, despite the fact that many took advantage of his largesse. In his mind, if the patient, for whatever reason, failed to pay the fee, then it was the patient—not Dr. Guyon—who had failed in his social, moral, and legal duty.

All Bear Lake County Physicians Were at Financial Risk

The problem of non-payment of fees was not limited to Dr. Guyon. In 1918, the local paper in Montpelier reported that besides setting minimum fees for obstetrics cases and cases involving contagious and non-contagious diseases, the Bear Lake County Medical Association (which included all Bear Lake County doctors) had passed a resolution that notified the public that all Bear Lake County practitioners would withhold treatment to "all parties . . . who have refused and neglected to make proper settlement of [their] indebtedness . . . until [their] unpaid accounts shall be satisfactorily arranged."[385]

In mid-1919, a resolution appeared in the local newspaper advising the public that Bear Lake County physicians would notify all patients delinquent in their payment of fees and allow them to settle their debts by May 16, 1919. The notice continued:

> By doing so will prevent us from putting their names on
> our blacklist. Those who refuse or neglect to do so will be

---

[385] "Medical Society Adopts Resolutions," *Montpelier (ID) Examiner*, December 20, 1918, p. 8.

refused professional services by the physicians of Bear Lake County.[386]

Later that same year, the Bear Lake County Medical Association notified the public of minimum charges for "day visits in city" and "country visits" along with mileage at one dollar per mile one-way.[387]

The countywide resolutions, signed by all five physicians practicing there, may seem out of character for the venerable medical professionals in view of their legal and ethical responsibilities to their patients. They also suggest a chronic failure on the part of the patients themselves that required an extraordinary response. What effect, if any, the resolutions had on the targeted audience is unknown.

Indigenous Economic Limitations

The next reason for Dr. Guyon's financial woes was his milieu in rural southeastern Idaho, a primarily agrarian economy with a limited number of potential patients who had a limited amount of cash. In 1880, the population of Bear Lake County was 3,235, which increased to 6,057 by 1890, and then climbed to 7,051 in 1900. By 1910 the population of the county had increased to 7,729, and by 1920 to 8,783,[388] but by 1930 it had decreased to 7,872.[389] Dr. Guyon's practice took him to places outside the demographic limitations of Bear Lake County, including Star Valley and Cokeville, Wyoming, but it does not alter the fact that the pool of potential patients was limited, and Dr. Guyon was not the only doctor to provide medical services.

The arrival of the railroad in Montpelier in 1882, with its employees and their families, probably accounts for much of the increase in population of approximately 2,800 between 1880 and 1890. Railroad employees injected their wages into the local economy, and that certainly strengthened what was otherwise purely agrarian. However, it did not change Bear Lake County's fundamental character as a large county with a relatively small population.

---

[386] "Medical Society Adopts Resolution," *Montpelier (ID) Examiner*, April 18, 1919, p. 8.

[387] "Doctors Establish New Rate Schedule," *Montpelier (ID) Examiner*, November 7, 1919, p. 4.

[388] In a form filled out in September, 1918, Dr. Guyon estimated the population in his area of practice at six thousand — with five doctors.

[389] US Decennial Digest, cited in "Bear Lake County, Idaho," Wikipedia, accessed August 18, 2016, https://en.wikipedia.org/wiki/Bear_Lake_County,_Idaho.

Efforts at Collection

It is not known how aggressively Dr. Guyon pursued the collection of unpaid fees, although there are a few indications that he occasionally utilized the legal process. In one lone example, his records of an unpaid bill show the notation "garnishee." On several of his "N.G." accounts, he wrote "bankrupt," or "gone," or "dead."

There are also a few notations in his ledgers that he charged interest on certain fees that were not paid at the time the services were provided, but there does not appear to have been a consistent policy to that effect. In other cases, he is known to have written off interest charges as part of an agreement to recover at least part of his fees. I have a hunch that Doc considered collecting unpaid fees from an unwilling patient unseemly.

Aside from charging interest on unpaid fees, there are few indications that Dr. Guyon made any significant efforts to collect earned, but unpaid, fees. A single surviving invoice for services, dated July 6, 1928—for $135—indicates that he sent out bills, at least on that recorded occasion, but it is not known whether he typically did so.

On ne Peut pas Faire des Merveilles à partir de Rien[390]

During the time period 1915–1918, Dr. Guyon began to seriously consider moving his medical practice and family from Montpelier to Salt Lake City. His motivation to move from Montpelier was primarily economic. He already knew that he was not making money, and the triggers for this anticipated change were the crippling lack of economic opportunity in Montpelier and the belated realization that if he was ever going to have a medical practice like the one he envisioned when he left medical school in 1891, he would have to go elsewhere to find it.

There were other circumstances he had to consider. He was sixty-two years old by the end of 1915, with a wife who was forty-one and three boys aged ten, eight, and six, all attending school in Montpelier. From a purely family standpoint, leaving the little town he and Effie chose as their home in 1903 was problematic.

---

390 French proverb: "You cannot make a silk purse out of a sow's ear."

By 1918, Dr. Guyon's medical practice appears to have gone from bad to worse. He had a total of only fifteen patient entries in his business ledgers for the entire year of 1918, the fewest known in any calendar year since he opened his practice in Oregon in 1892. The small number of patients could have been the result of any number of factors within or outside his control, but whatever the reasons, lack of patients equates to lack of money, despite all other considerations. It is not an overstatement to say that Dr. Guyon was barely hanging on financially during the latter part of the second decade of the 20th century.

Events teased him into believing circumstances in Montpelier would get better, if he could just hold on a little longer. In contrast to the abysmal year 1918, Dr. Guyon's ledgers for 1919 reveal that he saw at least eighty-five patients, more than five times as many as the previous year; that number increased to 158 in 1920, but dropped to ninety-five in 1921. In 1922, the number was 105 and in 1923 the number dropped to fifty. He had been practicing medicine for thirty years, and this roller-coaster lack of consistency and stability brought enormous pressures to bear. The anticipated peace and tranquility of retirement eluded him, bringing frustration and unhappiness.

When Grandpa and Effie sold their house in 1918, it may be more than coincidental that they were considering a permanent move elsewhere at the same time. The $1,250 realized from the sale may have been earmarked to finance the anticipated move. It may also be more than coincidental that the sale of their home in 1918 occurred during the year that money was probably the tightest. Taking the equity from their home may have been their way to protect themselves against other unknown financial conditions that might take place in their future. A letter to Maud[391] provides a clue:

> I have money standing out I must collect so as to pay some
> of my bills, without drawing on the money I sold my house
> for. I will have to stay until fall, at least, to get the money I
> need.

Exactly what the "need" was is unknown, although it seems highly likely that his objective was to have the financial wherewithal to move his family and medical practice to another location.

---

[391] E. F. Guyon to Maud Brown, 23 August 1918.

Chapter 11.

NEW LOCATIONS
MORE SERIOUSLY PONDERED

circa 1918–1924

Il n'est jamais trop tard pour bien faire. [392]
— French proverb

This chapter recounts the continued deterioration of Dr. Guyon's financial condition and his resolve to move his family and medical practice elsewhere; his attempt at active military service; the Guyon family's memorable 1923 road trip to Oregon; and the continuation of life in Montpelier.

Tantalizing Hopes

The possibility that increasing numbers of patients might lead to a more stable medical practice during the period 1919–1923 probably changed Dr. Guyon's mind about leaving Montpelier for the moment, but the idea was not dead. One of the reasons Dr. Guyon came to Montpelier in the first place was the apparent potential for economic growth evidenced by the large size of the county compared with a small population.[393] That potential, however, remained unrealized in the second decade of the 20th century. Had Dr. Guyon known in 1896 that the population of Bear Lake County would not top 9,000 well into the 21st century, he might never have come to Montpelier.

Another IOOF Honor Intervenes

In the midst of his financial difficulties, Dr. Guyon, along with two others, was chosen by the Grand Master of Idaho to represent the IOOF at the meeting of "The League to Enforce Peace" to be held in Philadelphia on May 16 and 17, 1918.[394] It was a significant honor to be

---

[392] "It is never too late to do the right thing."
[393] *Montpelier (ID) Examiner*, March 7, 1896.
[394] The League to Enforce Peace, founded in 1915, convened annually to promote public awareness of its objectives through speeches and magazines. The League called for an international organization that would ensure arbitration of disputes (as opposed to the carnage of World War I) and a guarantee of territorial integrity of its members by maintaining a military force sufficient to

chosen to attend the meeting, along with 6,000 representatives from the United States, Canada, and Europe.[395] The meeting touted speakers such as former president William Howard Taft, who would become chief justice of the US Supreme Court in 1921, and Charles Evans Hughes, who succeeded Taft as chief justice in 1930.[396]

After his return, Dr. Guyon reported on his journey to the editor of the *Idaho Odd Fellow*:

> The very air of the city [was] electrified with an intense war spirit. It is the consensus of opinion that the only way to World Peace lies in fighting this war to a finish and in forever crushing Prussianism.
>
> * * *
>
> This great meeting of Representatives from most all parts of the globe is the forerunner of a League of Nations which will be consummated at the end of the war and will be the instrumentality which will forever protect the world against the ravages and horrors of war. The peoples of the world will band themselves together in a brotherhood of mutual protection and enduring peace and all the Kings and Potentates of Earth shall not prevail against it. I am proud to have been one of the Representatives at this great meeting and I thank the Order of Idaho for sending me.

These events in Philadelphia occurred near the end of The Great War, and the emotions stirred by the imminent defeat of Germany may be difficult to fathom from the perspective of the 21st century. The United States had emerged from its own civil war sixty years before, but remained an unknown force in the arena of global conflict in 1917. Whether the Americans could or would play a definitive role in the hostilities in Europe was anything but a foregone conclusion. This lack of information about or appreciation for the vast resources of the United States may account for Germany's taking little note of the United States' April 6, 1917, Declaration of War against it.[397]

---

defeat any member.

[395] *Montpelier (ID) Examiner*, May 10, 1918, p. 5.

[396] E. F. Guyon to A. E. Gipson, Editor, *Idaho Odd Fellow*, 30 June 1918.

[397] The reluctance of the American public to become embroiled in a European conflict had been gradually eroded by, among other things, Germany's sinking of the *Lusitania* in 1915, the later

Perceptions aside, once aroused, the United States promptly mobilized and trained 4,000,000 men. By the summer of 1918, 1,000,000 doughboys were in France under the leadership of General Black Jack Pershing, with 10,000 fresh troops arriving daily. About 500,000 American troops eventually saw front-line service, which raised morale, particularly of French troops, and significantly affected the outcome of the war in favor of the Allies. Unfortunately, by the time the armistice was signed on November 11, 1918, 110,000 American soldiers had made the ultimate sacrifice, 43,000 of them because of an influenza pandemic.[398] These known and developing facts, and more, had brought emotions in the United States to a fever pitch, which Dr. Guyon personally witnessed in Philadelphia in mid-1918.

Patriotic Leanings

It was in 1918 that Dr. Guyon revealed something of his personal patriotism. In the fall of that year, he filled out a printed form entitled "Application for Membership in the Volunteer Medical Service Corps," which under its title states that it is "Authorized by the Council of National Defense [and] Approved by the President of the United States."

The form confirms in Grandpa's own handwriting certain background information already known about him, including his height (5'8"), weight (140 lbs), and medical experience, but also clarifies facts not generally known. In response to the question of the applicant's educational background, Grandpa answered that he had attended the "common schools of Portland, Oreg. and also high school, Whitman College, Washington, 2 yrs. No Degrees."

He also stated that he was familiar with chemistry and medicine and confirmed medical licensure in Oregon, Idaho, and Wyoming as of July 9, 1900. None of this information is particularly surprising except for his description of ophthalmology as his medical specialty, to which he said he devoted about 25 percent of his time on an "almost daily" basis. This document is the only known source of that information.

---

sinking by German U-boats of seven United States merchant ships, and the Zimmermann Telegram, clandestinely sent by Germany to Mexico to entice the latter to join Germany against the United States and thereby reclaim Texas, New Mexico, and Arizona, lost to Mexico seventy years previously.

[398] "United States in World War I," Wikipedia, accessed August 18, 2016, http://en.wikipedia.org/wiki/United_States_in_World_War_I.

In response to the request for "all past experience in industrial or railroad medicine and surgery," Doc Guyon identified his tenure as assistant surgeon for six years for the Oregon Short Line Railroad, the identical position at Diamondville Coal Co. for two years, and surgeon for Utah Construction for four and a half months. The latter position is un-known outside this document.

Chef Edwin (2nd from left) and unknown friends at IOOF picnic – August 12, 1918

Other parts of the application contain un-expected information. He was sixty-four years old in September of 1918, yet stated on the application that he was born in 1858 and was fifty-nine years old.[399] The cutoff for service was probably fifty-five, although that disability could likely be waived, at least up to age fifty-nine. In an attempt to get as close to that number as he could without attracting undue attention, he simply decided to be fifty-nine. His reasons for fudging on his age can be found in the remarks section:

> I desire to serve my country, and I don't care much about where I am placed so long as I can render the service I am best fitted to perform. I have a family wholly dependent on me. Three of my children are young, 8-10-12 years. I would rather serve on this account in U.S., but I am American enough to give all I have and go any where I am needed.

Even more unequivocal is his statement of religious affiliation: "Christian and 100 per cent American."

The application was accepted, and Dr. Guyon was issued certificate #6397 on October 14, 1918, as evidence of his membership in the Volunteer Medical Service Corps. Although he actively sought an appointment as a medical officer or assistant, he was never called to any

---

[399] In an era where many did not possess official birth certificates, and background investigations were nonexistent or at least ineffective, it may have been irresistible to make "adjustments" on applications such as this.

kind of active service, probably because the need for such volunteers disappeared with the end of the war in November, 1918.[400]

The Guyon Boys

Despite his financial problems, Doc Guyon's three sons inspired him. In a letter to Maud in early 1920, he commented about them:

L to R: Wendell, Royal, and Edwin – August 1918

I sent you a photo yesterday of my boys. They are not bad looking kids. The one with the long hair [Wendell] is one of the handsomest boys I ever saw, and he is the best boy you ever had anything to do with. He is affectionate and obedient and smart as a tack. The one in the middle [Buster] is the youngest. He is a good boy and smart as a cricket. The other [Edwin Fenimore] is the oldest and is a baby fellow. He would make a good preacher. He is mild and timid and fearful and just the kind of a boy to be imposed upon until you arouse him and then look out. The long haired boy I am going to put in the movies. I named him Wendell Shattuck Guyon. The oldest boy I named Edwin Fenimore Guyon and the little boy I named Royal Chatterton Guyon. They are fine boys, but full of vinegar and pepper and hard to control, but they are not mean or vicious or inclined to do wrong. If I live long enough I am going to make musicians out of two of them as a side issue and what else I will do for them I am not yet decided. They are brainy and can learn rapidly. Wendell is in the High School now[401] and he is very bright.

---

400 E. F. Guyon to T. M. Anderson, Chief of Staff, 104th Div., US Army, Salt Lake, Utah, 9 February 1925.
401 Born in 1907, Wendell would have not yet reached his thirteenth birthday when this letter was written. Grandpa Guyon probably meant Edwin Fenimore, who was born in 1905 and the only one of high school age in 1920.

Dr. Guyon was in a pensive mood in December 1920. Maud had sent Christmas presents, which he had not expected because "times are hard and people need their money to buy the necessaries with." He reciprocated by "sending a little present to [her] and a few good books for the children" and then said he was "going to have some turkey and try and forget the trials, troubles and disappointments of life." Finally, he gave Maud—and perhaps himself—some sage advice in the form of well-worn clichés:

> What is the use of lamenting over what cannot be helped. Do the best you can be satisfied with the result and be glad that it was no worse. Don't carry troubles to bed nor cross bridges before you come to them. Anticipation of trouble is much worse than the real trouble itself. Worry over the trouble of others and you will forget yours. "Tis easy to smile when life glides on like a song, but the man worth while is the man who can smile when everything goes dead wrong."[402]

By the spring of 1921, Grandpa's level of dissatisfaction with his circumstances in Montpelier had markedly increased, and he was more actively considering a move to Salt Lake City. That possibility created an entirely new set of concerns. Thoughts of paying higher rent in Salt Lake City for an office, developing a practice from nothing, and his advancing age all weighed heavily on him.[403]

His search for a place to relocate in 1921 was not limited to Salt Lake City. In that year he partially filled out an "Application for Physician and Surgeon Reciprocity Certificate" issued by the State of California. The parts of the application that are filled in confirm generally his medical school education and practice, but most of the detailed information that would have been required to complete the form is missing.

Clearly considering the possibility of a move, Dr. Guyon for the next two years continued his medical practice in Montpelier much as he had in the past, and his fortunes rose and fell as they had in the past. The erratic numbers of patients he was seeing fueled already existing anxieties about his financial condition and the welfare of his family.

---

[402] E. F. Guyon to Maud Brown, 22 December 1920.
[403] E. F. Guyon to Maud Brown, 8 April 1921.

The possibilities in Salt Lake City loomed large in his mind because of perceived new opportunities there. At the same time, the undeniable difficulties associated with such a move occupied a prominent position in his considerations and fueled his reluctance. At least five years had passed since he began to consider moving to Salt Lake City, and he must have been torn by the what-ifs: What if the family had left five years ago? Would they be settled in Salt Lake City and better off than they were now? Would he have passed the boards and be installed in Salt Lake City in the office practice he'd always dreamed about?

A Legal Challenge Looms

To make matters even worse, in February 1923, Dr. Guyon found himself named as a defendant in a civil lawsuit brought in Bear Lake County by the First National Bank of Weiser (Idaho). The bank's claim was based upon a delinquent $500 promissory note signed by Kent Placer Mining Company, a delinquent corporation, of which Grandpa Guyon was allegedly a director, along with S. W. Kent, John Bagley, Charles Barber, M. M. Kent, and W. W. Kent. None of the named defendants filed an answer or otherwise contested the complaint. The result was the entry of a default judgment in the amount of the note, $500.00, plus $245.84 interest, $100.00 in attorney's fees, and $20.45 costs.

There is no indication in the record that the judgment was ever satisfied or that the bank ever took any action to collect its judgment.[404]

Pendleton and Pilot Rock Revisited

During June or July, 1923, despite his financial and other difficulties (or perhaps to forget about them for a while), Dr. Guyon and his family started out on a road trip to Oregon. Grandpa's objective was to return to the Pendleton-Pilot Rock area where he grew up and in general to reminisce about his earlier life in Oregon.[405] The wary local newspaper mused that the "real" objective of the trip was otherwise and stated that "the family might very well make their home in Portland."[406]

For Effie and the three boys, the road trip was an opportunity to share parts of Doc Guyon's life that he had been unable to describe to them other than in the abstract. He was almost seventy years old at the time,

---

404 Official Records of Bear Lake County, Idaho, Judgment Book C, p. 53.
405 Edwin Fenimore Guyon, interview with author, Victor, Idaho, September 15, 1990.
406 *Montpelier (ID) Examiner*, September 27, 1923, p. 5.

Effie was about forty-nine, Edwin Fenimore eighteen, Wendell sixteen, and Buster thirteen.

The distance by automobile to Pendleton from Montpelier is approximately 540 miles, which can be covered today in eight hours on freeways and highways. Not so in 1923. There were no freeways for high-speed travel and no high-speed vehicles to drive on them if they had existed. In many cases the existing roads were unpaved. Circumstances must have been better by 1923, but in 1920 only 620 miles of roads in the entire state of Oregon were paved, along with only 297.2 miles of plank roads.[407] Traveling in Oregon by automobile in 1923 was risky. It is not likely that conditions in Idaho were much better.

Transportation Courtesy of Henry Ford

The family's automobile ride must have seemed to be on the cutting edge of comfort. The mode of transportation was probably a 1914–1915 Ford Model T Touring Car, affectionately and universally known as a "Tin Lizzie," which Dr. Guyon no doubt purchased from Bear Lake Motor Company of Montpelier. A promissory note dated December 31, 1921, reflects that Dr. Guyon paid $70 for a certain "Ford Touring Car,"[408] although the automobile's year of manufacture is not disclosed on the promissory note. The $70 was financed at 10 percent interest and marked "paid" as of January 4, 1923.

The Model T may have been a "pre-owned" vehicle, based on the price of a new Ford Touring Car in 1921, which was $370.[409] It is also possible that Dr. Guyon purchased a new vehicle in 1921, paid $300 cash as a down payment, and only financed $70 of the price. Buying the latest model was not as big of an issue in 1921 as it later became. There was little difference between the first Model T that rolled out of Detroit in 1908 and the last ones produced in 1927. All had bench seats in the front and back, a

---

[407] "Oregon Department of Transportation," Wikipedia, accessed August 18, 2016, http://en.wikipedia.org/wiki/Oregon_Department_of_Transportation.

[408] According to Edwin Fenimore, the Model T taken by the Guyon family to Oregon was manufactured in 1914 or 1915 and was not "straight-backed" like its predecessors, but was the first model to have rounded rear fenders.

[409] Conceptcarz, "1921 Ford Model T," accessed August 18, 2016, http://www.conceptcarz.com/vehicle/z1680/Ford-Model-T.aspx.

removable canvas top, a planetary transmission,[410] and a twenty-horsepower engine.[411]

The Model T allowed the driver and one passenger in the front seat and three in the back, all in relatively cramped conditions. This wouldn't have been an insurmountable problem in and of itself, except that there was the matter of the family's personal clothing and camping gear. One thing the Model T lacked was a trunk. Consequently, the family's luggage, tent, pots and pans, and other camping equipment were either sat on, piled on the floor, wedged between occupants, or hung on the inside or outside of the vehicle. Visions of the mythical Joad family in Steinbeck's *Grapes of Wrath* come to mind. Such a spectacle may seem out of place today, but it was hardly unusual in 1923.

Wendell, age sixteen, drove the Model T and its occupants the entire distance from Montpelier to Oregon and back again. The journey seemed to be ill-fated at first. The engine failed just when the clan reached Pocatello, approximately 100 miles from their starting point, but a handy mechanic by the name of Wagner, located at Fifth Avenue and Center Street in that city, fixed the problem in short order and the family was on its way again.

After the initial mechanical trouble, the car developed no further problems, despite being driven through Pendleton to the Dalles, Portland, and back to Montpelier.[412] According to Edwin Fenimore, after its initial repair in Pocatello, the Model T ran "like a Singer sewing machine" for the rest of the trip. Such a performance stands as a witness to the ruggedness of the family's Model T. The family members appear to have been no less rugged.

No Five-Star Hotels in the Firmament

The family stayed in camping areas where available, and where unavailable they camped along the road. No one kept a journal or diary of the journey, although Edwin Fenimore's recollections provide insights into the family's activities. In the Pendleton-Pilot Rock area, they stayed in a campground near the city of Pendleton. To earn money, the three boys hired out to pick hops, and found the job to be entertaining and fun. The

---

[410] Meaning rotation of several gears ("planets") around the central gear ("sun"), which allows changing gears while moving.
[411] Conceptcarz, "1921 Ford Model T."
[412] Edwin Fenimore Guyon, interview with author, Victor, Idaho, September 15, 1990.

family also attended the Pendleton Roundup, which even in 1923 attracted thousands of people.

Reminiscences in Pilot Rock

Dr. Guyon took time to re-familiarize himself with some of the places familiar to him when he lived in the area, and later gave the following poignant account:[413]

> I went by Wiley's old home on McKay creek and they were working on the dam then. I did not know the place. Everything was changed. All the way up to Pilot Rock everything was different and you could not find much that was familiar. Grand Pa's[414] home above Pilot Rock had been torn down several years ago, so I was told. I never went up there while I was in Pendleton. I only went to Pilot Rock and up to the Gilliam home and that was all I wanted as all the old familiar landmarks were gone and I felt that I was in a strange land. Well it is a very lonesome place to go to as all the old friends and chums of early years have vanished. All the people there are strangers. All the old houses have disappeared and strange houses have taken their place . . .
>
> * * *
>
> Our old house was still standing and looked just as it did when we left it, except the parties who were living there built a dormer window which extends out on the front porch about two or three feet. I did not go in and inquire who lived there, which I should have done. I regretted afterward that I did not go in and tell them who I was and that I built the house.

Grandpa's statement that he built the house in Oregon where the family lived reveals yet another skill and expertise in his seemingly never-ending stream of varied talents and accomplishments.

---

[413] E. F. Guyon to Maud Brown, 17 September 1928.
[414] "Grand Pa" in all probability refers to Madison Jones, Maggie's father and grandfather to both Maud and Fay.

174

The family returned to Montpelier in October 1923.[415] Several months later, in a letter to Maud, Dr. Guyon reported that during the trip to the Pendleton-Pilot Rock area:

> I did not see Frank and did not know where he lived and
> as I did not know him very well I did not make any effort
> to find him.

"Frank" may be the same Frank who was with Elizabeth Shattuck at her death in 1868. The possibility Frank was Grandpa Guyon's uncle is inconsistent with Grandpa Guyon's statement to his children that he had no living relatives after 1906, unless he meant only blood relatives and Frank was married to one of his aunts. Whoever Frank was, he was obviously known by both Grandpa Guyon and Maud, neither of whom used his last name in their correspondence.[416]

Semi-Retirement?

After 1923, there are no known patient ledgers reflective of Dr. Guyon's medical practice. It is certain that he continued it, but probably at a lower level of activity. Due to many factors over which he had little control, including the number of patients he was seeing and his advancing age, he may easily have defaulted into a state of semi-retirement.

During his younger years, Dr. Guyon practiced obstetrics, but gave it up in about 1918, or at least tried to give it up, because of being called out at odd hours and the resulting lack of sleep. As he got older, those considerations became more and more important. Edwin Fenimore recalled that during 1918–1925 , his father got telephone calls and personal requests at his front door at all hours of the night from patients for various reasons, to the point that Dr. Guyon, for his own mental and physical well-being, had to feign being out of town or otherwise unavailable. The unenviable assignment of explaining and excusing his unavailability usually fell to Effie.

Edwin Fenimore also recalled that his father had lapses of memory toward the end of his life. This prompted him to keep a record book, in alphabetical order, of the prescriptions he wrote for people. The fact that Dr. Guyon kept such a book is indicative that he continued practicing

---

415 "City and County Briefs," *Bear Lake County (ID) News*, October 9, 1923, p. 1.
416 Assuming that "Frank" was twenty years old in 1868, he would have been approximately seventy-five in 1923.

medicine almost to the end of his life, although his activity was significantly curtailed by his advancing age. His medical practice was the primary source of family income, and he lacked the luxury of a retirement plan or Social Security benefits.

It is unclear whether Dr. Guyon continued to actively look for a change in location from Montpelier in 1923–1924, but there is no apparent reason to think that he did not. Little had changed in his financial world. The overall economy, particularly in a rural area like Bear Lake County, got increasingly worse as the country moved closer to the beginning of the Great Depression in 1929. Economic conditions generally made him wonder whether it would make sense to uproot his medical practice and family for a new location that might easily be as economically depressed and unproductive as the one he was already in.

Dr. Guyon's financial condition was not helped by the failure of two banks in Montpelier in 1924, resulting in a loss to him of an indeterminate amount of money. These unhappy events had a ripple effect of negative financial consequences on the population at large, and caused the disappearance of another of an already meager set of alternatives. "If the bank here had not closed," he wrote to Maud, "we would have gone to some part of California for the winter at least, but without money you are helpless."[417]

Ever the optimist, Dr. Guyon hoped that the First National Bank would soon be back in operation with new people.[418] That optimism was tempered by lamentations over the passage of time: "What ever real happiness we have in our lives comes in our earlier years, but our later years are saddened by many a cloud we little dreamed of when we were young."[419]

The Mendoza Affair

In the midst of Dr. Guyon's financial difficulties and crises, a series of incidents[420] occurred to which I refer collectively as the "Mendoza Affair." The focal point of this melodrama was an Odd Fellow named A. J. Mendoza, a member of the lodge in Ft. Benton, Montana, who had the

---

417 E. F. Guyon to Maud Brown, 15 October 1924.
418 E. F. Guyon to Maud Brown, 9 March 1925.
419 E. F. Guyon to Maud Brown, 12 December 1924.
420 Generally speaking, the parts of the Mendoza Affair that precipitated Dr. Guyon's involvement occurred just prior to the family's 1923 trip to Oregon, although the real "action" took place after their return.

176

bad luck[421] to die within the jurisdiction of Montpelier's lodge. Acting on the written authority of the Montana lodge, the Montpelier lodge provided Mendoza a ritualistic Odd Fellows burial. When the Montana lodge was billed for the expense thus extended by the Montpelier lodge beyond a $75 death benefit, the former refused to pay it.

As secretary of the Montpelier lodge, Dr. Guyon was directly involved in the matter, and his actions and letters on behalf of the Montpelier lodge provide additional insight into his activities outside his medical career.

I include the history of the Mendoza Affair in Appendix III for several reasons. First, there is precious little information available to me about Grandpa's day-to-day involvement in the IOOF, and this story provides a limited window into his activities. Second, Dr. Guyon kept the documents in which I found the information, which is at least a modest indication that the matter represented something important to him. Third, and perhaps most important overall, is that it reflects ideals held by Dr. Guyon and his fellow brothers that seem to have diminished in importance in our present society. The IOOF Grand Masters of both Idaho and Montana were too timid, lacking in authority, or otherwise unwilling to take a stand in favor of doing the right thing, but that did not stop the Montpelier lodge from demonstrating its unwavering commitment to the stated ideals of the IOOF.

The Buena Park Sanitarium: A Likely Catastrophe Avoided

Dr. Guyon was presented what appeared on the surface to be a "fix-all" solution to his financial woes in mid-1924 via his son Fay, who pressured him to drop everything and come immediately to California to take over and manage a sanitarium-hospital in Buena Park.[422]

Aside from the fact that the apparent business opportunity came to naught, the urgency of Fay's letter to his father is a further indication that Grandpa Guyon's financial circumstances in Idaho were difficult, and the fact was known within the family. What Grandpa described to his daughter Maud as the possibility of a "fine opening for me" in Buena Park was this: a medical doctor by the name of Julian P. Johnson was leaving to do postgraduate work within a few days and had sold his sanitarium-hospital called the "Harmonie Sanitarium" to a private party, who in turn needed

---

[421] Even though it was bad luck for Mr. Mendoza to die, as it turned out, it was good luck for him to have died where he did.
[422] Lafayette Guyon to E. F. Guyon, 14 May 1924

someone "to take charge of it." That "someone" would be Grandpa Guyon.

The dilemma Grandpa found himself in was that to really evaluate the situation, he would need to travel to California, which he couldn't afford. In an effort to acquire additional information about the opportunity without physically going to California, Grandpa telegraphed his good friend Mr. H. M. Moore (the former manager of the Riter Bros. Drug Store in Montpelier, now living in Fullerton). He also asked Maud to "find out something about this proposition on the quiet" if she could.[423]

H. M. Moore responded to Grandpa Guyon's wire by letter on May 20, 1924, advising Grandpa Guyon that he knew something about the sanitarium before he received the wire. Mr. Moore's first statement was "[t]here is something fishy about this doctor that owns it. I understand he is pretty crooked," followed by "[h]e has been mixed up in domestic affairs with women." The bottom line to the Moore letter was that if the sanitarium was a good opportunity, it would have already been snapped up.[424]

Despite continuing significant pressure from Fay, coupled with his repeated unsuccessful attempts to make contact with the hospital's purported owners, Dr. Guyon resigned himself to the fact that he would not borrow the $75–$100 necessary to make the trip to California, and the matter was not pursued.

---

[423] E. F. Guyon to Maud Brown, 21 May 1924.
[424] H. M. Moore to E. F. Guyon, 20 May 1924.

Chapter 12.

OPPORTUNITIES AND OPTIONS DIMINISH

circa 1924–1934

For dust thou art, and unto dust thou shalt return.
— Genesis 3:19

This chapter discusses the last decade of Dr. Guyon's life, which was filled with more than its share of indecision, unhappiness, deteriorating health, and worsening financial conditions, although he somehow managed not to let his woes rob him entirely of moments of happiness.

Family Relationships

By 1924, Grandpa Guyon's three sons with Effie were in their teens. This presented a new set of challenges for the septuagenarian physician. In mid-1924 he was worried over his oldest son, Edwin Fenimore (almost nineteen), who was planning a trip to Salt Lake City "next Monday the 16th, provided his pass comes." Grandpa Guyon explained to Maud that Edwin "is a call boy and is now entitled to a pass and a lay off." He also subtly suggested that Maud's husband Dall might "keep his eye on him" and then voiced his first concern: "He is a good boy and is quite backward and bashful. He is 6 feet and 2 inches tall and his brother next to him is just about as tall."[425] Edwin Fenimore planned to see friends in Salt Lake who had recently left Montpelier. This prompted a postscript in the same letter reflecting Grandpa Guyon's overriding concern and something of his fathering instincts: "His friends name is Gertsch, they are Swiss. The boys are not bad, but Salt Lake has many temptations not found here, which are dangerous to young fellows."

Grandpa Guyon always had a warm relationship with his daughter Maud, but found it impossible to achieve with Fay. Contacts between Grandpa Guyon and his oldest son were few and far between and guarded. Grandpa Guyon complained in 1927 that he had not heard from Fay in three years.[426]

In his correspondence, Grandpa often discussed Fay with Maud, but it is very unlikely that he ever discussed Maud with Fay—at least on the

---

425 E. F. Guyon to Maud Brown, 14 June 1924.
426 E. F. Guyon to Maud Brown, 6 December 1927.

same level of trust and intimacy. Much of the correspondence from Grandpa to Maud that concerns Fay consists of venting over something Fay did or did not do, or lamenting how much Fay had cost him, or how much heartache Fay caused his parents.[427]

Another Attempt at Military Service

As discussed above, in 1918 Dr. Guyon was accepted in the Volunteer Medical Service Corps of the US Army, but never had an opportunity to engage in any active service. Seven years later, in early 1925, he again sought active involvement.

As he did in 1918, Dr. Guyon hedged on his application to avoid disclosing his true age, stating his age at nearest birthday as sixty-two.[428] However, to his certain chagrin, even subtracting almost ten years from his true age of seventy-one at his nearest birthday did not make him eligible for service, and his application was reluctantly denied because he exceeded the age limits.[429]

A Dangerous Collision with Polygamy

Early in 1925, Dr. Guyon learned of the death in Utah of Edith Parkinson, the wife of his friend Dr. Parkinson. Her death prompted a response from Grandpa to Maud[430] that reveals a surprising aspect of his relationship with Dr. Parkinson:

> I am sorry I could not have visited her before she passed away. She thought a good deal of me, as I was a friend to her husband when the U. S. Marshalls were after him for poligamy. [sic] He came to us when he was hunted and we

---

[427] Conflicts and unresolved issues between Grandpa Guyon and his firstborn son spilled over into his second family. Specifics were never discussed, but I heard enough comments about Fay during my childhood in the 1950s to know that hostility and animosity against him were alive and well long after Grandpa Guyon's death in 1934. In approximately 1957, Fay appeared at the door of our home at 160 South Ninth Street in Montpelier and requested to talk to my dad. My mother opened the door and talked to Fay, but my dad refused even to see him, despite my mom's encouragement. I was around twelve at the time, but I distinctly remember my mom telling me she thought my dad was wrong not to speak to his half-brother. I knew nothing of the level of animosity or the circumstances behind it, but I have often wondered since that incident what it was that generated such hostility in my father. Perhaps it is best for all concerned that the details not be known.

[428] E. F. Guyon to Major Samuel C. Gurney, 12 February 1925.

[429] Major Samuel C. Gurney to E. F. Guyon, 13 February 1925.

[430] E. F. Guyon to Maud Brown, 9 March 1925.

befriended him and protected him. I have often wondered if they would have done as much for me.[431]

No time frame or location is known for the events described by Grandpa, although it is likely they occurred in Montpelier. But it is not the location or time frame that begs discussion. Rather, it is that Dr. Guyon put himself and his family at risk of criminal prosecution for harboring a fugitive, interference with the legal process, obstruction of justice, or whatever other charges an imaginative prosecutor might dream up.

If these events occurred prior to 1891 in Oregon, it is easier to understand Grandpa's actions, but if they occurred later, the risk was enormous. The State of Idaho might have suspended his license to practice medicine, although that would also depend on when they happened, since the requirements for practicing medicine became progressively more stringent as time went on.

The fact that he took the risk accentuates the value Grandpa Guyon put on his friendship with Dr. Parkinson, even though the last sentence in the quotation above hints that he was not certain his loyalty was fully reciprocated.

The risk Grandpa accepted also says something important about his overall worldview. It was no secret that the Morrill Anti-Bigamy Act, the Edmunds Act, and the Edmunds-Tucker Act[432] were primarily passed in direct response to the practice of polygamy in the Territory of Utah, although the United States government was not unaware that "the principle" was practiced in other locations as well.

Many believed that the government's response amounted to selective prosecution and was otherwise unfair and unduly harsh,

---

431 William Brigham Parkinson, Sr., was born in England in 1852. His parents embraced Mormonism there and the family moved to Chicago, where his mother died. William's father then remarried and intended to move to Oregon with William's stepmother, but he died en route. William accompanied his stepmother to Oregon and lived there with her. Probably Grandpa Guyon and William were boyhood friends in Oregon until William ran away from his stepmother at age twelve (circa 1864), eventually making his way to Utah. Later on, William attended both Rush Medical College (est. 1837) in Chicago and the University of Louisville School of Medicine (est. 1837) in Louisville, Kentucky, and reportedly held degrees from each. He practiced medicine for many years in Utah and died in Logan in 1920. He had four plural wives: Elizabeth Bull (married September 8, 1873), Clarissa Marina Taggart (married December 6, 1875), Edith Benson (married January 27, 1886), and Margaret Wallace Sloan (married September, 1890).

432 The Morrill Anti-Bigamy Act, passed in July, 1862, criminalized plural marriage, but only as a misdemeanor. The Edmunds Act of March, 1882, increased the penalty to the level of a felony, which would have encouraged more aggressive prosecution by the United States. The Edmunds-Tucker Act, passed in 1887, declared the Mormon Church disincorporated, abolished women's suffrage, confiscated church property, declared children of plural marriages disinherited, and imposed other harsh measures against the church and its members.

whether they believed in the underpinnings of polygamy or not. The nation was not unaware of the Mormons' plight in Missouri and Illinois during the first half of the 19th century, and the idea of bullying a specific, identifiable group of people, for whatever reason, even for polygamy, did not sit well with many people. I believe my grandfather was one of them. It is unlikely that he supported polygamy at all, but to him the real issue was more political than religious. The government should not be allowed to persecute people for their religious views, practices, or otherwise, and I believe Dr. Guyon felt honor-bound and duty-bound to do what he viscerally felt was the right thing. That is not to say that he went looking for causes to support, but when Dr. Parkinson came to him in need, his response was both predictable and irresistible.

Relocation Becomes a More Serious Consideration

In early 1926, the winter in Bear Lake County had been uncharacteristically mild, but economically speaking, Dr. Guyon's outlook seemed no less than dismal. In a letter to his daughter he made the following observations:

> Things are dull & money scarce. I never was pinched as badly for money as I have been this last year. I would like to leave here and would if I had the money. When the cheap railroad rates are declared I may take a trip some place to look up something better than I have here.[433]

Dr. Guyon was trapped in Montpelier. Little or no money was coming in and there was no indication those circumstances would change anytime soon. Still, he held out hope that his economic circumstances would change for the better, and if that meant looking elsewhere, he seemed open to the possibility.

Outside Dr. Guyon's ledgers, little is known about his dealings with patients over medical issues. This is frustrating to a researcher, but not surprising. His oath as a physician demanded it. The details of a patient's condition and treatment were held inviolate, much like a sinner's confession to a spiritual leader. Luckily, there are a few tidbits of information sprinkled abroad that provide a small window into this

---

[433] E. F. Guyon to Maud Brown, 28 January 1926.

otherwise clandestine area of interaction with patients. One such example was Dr. Guyon's successful treatment of Deborah Rich, my friend John

Edwin at home – July 19, 1926

Sharpe's great-aunt, to whom John introduced me in about 1957. When she heard my last name, she immediately announced, "Your grandfather cured my ulcer," and happily went on to tell me how Dr. Guyon had put her on a diet of milk and bread, which ultimately led to the disappearance of her malady.

Another example was an operation performed by Drs. Guyon and Ashley in February, 1925, to surgically remove a woman's appendix that had grown onto her intestines. The operation was successful, but what may be more interesting than the operation itself is that certain of the patient's family members were allowed to witness the procedure in the hospital in Montpelier.[434]

In July 1926, Dr. Guyon and his medical comrades Drs. Ashley and King were forced to amputate a woman's arm above her elbow to save the woman's life. The arm was so badly injured or diseased that there was no alternative, which was little solace to the patient and her family. The three doctors sedated the woman with ether and collectively performed the operation, apparently with success.[435]

Dr. Guyon's practice was not necessarily limited to purely medical issues. In July 1926, Dr. Guyon, with the collaboration of Dr. Hooper, pulled a woman's teeth, which took over one and a half hours and a great deal of ether.[436]

The Camel's Back Breaks

As 1926 wore on, the family's economic circumstances continued to deteriorate, with no end in sight. Finally, Effie had had enough; she

434 Robert Schmid, personal journal, Bern, Idaho, 1926.
435 Ibid.
436 Ibid.

decided to take matters into her own hands and spearhead the family's migration to Salt Lake City to live and work. Armed with a letter of recommendation from Montpelier retailer Sam Lewis, [437] a previous employer, she in all probability intended to land a job as a secretary or a store clerk in retail sales.

Her move was the initial step in a process that was to include the entire family. The objective was to increase educational and employment opportunities for their children and allow Dr. Guyon to make the money that eluded him in Montpelier.

In correspondence to Maud in mid-August, 1926 Dr. Guyon attempted to confirm that Maud would be in Salt Lake City before "we start our trip . . . for two or three days visit."[438] The trip's objective was likely to take Effie to Salt Lake City to begin working there. Dr. Guyon probably characterized it as a visit because he was still attempting to talk Effie out of her plan. He eventually agreed with her decision, although he did so reluctantly.

By October 1926, Effie was in Salt Lake City and her husband was back in Montpelier, but preparing to go there himself. Where Effie lived in Salt Lake City is not known. Later correspondence reveals she did not live with Maud. As far as the public was concerned, "Mrs. E. F. Guyon and sons have moved to Salt Lake City for the winter, where the boys will attend college."[439] In all probability, the newspaper article accurately stated Effie's intent, except that she intended the change to be permanent. The same story was perpetuated two and a half months later when Doc went to Salt Lake City to see his family:

> Dr. E. F. Guyon is back from a two weeks visit with his family who are spending the winter in Salt Lake City, where the boys are attending school.[440]

The Anticipated Move Is Disquieting

Outwardly, Dr. Guyon went along with Effie's plan as he outlined in a letter to Maud:[441]

---

[437] Sam Lewis to "Whom It May Concern," 26 May 1926.
[438] E. F. Guyon to Maud Brown, 20 August 1926.
[439] "Locals," *Montpelier (ID) Examiner,* September 15, 1926, p. 12.
[440] "Locals," *Bear Lake County (ID) News,* December 1, 1926, p. 5.
[441] E. F. Guyon to Maud Brown, 10 October 1926.

I am going to Grand Lodge next Sunday morning at Pocatello and will be there 3 or 4 days and after that I will pack up and store my office furniture and library and go to Salt Lake for a time.

Once in Salt Lake, he said:

If I can get a license to practice in Utah I will move my belongings to Salt Lake and open an office there or get in with some other doctor as an assistant or consultant.

Such a move, however, presented a serious dilemma that he recognized and seriously grappled with:

I have to come to Salt Lake and have no license as I can't do anything else outside of my profession and I don't want to retire yet and be a burden and expense to my wife and family. Rather than do that I would prefer to stay here and do what I can to support myself and aid my wife to live in Salt Lake where the boys can have better advantages and more chance for employment.[442]

If he had his choice, Dr. Guyon and Effie would have moved to Salt Lake City together where he would have eventually opened up a practice that revolved around internal medicine. Before that was possible, however, he would have to pass the Utah medical board examination, and that would require full-time studying and preparation. Consequently, he would have no income from his medical practice, whether he stayed in Montpelier during that preparatory period or not.

By mid-December, 1926, Effie had been in Salt Lake City for four months at least, and her husband revealed to Maud that he was very concerned about her well-being:

I guess Effie is having a hard time making both ends meet. She would make the venture [sic] and I am worried almost sick about her, she is so frail that she isn't able to do the work she is doing to say nothing about the worry of it all.

---

442 It is unknown why Grandpa Guyon and Effie apparently did not consider a move to some other place in Idaho, such as Pocatello or Boise, where Grandpa was already licensed.

See her as often as you can and let me know how she is. She won't say much about herself.[443]

In the same letter, Dr. Guyon lamented his financial situation, telling Maud that his fees for services in Montpelier were sparse to begin with and, to make things worse, "nearly all is on credit."[444] Just two weeks later, he revealed to Maud more of the financial and personal pressures he was under:

I am as well as usual but awful lonely. I think we made a serious mistake in going to Salt Lake, but don't tell Effie. She has had her mind set on going there and I finally consented. If I had a license there it would be all right, but it will take a lot of study and review work before I could pass the Board.[445]

This is followed by the following poignant assessment of Doc's situation, eerily reminiscent of his comments to Maud eleven months earlier:

I never was in such a fix. I could come there and do my studying there but I would be an added expense and her expense now is too great to balance her proceeds. It may be better after the holidays. I am getting a little salary as County Physician and I.O.O.F. sec'y about $35.00 a month besides the practice I get here which nearly all is credit. If I turn this down and go down there I will be only a burden on her. I can't do it. So you can see where I am. I don't want to discourage her and hence keep my mouth closed. If either her or I should get sick or any of the family I would be on the County. It is a serious predicament to be in and one I was never in before.[446]

Financial Distress Continues Unabated in Montpelier

As suggested in Doc's letters to his daughter Maud, life in Montpelier as envisioned by Effie and her husband in 1903 when they married was far from the reality of 1925 and 1926 and the depressing economic con-

---

[443] E. F. Guyon to Maud Brown, 12 December 1926.
[444] Ibid.
[445] E. F. Guyon to Maud Brown, 26 December 1926.
[446] Ibid.

ditions they found themselves in. They had been forced by circumstances largely beyond their control to at least modify their expectations, if not rid themselves of them entirely. There was nothing positive on the horizon, and it was that reality that forced them to consider uprooting their family. Timing made it imperative. Although unknown to Effie or Doc at the time, in 1926, Dr. Guyon was eight short years from the end of his life; Effie was to live until 1965.

Effie's involvement in this family's attempt to better its circumstances must not go unnoticed or be marginalized. She was the one who got past the fence-sitting stage, insisted that a change be made, and then actually moved to Salt Lake City to implement her plan. She was the party who broke out of the family's comfort zone. She and her husband certainly were in conflict over her decision to move, but it is not known whether their marriage was in jeopardy over it. What *is* known is that Effie's mind was made up and Grandpa Guyon finally consented, even though he continued to have grave doubts about it. Dr. Guyon was the patriarch, but Effie's influence in her family was in no way uncertain. Her presence, usually behind the scenes, was there nonetheless.[447]

L-R unknown; unknown; Arthur Burke;
Doc Guyon – circa 1927

Effie's Attempts at Relocation Sputter

By mid-December 1926, Effie's attempt to move her family to Salt Lake City had come to naught. Her dreams of a life in the city, with all the experiences and opportunities she envisioned, had been wrested from her almost before they got started. She had taken upon herself the task of singlehandedly raising her family from its financial woes to what she felt was a higher plane, in a time when most women would not have considered

---

447 This was not the first time Effie had attempted to help her family financially. In collaboration with the composer R. G. Gradi, she had published a song entitled "Down by the Winding Stream" on November 8, 1913, and registered the copyright that same day with the Copyright Office of the United States, #323870.

such a venture. Her attempt stands as undeniable evidence of her unconquerable spirit and will.

In early 1927, the local newspaper reported, "Mrs. E. F. Guyon and sons have returned from Salt Lake, where they spent the last few months."[448]

The attempted relocation was certainly a bittersweet experience for Effie. Her experience in Salt Lake City had not been a positive one from a financial standpoint, but she had conquered the demons of fear by going there. She must have been justly proud of that fact. This intrepid lady would again have to delve into her supply of courage later on as a fifty-nine-year-old widow.

According to her husband, Effie soon began to recover from her experience. Grandpa Guyon, in an obvious attempt to make sure she stayed recovered, made it a point to arise at six a.m. every morning, start the fires, make the coffee, set the table, and take care of "many other little duties connected with a house maid's work."[449]

Life Goes On in Montpelier

In February 1927, Grandpa Guyon, Effie, and their three children were living with George Burke, Effie's brother. Edwin Fenimore, twenty-one, and Wendell, nineteen, were both working, presumably for the railroad, with shifts from eight a.m. to four p.m. in the case of Edwin Fenimore and from noon to midnight in the case of Wendell. Buster, sixteen, was not employed and, for the moment, had not "started to school yet."[450]

Because there are no business ledgers covering 1927, it is impossible to reconstruct from that source what happened in Dr. Guyon's medical practice in the late 1920s. Fortunately, there are other indicators of his professional activities. By February 1927, he had been reappointed county physician for Bear Lake County, a post he had held for the preceding four years, and which he had also held for a two-year term in the 1890s.[451]

As an aside, I cannot resist including in this biography a vignette from this same time period surrounding a drawing for an automobile in Salt Lake City. Grandpa Guyon reported to Maud that Effie would be sending three tickets to a drawing to be held at Auerbach's for an "Essex Four Door Sedan" and promised Maud that "if we win it the car we have in the shed there is yours."

---

448 "Locals," *Bear Lake County (ID) News*, February 2, 1927, p. 8.
449 E. F. Guyon to Maud Brown, 11 February 1927.
450 Ibid.
451 Ibid.

The exuberance over the possibility of winning the Essex was short-lived, however, and replaced by Dr. Guyon's almost comical reaction:

> I knew we would not get the car. If we had got all the tickets except one we wouldn't have won the car. It seems that I never can get something for nothing. I have always been unlucky in such matters.[452]

In mid-1927, Dr. Guyon remained busy, this time inspecting school buildings, which likely was one of his responsibilities as county physician. He also reported having visited Kemmerer over a period of three days, but it is not known whether that visit was professional or personal.[453]

In August 1927, he fussed to Maud over Edwin Fenimore's decision to go to Los Angeles, probably to look for a job. His son, age twenty-two, took $50 with him, which "won't last long there," according to his father. Grandpa had warned Edwin Fenimore that he already had a good job in Montpelier that paid him $100 per month, without the room and board costs of $40 to $45 per month that he would have to pay in Los Angeles. In Montpelier, he only paid his mother $5 to $10 per month for the same benefits. Overall, according to Grandpa, the $100 he made in Montpelier was equivalent to $150 in California, "to say nothing about his washing and mending."[454]

In 1927, Grandpa Guyon's health was good, and he showed no signs of slowing down as he neared the age of seventy-four. In a letter to Maud he proudly reported: "I sleep well, eat well and have no disability whatsoever." In the same letter he said he felt "just as well as when I was a boy, except I tire easily."[455]

In response to Maud's report of meeting a man whose eye Grandpa Guyon had saved earlier in his career, he couldn't remember the individual, but in a rare statement said:

> I am glad he appreciates what I did, so that is all that counts whether I remember it or not. I have saved many lives since I have been a physician, I have lost but few patients who

---

452 E. F. Guyon to Maud Brown, 27 February 1927.
453 E. F. Guyon to Maud Brown, 10 June 1927.
454 E. F. Guyon to Maud Brown, 15 August 1927.
455 Ibid.

came to me in time, and even if I do forget their names and faces a record is kept by One Who never forgets.

Correspondence in October 1927 between Dr. Guyon and the Intermountain Life Insurance Company reveals that Grandpa had examined George A. Ashley, who had died suddenly after purchasing a life insurance policy based in part on the medical examination. The life insurance company sought additional information from Dr. Guyon, who had also signed the proof of death. Grandpa's explanation of his diagnoses before and after death is clear and concise and reflects no apparent disability on his part.

A Gold Fever Relapse

In early 1928, Dr. Guyon caught a serious case of gold fever, and found himself engaged in another gold-mining venture on the Snake River.[456] "If the Fates are kind," he mused, "maybe I may yet have a few dollars in my old days."

It is unknown whether this operation involved the same principals or the same ground as his 1910 gold mining enterprise. The 1928 project was to recover flour gold, which was so fine it was impossible to recover economically using traditional methods. Dr. Guyon and his partners intended to overcome that obstacle with a recently manufactured machine that could recover the finest gold.

The venturers' new corporation was to have about eight hundred acres under lease, which had assayed from $0.44 to $4.20 in gold per cubic yard of material. The machine itself, which two of Dr. Guyon's partners had seen successfully tested, had already arrived in Montpelier at a cost of about $800, and would cost an additional $75 to become operational.

The testing machine could handle forty tons of material a day. If expectations were met, the initial machine would be replaced by a larger one, capable of handling 1,000 tons per day. Financing was to be through stock issues. At fifty cents per share, 1,600 pre-incorporation shares were sold initially for $800, with expectations that $2,500 would soon be realized from the sale of 5,000 shares.[457]

---

[456] As discussed above, Dr. Guyon's stepfather Henry C. Smith was at least an occasional gold miner, and it seems highly likely that Dr. Guyon caught gold fever from Skedaddle Smith during his younger years in Oregon.
[457] E. F. Guyon to Maud Brown, 20 February 1928.

The outcome of the 1928 gold mining venture is unknown, but it was apparently unsuccessful. The nature of the operation itself suggests that the highly touted machine did not perform as advertised.[458]

Illness Factors into Dr. Guyon's Practice

By September 1928, Dr. Guyon continued to work as he was able, but ill health curtailed his efforts. As he described it:

> I had a sore throat and a siege of La Grip [sic]. I am still weak and not able to do much. I am getting better slowly. I go downtown every day but do not stay long. I feel so tired all the time that it is an effort for me to do anything. I guess I will be all right soon.[459]

A scant two months later he reported to Maud that after a trip to Salt Lake, he "caught a severe cold and [had] been confined to the house ever since."[460]

Wheels Were an Important Commodity

In the midst of his bouts with various illnesses, Doc was somehow able to acquire a new automobile, an event that seems strangely out of place with the sluggish economy in general and his in particular. In late September 1928, he proudly announced to Maud, "Our new car is expected to arrive about next Monday or Tuesday,"[461] and ten days or so after the announcement, happily reported to her that "our car arrived a few days ago and is a dandy."[462] Nothing in later correspondence reveals the make, model, or year of the new automobile.

---

458 Historically, placer mining extracts gold from the earth by means of a sluice. Material is washed by water through the man-made channel and the gold, because of its weight, settles behind riffles and ribs, where it is later retrieved. That technology has not changed appreciably for hundreds, if not thousands, of years, and it is unlikely that the machine purchased by Dr. Guyon and his friends could retrieve flour gold as efficiently as contemplated. Probably the only party to make money was the manufacturer of the machine.

459 E. F. Guyon to Maud Brown, 17 September 1928.
460 E. F. Guyon to Maud Brown, 13 November 1928.
461 E. F. Guyon to Maud Brown, 30 September 1928.
462 E. F. Guyon to Maud Brown, 12 October 1928.

The Price of Aging Is Sometimes Hard Toupée

Dr. Guyon was seventy-five years old on November 7, 1928, and it may be that his birthday triggered a touch of vanity that his family had seldom seen before. His disappearing hair had prompted a visit to the Salt Lake Costume Company, where he was fitted for a hairpiece. Unfortunately, he later complained that they "took [his] measure and saw the color of [his] hair" and then sent "a toupée for a man of twenty one."[463] Dr. Guyon scrapped the hairpiece and swore he would not wear a toupée at all that didn't "suit." Whether Grandpa replaced the offending toupée is not known.

The loss of Grandpa's hair was probably not a subject that was acceptable dinnertime chit-chat during his lifetime. He may have been no stranger to toupées prior to 1928, although it is difficult to confirm. His wedding photograph to Maggie in 1878 exposes an already receding hairline at the age of 25, yet photographs thought to have been taken later show what appears to be a full head of hair.

Ill Health Persists, and Then Relents Temporarily

In early 1929, Dr. Guyon was unable to practice medicine due to ill health[464] that had persisted for a month or so. His condition was improving, however. This allowed him to go to his office every day and kindled his hopes that he would soon be able to return to his medical practice.[465] That hope was premature. Toward the end of March, 1929, he had not been able to return for about five months; "hence nothing coming in."[466]

Later that year, although not entirely recuperated, he ventured out on an automobile trip to Blackfoot, Idaho. The purpose was to accompany a patient, a "mentally afflicted" individual, Judge Goff, to the asylum there. The car, described by Grandpa as "a $2000.00 Buick," was driven by the patient's son-in-law. After successfully transferring Judge Goff to the institution, Dr. Guyon reported:

> On the way back as we were entering Pocatello, a truck struck our car and threw our car about 15 feet and turned

---

463 E. F. Guyon to Maud Brown, 28 November 1928.
464 E. F. Guyon to Maud Brown, 21 January 1929.
465 E. F. Guyon to Maud Brown, 3 February 1929.
466 E. F. Guyon to Maud Brown, 21 March 1929.

it over yet it never hurt me the least bit, nor did it hurt the driver. It was the luckiest accident I ever heard of. It took two men to get me out.[467]

The local paper reported Dr. Guyon made a visit to California for an indefinite period in early 1930.[468] He did not mention the reasons for or duration of this California visit in any of his known correspondence. Reportedly, he spent several weeks in Los Angeles and Santa Barbara.[469] The Montpelier paper mused that he had gone to California "for his health,"[470] but it is safe to assume that he was also exploring the possibilities of moving there permanently.

Doc Guyon's Health Continues to Deteriorate

By late 1930, at the age of seventy-seven, Dr. Guyon described himself to Maud as "melancholy . . . [m]y mind is weak and my memory is all to pieces. I forget nearly everything."[471] He may have continued to see patients occasionally, but at the very least was semi-retired. It is highly likely that his symptoms were in no small way exacerbated by his financial condition, his inability to find a reasonable alternative to his medical practice in Montpelier, and the anxiety they produced.

Over the next year Dr. Guyon's health deteriorated even more, and by late 1931 he had been compelled to discontinue his medical practice for the most part.[472] He reached his seventy-eighth birthday in November 1931. Just prior to that event he voiced a faint hint of despair in a letter to Maud: "All we can do is hope and pray for prosperity to smile upon us in the near future."[473]

Just three days later, he painted a dismal picture of life, but not only in Montpelier:

> It is very dull here as it is everywhere and no signs of a change very soon.

* * *

---

467 E. F. Guyon to Maud Brown, 12 July 1929.
468 *Montpelier (ID) Examiner*, February 20, 1930, p. 1.
469 "Local Happenings," *Bear Lake County (ID) News*, February 21, 1930, p. 5.
470 *Montpelier (ID) Examiner*, March 13, 1930, p. 5.
471 E. F. Guyon to Maud Brown, 11 December 1930.
472 Charles E. Harris (Dr. Guyon's Montpelier lawyer) to Senator Borah, 2 December 1931.
473 E. F. Guyon to Maud Brown, 25 October 1931.

There is no news to write as it is destitute of activity of all kinds [,] here as well as everywhere.[474]

Despite his circumstances, he seemed to be far from giving up or giving in to his ailments. In a letter to Maud in mid-1931 he mentioned a trip by rail to California,[475] which in all likelihood was to look for a better professional location and better opportunities, as he had done in early 1930. It is likely he found that California was in no less economic distress than Idaho.

The Saga of the Indian Wars Pension Begins

On October 13, 1931, Dr. Guyon applied for a pension for his service in 1878 in the Bannock War, based upon a law passed by Congress on March 3, 1927 (the "1927 Act"), which purported to pension veterans of the Indian Wars. According to the government, his application was deficient because there were no official records from which his service could be confirmed, and the sworn testimony of his comrades lacked the details necessary prove his entitlement in lieu of such official records.

The compatriots who filed affidavits supporting Dr. Guyon's application had themselves been granted pensions through special acts of Congress prior to 1929, and when Grandpa's 1931 application failed, his next move was to adopt his friends' strategy in 1932 and 1933. His death in early 1934 apparently mooted his attempts to secure a special act.

After Dr. Guyon's death Effie, as his surviving spouse, continued the fight for the pension in the halls of Congress. Those attempts culminated in a presidential pocket-veto of the bill introduced for her. Undaunted, Effie made two subsequent applications in her own behalf, both of which failed because of her inability to establish the details of her husband's service.

The odyssey eventually ended in 1953. Over the more than twenty years in the meantime, the efforts of both Dr. Guyon and his widow involved several Idaho senators along with the unforgiving and perhaps overly-punctilious Washington bureaucracy. The details of this sad and unproductive adventure are contained in Appendix VI.

---

474 Ibid.
475 E. F. Guyon to Maud Brown, 20 July 1931.

In late 1931 and in the midst of worrying about his financial condition and considering relocating his office and family, Doc Guyon took time to write a letter reminiscing about things he had seen and events he had experienced in Oregon in the 1860s. His actual letter has apparently not survived, but luckily was answered by George W. Done, a Pilot Rock councilman, in two surviving letters dated December 20, 1931, and January 24, 1932. Mr. Done provides the following colorful response:

> Our old friend Oscar DeVaul died some few years ago, after practicing medicine here and in Portland for several years. I was going to his school when a fellow by the name of McCarty was shot and killed by one John Alexander, up on Birch Creek, and after McCarty was buried for about two weeks it was decided to take him up and hold a postmortem to determine the location of the first bullet wound.

> Oscar was teaching school at the time and he gave Alex Manning and myself a half day off providing we would go up and dig up McCarty for examination.

> I remember quite well that you and Dr. C.J. Smith done the dissecting of McCarty. I looked on and it was quite a sight for me and I remember well the course of the bullet you were looking for, and found lodged on the inside of his hip bone.

> Those were the good old days, when we went to school and only our lessons to worry about, and many of the pupils did not even worry about them.

Mr. Done also commented on some of the information provided in Dr. Guyon's earlier letter:

> Although I have been in Umatilla County for about 54 years you have many things in your letter of the early days in this section that I had never heard, for instance the history of our cemetary [sic] and the Hicks children being the first burried [sic] there. And to see in print by one who

really had seen flour sell at $20 per sack and wood at $50 dollars per cord during the first part of the sixties.

Grandpa Guyon Investigates a Possible Return to Pendleton

Grandpa's anxiety about his circumstances in Montpelier led him to consider returning to Pendleton, despite his physical frailties. Pendleton druggist J. V. "Joe" Tallman, in response to a query from Dr. Guyon, painted a dismal picture, including the failure of Pendleton's only bank, and advised:

> I would warn you against returning to Pendleton now and I think several years will pass before the town will be a fit place to locate in. If I get an opportunity to sell out I am going to do it at my first chance. It isn't in the cards here. There isn't a doctor making it today.[476]

Desperation and Despair

In late July, 1933, Grandpa Guyon's overall circumstances and those of his family continued to deteriorate:

> I am not very well now days and don't know how matters will shake up later on. I am broke flat and don't see how I am going to make it. I am not able to practice medicine and too poor to live without money or not. Effie and Buster and myself are soon going to try and find a better locality & a warmer place to live. I am pretty old to do this, but when you are destitute what else can we do. I am a very unhappy man. We certainly don't deserve such a fate. We are going to try and find a warmer climate and a better practice if possible. Otherwise I will have to go to the poor house and that right soon. We don't know where we will go.

***

---

[476] J. V. "Joe" Tallman to E. F. Guyon, 25 March 1933.

I don't know when we will start on our hunt for a location. It must be a warmer place than this one and with more money. We have but little money to go on and if we can't find what we want I don't know what will become of us. We will stop off at Pocatello where we start on our investigation and we will have to make a hurried investigation and just how it will end I can't say.[477]

Doc had corresponded with his friend H. M. Moore in Anaheim in hopes of finding a position in California, but the Depression had made any such option impossible.[478]

Several days later, in a return letter to H. M. Moore, Grandpa Guyon commiserated over the death of Moore's wife, among other things. This letter less than five months before his own death reveals circumstances in Montpelier that are best conveyed by his own words:

> Conditions are very dull here and being under the weather for 3 years and unable to do anything, I am about ready for the poorhouse. I am broke and don't know what to do. My health has declined so that I am not able to do any strenuous work. So I confine my work to the office. There is no money here yet, but we are trusting it will soon come back.[479]

Dr. Guyon, Effie, and Buster lived in Montpelier at least through August, 1933, as evidenced by an empty envelope from the US Department of the Interior with a postmark of March 30, 1933. The letter to Edwin Fenimore quoted above bears the inside address "Montpelier, Ida.," and a later letter from Grandpa Guyon to Maud of August 13, 1933, shows "Montpelier" as the return address. In the letter to Maud, Grandpa stated:

> We are destitute. I never was so destitute and don't know just what to do. We have decided to investigate California and Nevada. If we had the money we might find a suitable location. I am at my wits end and am discouraged. It is too

---

477 E. F. Guyon to Edwin Fenimore Guyon, 29 July 1933.
478 H. M. Moore to E. F. Guyon, 12 August 1933.
479 E. F. Guyon to H. M. Moore, 15 August 1933.

cold here and the weather too hard for us poor people. I am just too feeble & old to endure another winter here.

Doc Guyon and his family had few options. In the fall of 1933, just four years into the Great Depression, poverty was common. The circumstance that finally triggered a move was the impending winter in Bear Lake County—not a trivial consideration. The quest for a warmer clime began sometime in September, 1933. The date is not known with certainty, but the family would have wanted to avoid possible snowstorms in October and November.

Whether the trio went as far as California or Nevada in their search is unknown, but Dr. Guyon and Effie were in Pocatello on January 8, 1934, and may have been there for several months.[480] The decision to land in Pocatello may have been mandatory because of lack of money, Dr. Guyon's deteriorating health, or other factors. One important advantage to Pocatello was that Edwin Fenimore lived there. What happened to Buster after leaving Montpelier is unknown. He was twenty-four years old in the fall of 1933 and likely was working to help support his parents, but whether he was also living with them is not known.

Grandpa Guyon's Death in Pocatello

Grandpa Guyon died suddenly on January 8, 1934. He and Effie were living in the Quinn Apartments at 580 West Clark Street in Pocatello at the time. Upon their return from a long walk they had taken together, Grandpa sat down in a chair and gently passed away without saying a word and without showing any outward signs of suffering or distress. Effie promptly notified Edwin Fenimore, who came immediately to comfort his mother.[481] A local physician was called, who confirmed the death due to "mitral insufficiency." [482] As arrangements were made for his funeral, other family members were notified. Due to a misunderstanding, Dr. Guyon's body was taken to the Woodard funeral home in Pocatello, where it was embalmed, rather than to F. M. Williams in Montpelier, as Effie and Edwin Fenimore had intended.

---

[480] Dr. Guyon's obituary states that he "had been living in Pocatello for the past three months, following a trip to California for his health" and that he was "actually engaged in the practice of his profession [in Montpelier] until a few years ago, when ill health compelled him to retire."
[481] It is also possible, although unconfirmed, that Edwin Fenimore was present at the death of his father.
[482] Years later, Effie reported that Grandpa Guyon also suffered from chronic bronchitis at the time of his death.

Fay asserted that his father had wanted to be buried in Pilot Rock next to his mother. Grandpa Guyon had apparently never voiced that desire to his second family, and the cost associated with sending his body to Pilot Rock for burial was an expense the family could ill afford. Dr. Guyon's funeral took place in the Presbyterian Church in Montpelier and he was buried in a plot, with no other resident than himself, in the Montpelier cemetery according to the rites of Odd Fellowship.[483] Eventually, Effie and their son Royal joined him there. Dr. Guyon's headstone, chosen by his daughter Maud, is a small bronze plate on a stone base that reads: "Dr. Edwin F. Guyon, November 7, 1853 [–] January 8, 1934."

An article in the *Montpelier Examiner*[484] announced his passing locally, and outlined in some detail his life in Oregon, his move to Montpelier, his affiliation with Odd Fellowship, and his long service as a physician. The article expressed what many locals were likely feeling:

> His passing will give many of the old timers a pang of keen regret, especially those whose family physician he had been for so many years. The doctor was a good citizen and a fine neighbor, and numbered his friends by the scores throughout this section of Idaho. He gave freely of his time and professional services to the community, and many hearts were saddened when news of his death reached this city.

The *Bear Lake County News* reported his death on January 12, 1934,[485] and, a week later on January 19, 1934,[486] described his funeral services as "impressive."

Dr. Guyon's passing coincided with the end of an era. The Guyon family's link to the pre–Civil War Deep South was severed. The world he had known most of his life had passed with him. The bumpy, dusty, unpaved roads imbedded with wagon ruts that he was so familiar with in his youth and earlier years would soon be but a memory, along with the smoke- and steam-belching locomotives that pulled passengers and freight from coast to coast. The trips he had taken by train would soon be taken in private automobiles, on asphalt and concrete roads, at speeds and with

---

483 *Bear Lake County (ID) News*, January 19, 1934, p. 1.
484 *Montpelier (ID) Examiner*, January 11, 1934, p. 1.
485 *Bear Lake County (ID) News*, January 12, 1934, p. 1.
486 *Bear Lake County (ID) News*, January 19, 1934, p. 1.

comforts he'd never dreamed of. Not long after, those distances could be covered in airplanes. Horse-drawn buggies and sleighs would soon become mere curiosities.

He started life with little, save the love of a devoted mother and her extended family, soon supplemented by a loving and supportive stepfather. His parents encouraged his formal education during his formative years, and he leveraged his initial training into a lifelong love affair with education, both as a student and as a teacher. His search for knowledge eventually led him to medical school, where he opened the door to national and international acclaim as a warrior in the struggle against tuberculosis.

E. F. Guyon's legacy is his example. He was a self-made man, a humanitarian, a patriot, and a father. A religious and moral conservative, he was also broad-minded, liberal and progressive in his views socially and politically, and a champion of the less fortunate members of his world. He earned the esteem of political leaders, his colleagues in the medical profession, his brothers in the IOOF, his patients, and last but not least, his family. He made his mark in the world under often unfavorable conditions, guided as he was by his personal belief there was a sharp difference between right and wrong. His honesty and integrity ensured his success as a venerable human being and fond memories of him after his passing.

After his death, his surgical instruments, sundry equipment, and a small collection of medicines and chemicals lay in my parents' basement for many years until they were donated by our family to the Rails and Trails museum in Montpelier, where they can be viewed. Reportedly, Dr. Guyon had a large library at the time of his death that was eventually donated to the medical school at the University of Utah.

APPENDICES

THE HUGUENOT DIASPORA

Religious Persecution in France

Protestantism[487] in the 16th, 17th, and 18th centuries was known in France as "la Religion Prétendue Réformée," or "the Pretended Reformed Religion." The fact that the movement was christened "pretended" by its opponents gives an inkling of the antagonism and contempt directed toward it, but hardly scratches the surface of the lengths to which its enemies, ultimately including the French state, would go to suppress and eradicate it.

The institutions in France, particularly the clergy, were so entrenched in the exclusive accuracy of the theology of Catholicism that the perceived threat of Protestantism somehow altered the state's national and world view and in no small way skewed its national interests. There appeared to be no price the government of France would not pay in its frenetic attempts to stamp out the perceived threat. The French State readily sacrificed the lives of its soldiers and its loyal Protestant citizens in civil war. It ignored human rights and religious freedom on a vast scale. It ultimately embarked upon a self-destructive national policy that prevented it from establishing itself as a major power in the western hemisphere, which could have materially altered the balance of political power in North America in France's favor forever.

The eventual transplantation of French Protestants to the eastern seaboard of the United States after the Revocation of the Edict of Nantes in 1685 is to Americans the best known, but not the only migration to this country, and even to this hemisphere. As early as 1555, French adherents to the doctrines of the Reformation had unsuccessfully attempted to establish themselves first in Brazil, and then in Florida.[488] Other, successful, migrations to Acadia, Nova Scotia, the French West Indies, the Dutch possession of New Netherland (now New York), and Canada also occurred during the pre-1685 period.[489]

---

[487] The terms *Protestantism* and *Calvinism* are sometimes used interchangeably, but doing so may be misleading. Calvinists, Lutherans, and others dedicated to the reformation of certain elements of the Catholic Church are all Protestants, but there are significant theological differences between them that are beyond the scope of this discussion.

[488] Baird, *History of the Huguenot Emigration*, 1:21.

[489] Ibid.

François I (approximate pronunciation "frawn-swah pruhm-yay"), known to the English-speaking world as Francis I (b. 1494, d. 1547; reigned 1515–1547), is widely acknowledged and admired as France's first Renaissance king. Initially, he was not unsympathetic to the idea of personal religious freedom, and at one point in time was even said to have been in favor of curbing acknowledged abuses of the Catholic Church.[490] His initial warmth to the cause of Calvinism was in part politically motivated by a need to befriend Protestant allies and placate his own Protestant subjects. When the importance of those practical considerations waned, the initial flash of apparent enlightenment turned into outright hostility.[491] During the last years of his reign, he engineered legislative enactments that criminalized heresy[492] upon penalty of death; Protestant citizens in twenty-two towns and villages in southeastern France were massacred, and fourteen members of the newly organized Protestant Church at Meaux were burned at the stake.[493]

Protestant life in France under François I was difficult, but became almost unbearable under his son Henri II (b. 1519, d. 1559; reigned 1547–1559). The Edict of Chateaubriand, which became law on June 27, 1551, was passed under Henri's watchful eye. Among other things, this draconian act combined civil and ecclesiastical courts that were vested with the exclusive power to detect and punish heretics. Those convicted of heresy had no right of appeal from the trial courts. This meant that there was no legal mechanism that allowed for the correction of inevitable errors in the legal process. This, in turn, ensured that trial judges had no fear that their orders and decrees, however extreme or ill-advised, would ever be overturned, much less reviewed, or that they would have to answer to a higher legal authority.

Persons merely suspected of heresy found themselves disqualified from academic honors and public recognition. Anyone found aiding or abetting them in any fashion might well find one-third of their goods confiscated and awarded to their informers. Those actually fleeing the country suffered the confiscation of all their property.[494]

Censorship provisions forbade the importation of so-called heretical literature as well as its production within the realm.[495] The fact that the

---

[490] Ibid., 1:23.
[491] Ibid.
[492] "Heresy," of course, meant anything contrary to the theology and doctrines of Catholicism.
[493] Baird, *History of the Huguenot Emigration*, 1:23.
[494] Ibid.
[495] Ibid, 1:24.

Protestant faith continued to flourish in France despite the repressive measures of the Edict of Chateaubriand attests to the depth of the faith and devotion of those early adherents to the cause of religious freedom.

Unsatisfied with the effects of the already extreme measures imposed by the law against the Protestant faith, its enemies plotted to impose even harsher punishments. A proposal to introduce the singularly effective Spanish Inquisition in France was pending before the Parliament of Paris in 1555.[496] Luckily for Protestantism, that particular measure was not adopted.

The Protestant movement persisted, notwithstanding the continued efforts of the government to suppress it via edict after edict imposing imprisonment, confiscation of goods, and death for those convicted of heresy. The Edict of July 1561 is recognized as the most severe and most sweeping.[497] Under its proscriptions, any person who attended a Protestant worship service, public or private, whether the person was armed or not, was subject to imprisonment or confiscation of his property.[498] By the time the law came into effect, however, there were already 2,150 Protestant churches in France,[499] making their members a force to be reckoned with. The measure brought the country to the brink of civil war.

War was temporarily averted when Catherine de Medici, then acting as regent for her son Charles IX during his minority, chose tolerance over oppression on the advice of her minister Coligny, a farsighted and tolerant pacifist and friend to Protestantism.[500] The result was the passage of the Edict of January 1562, which marked the first time in France that the Protestant religion was recognized as legal and was granted some measure of protection under the law.[501] The penalties imposed previous to its passage were provisionally repealed, pending the settlement of all questions of religious faith via a general Council of the Church.[502]

The Edict of Nantes Finally Becomes Law

If Protestants were encouraged by the Edict of January, 1562, to believe that their religious worries and struggles were over, or at least

---

[496] Ibid.
[497] Ibid, 1:58.
[498] Ibid.
[499] Ibid, 1:59.
[500] Ibid.
[501] Ibid.
[502] Ibid.

lessened, it was not long before their dreams were dashed by cruel reality. A scant six months after its passage, the Duke of Guise caused the unprovoked massacre at Vassy of fifty to sixty Protestant worshipers. This event triggered the outbreak of the First Civil War.[503] The chain of events thus begun kindled conflicts that would last forty years in the form of eight civil wars[504]—the Wars of Religion—with the attendant deaths, ruined and impoverished villages and cities, and farms laid waste.[505]

Finally, on April 13, 1598, the Edict of Nantes was signed. This event had an almost immediate positive effect upon the political and economic conditions of the country. The edict guaranteed certain religious and civil rights to Protestants in France, also had the effect of reviving public confidence in general, and signaled the return of economic prosperity.[506]

The level of tolerance embodied in the new law was not in any way a general acceptance of Protestantism. The Edict of Nantes continued to limit the exercise of the Religion Prétendue Réformée, although in a somewhat less draconian fashion than its predecessors. Any function of the Protestant faith was forbidden within the court or its retinue, in the crown's lands and territories beyond the mountains, and within five leagues of the city of Paris.[507] No books concerning the religion could be printed or sold, except where the public exercise of the religion was specifically permitted. It did grant rights theretofore unknown to the Protestant faith, but it did so reluctantly and with a spirit of malevolence that would reappear with a vengeance before a century had passed.

The passage of the Edict of Nantes into law was, to say the least, a severe blow to the enemies of Protestantism in general, and a particularly bitter event to the more extreme elements of the Roman Catholic political party and the clergy of the Roman Catholic Church.[508] Negative internal pressure from these elements was so great that the parliaments charged with the registration of the decree initially refused to enter it as law, and only capitulated to the specific command of the king that it be done.[509]

The political and religious influences in France that had temporarily yielded to the passage of the Edict of Nantes were not spent, and the

---

[503] Ibid., 1:62.
[504] Huguenot Society of Great Britain and Ireland, "Huguenot History," accessed August 19, 2016, http://www.huguenotsociety.org.uk/history.html.
[505] Baird, *History of the Huguenot Emigration*, 1:79.
[506] Ibid.
[507] Edict of Nantes, Section XIV.
[508] Baird, *History of the Huguenot Emigration*, 1:83.
[509] Ibid.

fearsome influence of the Jesuits, who had been banished previously, was again being felt at court.[510] Persecution, although wounded, was not dead, and would yet again rear its ugly head against those who would presume to embrace Protestantism.

Huguenots Begin to Colonize America

The specter of renewed persecution was foreseen by the cagey Coligny, who continued to encourage the establishment of places of refuge outside France where Calvinists and their descendants might enjoy freedom of conscience in the event the "irrevocable" confirmation by the Edict of Nantes of all citizens' religious and civil rights were ever to be reversed.[511]

In 1599, Henri IV commissioned Pierre Chauvin, seigneur de Tontuit, a Protestant, to establish colonies in America.[512] Chauvin, with a force of five hundred men accompanied by ministers entirely Calvinistic, established a trading post at Tadoussac on the northern shore of the St. Lawrence.[513] The attempt at settlement was ultimately unsuccessful, but it may have paved the way for Pierre du Gua, sieur de Monts, a Huguenot who was granted a commission on November 8, 1603, to possess and settle that portion of North America between the fortieth and forty-sixth parallels of north latitude, along with a trade monopoly between Cape Race and the fortieth parallel.[514] The coasts of these same lands had been visited by the famous French explorer Jacques Cartier almost seventy years prior, and an unsuccessful attempt at colonization had been made during the reign of Francis I.[515] Early in 1524, the explorer Verrazzano had planted the flag of France in these vast territories, but it was not until the early part of the 17th century that attempts to settle them began to be successful.

Le sieur de Monts became the lieutenant-general as well as viceroy of Henri IV over an enormous territory that included present-day Canada and a large part of the rest of the continent.[516] He was particularly attracted to the peninsula south of the Gulf of St. Lawrence as a place for his colony.

---

[510] Ibid.
[511] Ibid.
[512] Ibid., 1:84.
[513] Ibid., 1:85.
[514] Ibid., 1:84.
[515] Ibid.
[516] Ibid., 1:101.

Originally named La Cadie,[517] the English equivalent of which is Acadia, it was later called Nova Scotia (New Scotland), as it is known today.

For our purposes, perhaps the most important fact, at least in the abstract, is that religious freedom and tolerance were rights secured by the government of New France from its inception.[518] Despite the wording of the king's commission, however, there were attempts in France to withhold its confirmation. In the case of the Parliament of Rouen, its foot-dragging required an unequivocal royal command, which was speedily complied with.[519]

The Death of Henry IV and Renewed Persecution

A number of settlements eventually appeared in New France, including Port Royal in 1604 and present-day Quebec City in 1608, the latter by the explorer Champlain under authority of De Monts. [520] Unfortunately, however, the even-handed approach to religion that had earlier existed, if only in theory, disappeared virtually overnight with the assassination of Henri IV in 1610. The protector of Protestantism was gone, and in the New World, through the machinations of one Antoinette de Pons, marquise de Guercheville, the authority over half a continent to make such determinations fell from the hand of a Huguenot into the hands of the Jesuits—the Society of Jesus.[521]

The die was cast in the religious sense. On May 23, 1633, Champlain was reappointed as governor and received the keys to the fort of Quebec from the Protestant De Caen, and Canada was formally closed to colonization by Protestants.[522] This exclusion of Huguenots from New France, sanctioned as it was by the powerful Cardinal Richelieu, not only barred Protestants as colonists in what is present-day Canada, but also sounded the death knell to the French colonial system in America. It has been characterized as "one of the most stupendous blunders that history records."[523]

At the time, the Huguenots constituted not only the most available, but also the most desirable, class of persons capable of succeeding at the gigantic task of colonization. Motivated by religious fervor and possessing

---

[517] The word is Scottish in origin and denotes an errand boy, porter, or messenger.
[518] Baird, *History of the Huguenot Emigration*, 1:87.
[519] Ibid., 1:99.
[520] Ibid., 1:101.
[521] Ibid., 1:102–3.
[522] Ibid., 1:115–16.
[523] Ibid., 1:116.

industrial skill, intelligence, moral worth, and an unsurpassed work ethic, they were essentially "made to order" for the task of creating a vast Gallic empire in North America.[524] France's mind-boggling decision to exclude them from the process of colonization underscores the price France paid for its religious extremism, particularly in view of the resulting loss of the human capital embodied in its hundreds of thousands of Protestant Frenchmen and Frenchwomen, who instead enriched the Protestant countries of northern Europe and the British colonies of the United States.[525]

The Edict of Nantes Is Revoked

For all of its mind-numbing wrongheadedness, this repressive policy was followed by France for the next fifty-plus years, and would culminate in the revocation of the Edict of Nantes (hereafter the "Revocation") on October 22, 1685.[526] In-depth analysis of the political and religious forces at work in France and abroad during the 17th century that brought about the Revocation is beyond the scope of this short history. However, it is important to grasp the depth of fidelity and commitment to their religious consciences that impelled hundreds of thousands of loyal Frenchmen and Frenchwomen to leave their ancestral homes and property and to risk their lives and futures in doing so.

The document embodying the Revocation is less than three 8½" x 11" pages in length, with twelve sections, each in Roman numerals. The Edict of Nantes itself is almost twenty-five 8½" x 11" pages in length, with ninety-two sections, also in Roman numerals. The disparity in length reflects the care in the edict itself to carefully limit the scope of the rights being granted. The Revocation pretends no such care in taking them away.

The Revocation is an extremely mean-spirited document. It leaves no lingering uncertainty about its objectives. It contains the flowing and flowery language typical of official French documents of the 17th century, but no amount of legerdemain can soften, much less conceal, its meaning and its malevolent intent.

In Section I, the Revocation nullifies the Edict of Nantes and the Edict of Nimes of July, 1629, with the following language:

---

[524] Ibid., 1:116–17.
[525] Ibid., 1:117.
[526] Ibid., 1:116.

We declare them null and void, together with all concessions, of whatever nature they may be, made by them as well as by other edicts, declarations, and orders, in favor of the said persons of the [Pretended Reformed Religion], the which shall remain in like manner as if they had never been granted; and in consequence we desire, and it is our pleasure, that all the temples of those of the said R.P.R. situate in our kingdom, countries, territories, and the lordships under our crown, shall be demolished without delay.

The Revocation in Section II states: "We forbid our subjects of the [R.P.R.] to meet any more for the exercise of said religion in any place or private house, under any pretext whatever."

In Section III, noblemen are declared subject to "imprisonment and confiscation" who allow subjects of the R.P.R. to hold religious exercises in their houses or fiefs.

Protestant ministers were immediately enjoined in Section IV from "preaching, exhortation, or any other function" and ordered "to leave our kingdom and the territories subject to us within a fortnight of the publication of [the Revocation] . . . on pain of being sent to the galleys."

Protestant parents were ordered by Section VII to have their children baptized and brought up in the "Catholic, apostolic, and Roman religion," under penalty of a fine of five hundred livres, which might be "increased as circumstances may demand."

Section X contains the "express prohibition" against any subject's leaving "our kingdom, lands, and territories subject to us, or transporting their goods and effect therefrom under penalty, as respects the men, of being sent to the galleys,[527] and as respects the women, of imprisonment

---

[527] Galleys were primarily fighting vessels used on the Mediterranean, propelled by human oarsmen, but also having masts and sails as options. They were capable of short bursts of speed, enabling them to catch and ram enemy vessels. Being "sent to the galleys" is a punishment one might expect to see in ancient times, and seems curiously out of place in the 17th and 18th centuries. Nevertheless, Louis XIV created a galley corps in 1665, the individual ships of which were commanded by handpicked court favorites and carried French infantry as fighting forces. The French galleys of the era were approximately 150 feet in length, 40 feet in width, and 7 feet in depth. Because of their shallow draft, the galleys were advantageous in calm waters, but extremely unseaworthy in rough seas. The oarsmen, about three hundred in number, were chained to each other on the deck, where they sat on benches six abreast and pulled their oars against a wooden beam parallel to their benches. A sentence to the galleys was meant to be servitude for life. The experiences of one Protestant victim of the galley system may be found in Jean Marteilhe, *Galley Slave* (Barnsley, UK: Seaforth, 2010).

and confiscation." The underlying reasoning was, of course, to force those inclined to leave the catholic faith back into the fold.

In view of the religious and property rights guaranteed by the United States Constitution, which had had their genesis in the chaos of the French Revolution and the Declaration of the Rights of Man in the 18th century, it is difficult to comprehend the almost perfunctory way the Revocation strips away rights modern Americans take for granted, and which Protestants in France had enjoyed for almost one hundred years. It must be remembered that these events took place almost a century before the French Revolution rewrote the relationships between those who govern and the governed. Despots in the 17th century were rarely benevolent, and they made the law. The iconic Louis XIV is often quoted as saying, "L'état c'est moi,"[528] and he doubtless meant it.

The Revocation Triggers Emigration

What is *not* so difficult to understand are the feelings these beleaguered Protestants must have felt when they became aware of the Revocation and its requirements. Faced with the immediate and institutionalized destruction of their houses of worship and their religion, it is little wonder that the many Protestants in France sought more receptive religious climes. The current estimates are that approximately 200,000 Huguenots left France after the Revocation. Of that number, 50,000 went to England, and about 10,000 of that number moved on to Ireland. Approximately 10,000 went to America directly, and the balance went to the Netherlands (50,000 to 60,000); northeast Europe (2,000); Germany (25,000 to 30,000); Switzerland (22,000); and a small contingent of 400 around the Cape of Good Hope, sent there by the Dutch East India Company to develop vineyards in southern Africa.[529] The numbers are necessarily estimates because many left France in secret, and there was little official record-keeping machinery in place at the end of the 18th century that could memorialize their entry into foreign lands.

La Rochelle

Much can be said of La Rochelle in both the secular and ecclesiastical senses, but must necessarily be abbreviated here. For over five hundred years it had enjoyed a number of extraordinary royal favors, including the

---

[528] "I am the state."
[529] Huguenot Society of Great Britain and Ireland, "Huguenot History."

right to elect its mayors and magistrates, not to mention exemption from taxes, all of which came as a result of the loyalty of its citizens to successive kings of France.[530]

La Rochelle also became the rallying point for French Protestantism, and its importance to the Reformation in France can scarcely be overstated.[531] Such was the religious climate in La Rochelle that when the Revocation was published in 1685, the Roman mass had not been celebrated in La Rochelle for almost forty years.[532]

During the civil wars that followed the Edict of January 17, 1562, the walls of La Rochelle protected its inhabitants from a siege by the royal army that lasted nine months (November, 1572–July 10, 1573) and for the next fifty years allowed and promoted a free intellectual life within.[533]

The terrible second siege (August 15, 1627–November 1, 1628) decreed the abrupt end of La Rochelle's independence and importance as the "Western Geneva" of Protestantism, from which it was never to recover.[534] Under the heavy hand of Louis XIII, the fortifications that had so plagued the royal soldiers and engineers were razed to the ground and the royal favors La Rochelle had enjoyed for centuries were abrogated.[535] Nevertheless, La Rochelle continued to be a sanctuary of sorts to French Protestants. By gathering there, many avoided afflictions suffered by their religious compatriots elsewhere in France.[536] Sadly, many would later suffer a pitiless expulsion from this once great center of Protestantism.

In 1628, one of the provisions imposed by Louis XIII was that no Protestants not already living in La Rochelle at the end of the second siege could thereafter be admitted. This provision was not enforced for more than thirty years immediately following 1628, but was suddenly revived in 1661 through a civil ordinance.

During the intervening period of thirty-three years, many Protestants had come to La Rochelle to live. Some knew no other home. Regardless of individual circumstances, those in violation of the ordinance were given fifteen days to leave (always with the exemption a change of religion would bring). More than 300 families complied with the ordinance.[537] The rest

---

[530] Ibid.
[531] Ibid.
[532] Baird, *History of the Huguenot Emigration*, 1:266.
[533] Ibid., 1:267.
[534] Ibid., 1:267–68.
[535] Ibid., 1:268.
[536] Ibid.
[537] Ibid., 1:269.

were forcibly removed, their property either confiscated by government officials or thrown into the streets during a torrential rain that history records as lasting three consecutive weeks.[538] There were no exemptions for infants in cradles, the aged, the sick, and the bedridden, some of whom died during the process.[539]

As reported above, at some point prior to 1685 Huguenots had settled in what was New Netherland and later became New York, and there is some evidence that a number of immigrants came to America straightaway after the expulsion from La Rochelle. A petition sent by one Jean Touton on his own behalf and on behalf of others to Governor Endicott of the Commonwealth of Massachusetts requests permission to relocate in what would become the United States, although the names and number of those signatories have been lost. Touton himself is known to have been a resident of Rehoboth, Massachusetts, in 1675.[540]

The existence of French Protestant communities may have beckoned to the immigrants of the post-1685 period at the very least because of the obvious religious and linguistic similarities. However, those similarities do not necessarily mean that post-1685 Huguenots came straight from France to the United States. Many by far first went to Holland, the British Isles, and Germany. There are a number of reasons why, but doubtless economics played a part. Travel was expensive, and the cost to Holland or the British Isles was less. Second, and perhaps even more importantly, Britain, Holland, and even Germany, all Protestant countries in their own right, welcomed these escapees from religious persecution with open arms, in sharp contrast to the French authorities.

---

[538] Ibid.
[539] Ibid., 1:269–70.
[540] Ibid., 1:270–71.

APPENDIX II

DEVELOPMENT OF THE PANAMA ROUTE

The Panama Route in all its variations came about as the result of the convergence of a number of important historical events and developments. Chronologically, the first was the successful application of steam power to oceangoing vessels ("steamers").[541] The size of steamers varied greatly, as did their passenger accommodations. Generally speaking, they were wooden side-wheeled ships (i.e., one paddle-wheel on each side) with one to four decks, two or three masts, and accommodations for up to five hundred people, including first-class, second-class, and sometimes third-class cabins along with room in steerage.[542] Most of these vessels were 200 to 300 feet in length and weighed 1,200 to 2,700 tons, although smaller ones might weigh 500 tons and the largest 4,000 tons.[543] The major advantages of steamers over sailing ships were time and predictability. Sailing ships were slaves to the vicissitudes of wind and weather, but the steamer had the enviable ability to maintain a relatively straight course to its destination, despite the direction of the wind, and despite the weather—within reason. The tradeoff was that travel by steamer was more expensive than by sail.[544] For that reason, the advent of the oceangoing passenger steamer had little effect on the shipping industry, where cost was more important than time.[545]

Second was the acquisition by the United States of title to vast tracts of territory in the West, the possession of which was theretofore in question for different reasons.[546] The first of these was the settlement of the question of ownership of the Oregon Territory south of the forty-ninth parallel in favor of the United States by the Oregon Boundary Treaty of 1846.[547] Concurrent with that event was the initiation in 1846 of hostilities

---

[541] Kemble, *Panama Route*, 11.

[542] "Steerage" describes the lowest deck of a ship where cargo is stored. Space not occupied by cargo was sold to travelers at the lowest prices, with correspondingly fewer comforts. Typically, they had no bathroom facilities except for pots and pans, no privacy to speak of, poor food, and bunks for sleeping.

[543] Kemble, *Panama Route*, 213–52.

[544] Steamers, unlike sail-powered ships, needed to carry coal or other fuel, and often intermittently resupply during their journeys.

[545] Kemble, *Panama Route*, 11.

[546] The United States had already doubled its size in 1803 with the Louisiana Purchase, comprising some fifteen million acres, purchased at the fire-sale price of approximately four cents per acre.

[547] Kemble, *Panama Route*, 7.

with Mexico by the United States, culminating in the Treaty of Guadalupe-Hidalgo in 1848, which confirmed the United States' ownership of lower California and the whole of the Great Southwest.[548]

With these huge tracts of land, now unarguably part of the United States, came their inhabitants, who demanded reliable mail service, the timely delivery of goods, and reasonable travel accommodations.

The third important condition that contributed to the development of the Panama Route was the demand created in 1848–1869 by the flow of more than four hundred thousand persons through the Isthmus of Panama en route from New York City and other points on the Atlantic to San Francisco.[549]

This unprecedented influx of people to the West was triggered by the discovery of gold in California on January 24, 1848. During that year, only 335 individuals traveled the Panama Route to San Francisco. The next year, 1849, however, saw 4,624 make the journey, followed by 11,229 in 1850, 17,395 in 1851, 31,826 in 1852, and 26,701 in 1853. The year 1854 witnessed 31,508 make the trip, the largest number except for 1852. In 1855, 26,449 followed their predecessors. In 1856, 22,613 made the voyage and in 1857, 13,593. From 1858 through 1869 the number of travelers varied from a low of 12,744 to a high of 40,395, but mostly reflected numbers in the 17,000 to 20,000 range.[550]

The figures are necessarily approximate because of the way records were kept or, to be more precise, were not kept. First-class, second-class, and, where available, third-class passengers were usually documented in lists of individual names, but those lists might conclude with the statement "and many others" rather than even a specific number.[551] Steerage passengers were never identified individually. Contributing to the inaccuracy of passenger lists was the fact that most steamers on the Atlantic side began their voyages in New York City, but made intermediate stops at Charleston, Savannah, Havana, and New Orleans,[552] where additional passengers might be added. The original passenger lists from New York City appear to be relatively complete, but records of those joining the voyage at the intermediate stops are incomplete, if not nonexistent.

---

[548] Ibid.
[549] Ibid., 254.
[550] Ibid.
[551] Ibid., 253.
[552] Ibid., 13.

Congress, sympathetic to the increasing needs of the populace as the country expanded, had as early as 1819 entertained proposals for the construction of wagon roads across the continent. [553] However, the realities of winter weather and hostile Indian attacks, among others, seemed to make such a venture ill-advised. [554] Such dangers and inconveniences were non-existent on a route across the Isthmus. This led Congress to conclude in 1845 that it should promote a passenger and mail route to the Northwest via Panama, soon followed by its invitation of proposals from private individuals and companies to accomplish that objective. [555] The need for such a service would shortly become much more acute as a direct result of the California gold rush.

Aside from its solicitation of proposals from the private sector, Congress itself made attempts to develop the Panama Route for mail and passengers. It offered subsidies for various periods of time for mail contracts, and eventually gave the power to the Department of the Navy as well as the Post Office Department to let contracts. [556] By the end of 1848, the stage was set for the mail service Congress envisioned, implemented by subsidized steamers that would operate from the Atlantic to the Pacific. [557] Between the public and private sectors, during the period from 1848 to 1869 a total of 104 steamers plied their trades on both sides of the Isthmus. [558]

---

[553] Ibid., 7.
[554] Ibid., 8.
[555] Ibid.
[556] Ibid., 11-15.
[557] Ibid., 30.
[558] Ibid., 213–52.

APPENDIX III

THE MENDOZA AFFAIR

Mendoza, reportedly of Portuguese descent, died unexpectedly and from unknown causes on June 3, 1923, at a sheep-shearing corral north of Georgetown, Idaho (about thirty miles from Montpelier), where he was working. The undertaker in Montpelier, F. M. Williams, was summoned and removed the body to Montpelier. Mendoza's coat bore a pin with the Three Links of the IOOF, and a paid-up membership card identified his affiliation with the lodge in Ft. Benton, Montana, which caused the undertaker to contact the Montpelier lodge. Information hurriedly obtained by Dr. Guyon as secretary of the Montpelier lodge via telegraph from the Ft. Benton lodge confirmed the availability of a death benefit from the lodge in the amount of $60,[559] and based on that fact and the undertaker's personal knowledge of the local (Montpelier) lodge, he embalmed the body, pending notification from Mendoza's California relatives.[560]

Eventually, the Ft. Benton lodge instructed the Montpelier lodge to bury Mendoza and to have the undertaker send an itemized statement of expenses beyond the $60 death benefit, which the Montana lodge agreed would be paid from the deceased's estate. Luckily, the public administrator of the county in Montana where Ft. Benton was located was also an IOOF brother and personal friend of Mendoza. Dr. Guyon was assured that Mendoza's "estate will pay all the expenses not covered by his lodge memberships." Furthermore, Dr. Guyon was advised that "the funeral expenses are preferred claims against the estate and will be paid out of the first monies received."[561] Based on these promises, Mendoza's remains were interred according to the IOOF's rituals.

The undertaker's unpaid bill, which totaled $232.20, was sent to Wm. H. Jenkinson, the public administrator of Chouteau County, Montana, who acknowledged receipt and responded, "I will see that you are paid this bill as soon as possible and I have every reason to believe that there is more

---

[559] Actually, the death benefit turned out to be $75, but was represented to be $60 in an apparent attempt by the Ft. Benton lodge to reimburse itself from the difference for its own expenses of contacting Mendoza's relatives.

[560] F. M. Williams to E. F. Guyon, 26 October 1926.

[561] Pettit to E. F. Guyon, 16 June 1923.

than enough to take care of all outstanding indebtedness against the estate."[562]

Months later, and apparently in response to at least one other request for payment by the undertaker, Mr. Jenkinson's previous positive assessment of the availability of funds from Mendoza's estate to pay funeral expenses was replaced by a decidedly negative one:

> I will say that things regarding this estate are in much worse condition than I even dreamed they could have been, in fact most everything that Mendonza [sic] owned was mortgaged. However there is [sic] some lots and a little personal property that is clear and as soon as possible we will dispose of it and as your bill is a perferred [sic] claim it will be taken care of first.[563]

Unfortunately, even Mr. Jenkinson's gloomy report of November 10, 1923, was overly optimistic, as evidenced by the fact that three years passed and the undertaker's bill remained unpaid. Those circumstances prompted a letter to Dr. Guyon from F. M. Williams, the undertaker, who stated:

> This account has been riding on my books for over three years, and I might say it does not set right with me to see this acct as it is, when I took the chance and buried him under the direction of the Local Lodge, who had the authority from his home lodge to give him a fitting burial.

Williams then recounted the history of the matter, and pointed out that without the intervention of the IOOF, the county would have paid for Mendoza's burial as a pauper, and would even have reimbursed Williams for his mileage to pick up the body, ending the letter with "I would appreciate it if you would take this matter up through your local lodge, and see if I can get this off my books."[564]

In response to Williams' entreaty, Dr. Guyon wrote to the Grand Master in Boise, "with the request that you take it up with the Grand Master of Montana and have him ascertain if they intend to flatly repudiate

562 Wm. H. Jenkinson to F. M. Williams Co., 28 June 1923.
563 Wm. H. Jenkinson to F. M. Williams Co., 10 November 1923.
564 F. M. Williams to E. F. Guyon, 26 October 1926.

this obligation and leave us to reimburse the Undertaker for his services?"[565]

In response to a contact from the Grand Master of Montana, the Ft. Benton lodge submitted its report that detailed the distribution of Mendoza's estate under the auspices of the administrator, including the sum of $2.86 as a pro-rated amount "after the appraisers, attorney and administrator has been paid in full."[566] The report also referenced a Montana statute that gave priority to funeral expenses, and observed that "claims against the estate was [sic] not paid in compliance with this statute, ~~and it appears to us that in a case of this kind the Administrator should be held responsible~~."[567] Finally, the report references the minutes of its meeting from June 3, 1923, three years earlier:

> Motion made and carried that Montpelier, Idaho Lodge be notified that our death benefit is $75.00 and we will be responsible for no more.

Curiously, neither Grand Master took a stand one way or another. This triggered a letter dated August 29, 1927, on behalf of the Montpelier lodge to the Ft. Benton lodge and signed by E. F. Guyon. The missive is surprisingly benign in tone and reflects a position that can only be characterized as "taking the high road." In sum, the Montpelier lodge paid the full balance due the undertaker, but felt compelled to explain its actions as follows:

> We have no regrets for giving Bro. Mendoza a Ritualistic burial, which he deserved and was entitled to and this Lodge would do the same again, under the same circumstances, regardless of it's experience in this case.
>
> The County would have buried him and paid the expenses of the same, but as Oddfellows, we objected to having a member of this great Fraternal Order buried in a Potter's Field, among the unfortunates who fall by the wayside, unhonored, unsung and unknown. Brother Mendoza did not deserve such treatment and thank God he didn't get it.

---

565 E. F. Guyon to Carl O. Johnson, 5 February 1927.
566 Ft. Benton report, May 4, 1927.
567 Interlineation in original.

We had no acquaintance with this brother prior to this death. He never visited our Lodge, or made himself acquainted with any of our members, but after his death he was found to be a member of this Order in good standing, in your Lodge. We then took charge of his remains and notified your Lodge by wire asking your pleasure in the matter of his burial. You informed us to bury him in Montpelier, which was done with the burial service of the Order and he was buried in the I.O.O.F. Cemetery.

If your lodge thinks we should suffer this injustice we will do so. We did our duty and are glad of it. We leave the matter to your sense of justice.

APPENDIX IV

DR. GUYON'S IOOF ACTIVITIES

Representative, Twenty-Second Annual Session, Grand Lodge, Nampa, October 18, 1904

Representative, Annual Session, Grand Encampment, Lewiston, October 16, 1905

Representative, Twenty-Third Annual Session, Grand Lodge, Lewiston, October 17, 1905

Grand Lodge, Coeur d'Alene, October 16–18, 1906

Grand Encampment, Coeur d'Alene, October 16–18, 1906

Member, Grand Lodge, Caldwell, October, 1907

Member, Grand Encampment, Caldwell, October, 1907

Representative, Twenty-First Annual Session, Grand Encampment, Boise, October 19, 1908

Representative, Twenty-Fifth Annual Session, Grand Lodge, Boise, October 20, 1908

Annual Session, Sovereign Grand Lodge, Denver, September, 1908

Representative, Twenty-Second Annual Session, Grand Encampment, Grangeville, October 18, 1909

Representative, Twenty-Seventh Annual Session, Grand Lodge, Grangeville, October 19–22, 1909

Representative, Annual Session, Grand Lodge, Sandpoint, October 18, 1910

Representative, Annual Session, Grand Encampment, Sandpoint, October 17, 1910

Delegate, Annual Session, Grand Lodge, Twin Falls, October 16, 1911

Annual Session, Grand Encampment, Twin Falls, October 16, 1911

Representative, Annual Session, Wallace, October 14, 1912

Representative, Thirtieth Annual Session, Grand Lodge, Wallace, October 14–18, 1912

Representative, Twenty-Fifth Annual Session, Grand Encampment, Wallace, October 14, 1912

Sovereign Grand Lodge, Winnipeg, 1912

Annual Session, Grand Lodge, Weiser, 1913

Grand Lodge, Boise, 1914

Grand Encampment, Boise, 1914

Representative, Annual Session, Grand Lodge, Idaho Falls, October 19, 20, 21, 1915

Grand Lodge/Grand Encampment, Coeur d'Alene, October 16, 17, 1916

Representative, Twenty-Seventh Annual Session, Grand Lodge

Delegate, Grand Lodge, Nampa, October 15–18, 1917

Thirty-Second Annual Session, Grand Encampment, Boise, October 20, 1919

Department Council, Nampa, October 15–18, 1917

Twelfth Annual Session, Department Council, Boise, October 20, 1919

Thirteenth Annual Session, Department Council, Caldwell, October 18, 1920

Thirty-Seventh Annual Session, Grand Lodge, Boise, October 21, 1919

Forty-Third Annual Session, Grand Encampment, Idaho Falls, October 20–21, 1930

Forty-Eighth Annual Session, Grand Lodge, Idaho Falls, October 21, 22, 23, 1930

Representative [undated and unidentified]

.

APPENDIX V

SELECTED POEMS

The Fleet
1st

1.   "Uncle Sam" has sent his fleet
Out upon old Oceans deep
Just to limber up and take some exercise
And he has a gallant crew
Big and strong and brave and true
Just the lads the yankees like to idolize

2.   And I do not give a rap
Whether every nosey Jap
Hates to see old Bobby Evans sail about
But I'd like to kindly say
Better not get in his way
For it's hazzrdous [sic] to interrupt his route

3.   He's a jolly sailor lad
But he's <u>awful</u> when he's mad,
And he never turns his back to any foe
You will always find him stay
In the thickest of the fray
And defeat's a thing that Bobby doesn't know

4.   He will go where he is sent
There are none who can prevent
And the Japanese had better tremble now
For we'll have them understand
That we'll always be on hand
And be ready when they want to start the row.

5.   So let freedom's good old flag
With it[s] stars and stripes wig-wag
In every breeze that blows across the sea
It's the finest rag in sight

And it stands for truth and right
And forever it shall wave above the free

An undated and untitled poem that could easily bear the name "The Valentine":

That valentine I showed to you,
Back in the years of long ago,
How sad it was I never knew,
The girl who truly loved me so.

I asked you, candidly, to tell,
The one you thought I ought to blame,
And with your secret guarded well,
You hid behind another's name.

Our paths laid sweetly near that day,
And, smiling closely by, stood Faye,
But you refused to point the way,
To where my soul might find it's [sic] mate.

Not bound, that day, by any ties,
My heart was free to claim it's [sic] own,
And there before my very eyes,
She rode, unrecognized, unknown.

That valentine you sent to me,[568]

Another example is the following handwritten but undated poem, which introduces an element of fatalism:

And who shall walk some narrow path of life,
So nearly side by side that should one turn even so little
space,

---

[568] It is unclear whether the last line was meant to be the beginning of a new verse, whether it was meant to be unfinished, or whether the balance of the poem is simply lost.

To left or right, they needs must stand acknowledged face
    to face.
And yet, with wistful eyes that never meet,
And groping hands that never clasp,
And lips calling in vain to ears that never hear,
They seek each other all their weary days,
And die unsatisfied – <u>And this is Fate</u>.

The following typewritten and undated poem laments the inevitable
loss of youth and love in a decidedly fatalistic way:

I can see the shady woodland where the twillight [sic]
    shadows fall,
Where the soft wind whispers gentle through the trees so
    straight and ta[ll?].
My sweetheart stands, again beside me as in those days
    long past,
Happy days, which come, but once to you, and far too
    sweet to last.
In my dreams I travel back beneath a sky of blue and
    gold,
And a Lark's note long and pensive seems to thrill me
    through and thr[ough.?]
And my soul will always linger near the old familiar scene,
    Where once I wandered with my sweetheart
    beneath the twilights gleam.

A short poem entitled "Life" seems to be particularly fatalistic and
poignant:

Just a little pleasantness,
Then just a thousand pains.
Just a little sunniness,
Then just a flood of rain.
Just a little merriness,
Then just a million tears.
Just a little hopefulness,
Then just a surge of fears.
Just a little happiness,
And then a flood of cares.

Just a little garnered wheat,
And then a field of tares.
Just a little trustfulness,
And then deceptions [sic] blight.
Just a hint of Angels [sic] wings,
And then the gloom of night.

The following typewritten and undated poem suggests a love gone awry, perhaps one of more than passing importance:

'Tis sweet to keep on telling you,
The things I know you know,
To let the heart reveal it's [sic] heart,
To tell "I loved you so".

It is sweet to just remember
Some things we cant [sic] forget,
And yearn each day for what we lost
And hug the fond regret.

I truly thought you did not care,
You thought the same of me,
And thus be drifted blindly on,
With eyes that did not see.

We did not know each other then,
And senses not Love's appeal,
We both refused to let our hearts,
Their secret love reveal.

And hence, we made an empty life,
Of yours as well as mine,
And missed the joys "love" held in store,
Nor drank it's [sic] secret wine.

The only poem in my possession that is both dated and titled is also the longest one. "In the Green Fields Where the Meadow Larks Were Singing" is dated April 24, 1917, but is also different from the other poems in that the inclusion of a "refrain" may indicate it was intended to be a song:

How oft my heart goes back again,
To those green fields I loved so dear,
How oft in dreams the lark's refrain,
Comes gently to my sleeping ear.

Oh just to be a boy once more,
To roam those fields all fresh with dew,
To live again those days of yore,
When all was joy and life was true.

Come back, Oh Youth, with your sweet charms,
Make me once more a barefoot boy,
Oh, Come, and clasp me in your arms,
And bring me back my boyhood's joy.

Farewell, green fields I loved so well,
Amidst thy charms no more I'll roam,
But in my soul you'll always dwell,
Until from earth God calls me home.

Farewell, sweet larks, that sang for me,
When life was young and held no sighs.
I'll hear again your songs of glee,
In greener fields beyond the skies.

REFRAIN.

In the green fields where the meadow larks were
      Singing,
There is where my heart is ever fondly clinging,
Where my boyhood[']s shouts and laughter oft were
      ringing,
In those sweet fields where the meadow larks were singing.

An expression of Doc's patriotism arising from the Great War can be found in the following:

They say, on Flander's field the poppies bloom,
With drooping heads and petals white and red,

To drive the sadness and dispel the gloom,
From Glory's field where rest our sacred dead.

For Freedom's cause those heroes sought the fray,
And sailed, with eager hearts across the sea,
They counted naught, the price they were to pay,
But gave their all, that mankind might be free.

Through all the years of Time's unmeasured way,
The mem'ry of their deeds shall never die,
And when the sun and moon and stars decay,
They'll dwell in Glory with the Saints on High.

So may those humble poppies always live,
And bloom in Flander's field across the sea,
And to each mourners heart a solace give,
And be a chosen emblem of the Free.

O, mothers, wives and sweethearts, don't forget,
To grow these simple flowers of white and red,
For they will soothe and soften your regret,
And case a smile of sunshine on your head.

APPENDIX VI

THE SAGA OF THE INDIAN WARS PENSION

*Two things are infinite: the universe
and human stupidity; and
I'm not sure about the universe.*
— Albert Einstein

Congress Purports to Reward White Survivors of the Indian Wars

Grandpa Guyon's participation in the Bannock War near Pendleton, Oregon, beginning on July 3, 1878, described earlier in this biography, gave rise to an interesting, if unproductive, odyssey that began for Dr. Guyon and his family in 1931 and continued until 1953, notwithstanding his death in 1934. The adventure was triggered by a law passed by Congress on March 3, 1927 (the "1927 Act"), which purported to pension veterans of Indian Wars under the following circumstances:

INDIAN WAR SURVIVORS

The act of March 3, 1927, grants pension to any person who served thirty days or more in any military organization, whether such person was regularly mustered into the service of the United States or not, but whose service was under the authority or by the approval of the United States or any State or Territory in any Indian war or campaign, or in connection with, or in the zone of any Indian hostilities in any of the States or Territories of the United States from January 1, 1817, to December 31, 1898, inclusive, and who is suffering from any mental or physical disability or disabilities of a permanent character not the result of his own vicious habits, which so incapacitate him for the performance of manual labor as to render him unable to earn a support. Rates range from $20 to $50 per month proportionate to the degree of inability to earn a support, and pension commences from the date of filing of the application in the Bureau of Pensions, after the passage of this act, upon proof that the disability or disabilities then existed, and continues during the existence thereof.

Any person above referred to who has reached the age of sixty-two years shall, upon making proof of such fact, be placed upon the pension roll and entitled to receive a pension of $20 per month; in case such person has reached the age of sixty-eight years, $30 per month; in case such person has reached the age of seventy-two years, $40 per month; and in case such person has reached the age of seventy-five years, $50 per month.

The Value of the Pension

Grandpa Guyon first applied for this pension in on October 13, 1931, less than a month short of the age of seventy-eight, and therefore would theoretically have been eligible for the maximum authorized payment of $50 per month. That $50 had value in today's dollars of somewhere between $716 and $9,490, depending on the method used to calculate it.

The $716 figure can be ascertained by calculating the value of $50 against the increases in the Consumer Price Index between 1931 and the present, but that value may not be the most accurate. The Contemporary Standard of Living value of the $50 is $1,530. The Economic Status value is $3,800 and the Economic Power value is $9,490.[569] Assuming that the smallest figure, $716, is the correct figure, Dr. Guyon's yearly income would have increased by $8,592, had he been granted the pension. Whatever the value, there is no doubt that the pension would have had a significant positive financial impact on Dr. Guyon and his family.

The following is a discussion and review of part of the contents of the file created in response to Dr. Guyon's initial application in 1931 (the "File").[570] The File contains eighty-six separate pages of additional applications, memoranda, correspondence, and notes ranging from the initial filing in 1931 to the most recent document, filed in 1953. It recounts the tortuous path followed first by Dr. Guyon and then by his widow Effie

---

[569] See, for example, MeasuringWorth.com.

[570] I have opted to include the entire text of certain documents, usually correspondence, in hopes that the flavor of the documents will be more accurately presented. In other cases, where the entire text did not seem mandatory, I have paraphrased the documents or quoted selected portions. I have refrained from making any personal comments concerning the events reflected in the File until after the actual review. Although I have developed some strong feelings about the fairness of the process, I wanted readers to come to their own conclusions.

Myrtle Guyon in their efforts to secure the pension, along with the frustrating bureaucratic hurdles and their own misunderstandings and confusion that stood in their way.[571]

The Application Is Filed

The first document submitted by Grandpa Guyon was a government form entitled "Declaration for Survivor's Pension—Indian Wars" dated October 13, 1931 (the "Declaration"),[572] supplemented by a shorter form entitled "3-027 Declaration for Survivor's Pension—Indian Wars" (the "Supplementary Declaration"). The Supplementary Declaration seems to serve no particular purpose, but does add the following information concerning Grandpa Guyon's whereabouts after 1878: "Pendleton, Oregon, until 1896 and from 1896 in Montpelier, Idaho, to date" and states the following concerning his occupation: "at time of service was school teacher and since 1891 occupation has been surgeon and physician."

To digress slightly from the objective of the Declaration to the Declaration itself, it confirms Doc Guyon's age (seventy-seven) and date and place of birth (November 7, 1853, New Orleans, Louisiana), but also reflects other information not necessarily common knowledge. His personal description, for instance, "at the time of first enlistment" [1878] was as follows: height 5'8"; complexion dark; color of eyes brown; color of hair black; and occupation schoolteacher. His justification for his need of a pension, as required by the Act of March 3, 1927, states that his occupation has been "physician," but that he is "wholly" unable to earn a support because "due to my age I am unable to carry on my profession."

Accompanying the Declaration were five affidavits signed, respectively, by C. E. Finch (the "Charley Finch Affidavit"), J. T. Arrasmith and Maggie M. Finch (the "Arrasmith/Finch Affidavit"; both signed the same affidavit), and Edward W. Jones and Laura G. Jones (the

---

571 I commenced my quest to obtain a copy of Dr. Guyon's application and related documents not later than 2008. After a number of telephone calls and correspondence from the National Archives saying that the file was lost, misplaced, or otherwise unavailable, in March, 2012, on a Friday, I received a telephone call from an affable gentleman stating that he had found the file, had copied it, and at that moment was sending the copy to me, along with his apologies that it had not happened earlier. This telephone call was particularly well received, although not readily believed, since I had received a letter only several days prior expressing regrets that they were still unable to retrieve the records. The following Monday I received the promised package, containing approximately eighty-six separate pages of information, from whence this part of the biography comes.
572 "Declaration for Survivor's Pension — Indian Wars," Department of Veterans Affairs, 313/21/RA; CSS: 12-02244-F.

"Jones Affidavit"; both signed the same affidavit). At times hereafter, the five affidavits are collectively referred to as the "Supporting Affidavits."

Collectively, the Supporting Affidavits recount that in response to the apparent threat of an Indian uprising, Grandpa Guyon took refuge in Pendleton; that within a few days he volunteered for military service, was mustered in for guard and picket duty, and acted in that capacity for six weeks to two months; and that each affiant had daily contact with Grandpa Guyon. The Declaration, Supplementary Declaration, and Supporting Affidavits are sometimes hereafter collectively referred to as the "Application."

Why Dr. Guyon did not apply for a pension earlier is not evident from the record, although as explained below, the penalty for the delay was likely the loss of the pension itself, due to congressional and presidential tinkering. He was probably unaware of the 1927 Act until just prior to his Application filed in late 1931, or would have applied for it earlier.

The Application Proves Unsuccessful

The government's response to the Application was swift and decisive. In letters dated November 27, 1931, to both Senator Borah and Grandpa Guyon (hereafter the "Rejection Letters"), Mr. Morgan, the director of pensions, stated that the information in the Application was insufficient. To establish his service, Grandpa Guyon would have to supplement the application with the following information (hereafter collectively referred to as the "Required Supplement"):

[1]   a correct designation of the organization in which Grandpa Guyon served;

[2]   dates of enlistment and discharge;

[3]   the name of Grandpa Guyon's captain and names of some of Grandpa Guyon's comrades;

[4]   the amount of pay received by Grandpa Guyon by day or month;

[5]   the name of the official by whom Grandpa Guyon was paid;

[6]   stations of his company (presumably   locations where his company was stationed);

[7]   engagements (battles) in which Grandpa Guyon participated; and

[8] any other incidents that may have become matters of record.[573]

If Mr. Morgan's Rejection Letters seem harsh, from his standpoint it could hardly have been otherwise. For reasons unknown, there was apparently no official record in the War Department of Captain Emmett Wheeler's organization of Oregon Volunteers or its involvement in the Bannock War, much less the names of those who were mustered to serve in it in 1878. Therefore, there was no way that Mr. Morgan could independently confirm the validity of Dr. Guyon's Application. Consequently, in theory none of the Oregon Volunteers could have successfully secured a pension under the 1927 Act because of their inability to establish their membership and military service in an organization that officially did not exist.

A benevolent Congress allowed, for a time, pensions where official records were inadequate, but where claimants were able to prove membership and military service through affidavits and sworn testimony via private "special acts" of Congress.

Through special acts, two of Dr. Guyon's friends and compatriots, Charles E. "Charley" Finch and Jacob T. Arrasmith, had already received pensions (Finch's on May 15, 1928, and Arrasmith's on February 20, 1929)[574] for service in the Bannock War that was similar to Dr. Guyon's service.

Whether the denial of Finch's and Arrasmith's applications on an administrative level was a condition precedent to applying for special acts of Congress is unknown, although if true it would explain why Dr. Guyon filed his Application first, and only then applied for a special act of Congress after the Application was denied. What is certain is that Finch's and Arrasmith's pensions were both granted via special acts of Congress even though their applications themselves were deemed deficient by the government.[575]

---

[573] The Rejection Letters appear to request information inconsistent with the requirements of the Act. With the sole exception of the request for the "correct designation of the [military] organization in which [Grandpa Guyon] served," the requests are for indirect, circumstantial information that is not required on the face of the Act; is not required by the government form submitted as Grandpa Guyon's Declaration; and is information that is unlikely to be remembered more than fifty years after the events. The resolution of this apparent conflict between the language of the Act and the requests for additional information was critical to the eventual failure of Dr. Guyon's Application.

[574] Report of Contact, Department of Veterans Affairs, 313/21/ra, 12-02244-F, dated November 3, 1944.

[575] R. J. Hinton reported to Idaho Senator Bert H. Miller that the applications of both Finch and

The Finch and Arrasmith pensions were successfully obtained during the administration of Calvin Coolidge (1923–1929), which seems to have made all the difference. By the time Grandpa Guyon attempted to do the same thing in 1933–1934, the administrations had changed twice,[576] and the apparent favorable attitude in the Coolidge administration toward veterans of the Indian Wars had diminished, if not disappeared altogether.

Dr. Guyon Pursues the Pension through Special Acts of Congress

Like Finch and Arrasmith years before, Grandpa Guyon's next move was to attempt to secure the pension by special act of Congress. Senator Borah introduced Senate Bill S-5222 in the Seventy-Second Congress on December 8, 1932,[577] and Senate Bill S-711 in the Seventy-Third Congress on March 9, 1933,[578] both seeking a pension for Dr. Guyon as a special act of Congress. Why separate bills were introduced in 1932 and 1933 is unclear from the record, although it may be that the earlier bill was introduced too late in 1932 to be acted upon before Congress adjourned, and was then reintroduced, with a different number, at the beginning of the Seventy-Third Congress in 1933. As S-711 made its way through Congress and before any final action granting it, Dr. Guyon died,[579] which event apparently rendered the Application moot.

Effie Tries to Exercise Her Own Rights to the Pension

Effie, left high and dry by the death of Dr. Guyon in early 1934, accepted the challenge of pursuing the pension on her own. Senator Borah introduced S-3454 in the Seventy-Fourth Congress at some unknown point between January 3, 1935, and January 3, 1937,[580] this time on behalf of Effie as Grandpa Guyon's widow. S-3454 was rejected for unknown reasons, whereupon Senator Borah introduced S-214 in the Seventy-Fifth Congress on January 6, 1937, where it was "read twice and referred to the Committee on Pensions." According to a later field examiner's report, no

Arrasmith had been reviewed in an attempt to uncover evidence of Dr. Guyon's service, but even "their service could not be established for pensionable purposes by this Administration within the legislation providing pension at that time." R. J. Hinton to Senator Bert H. Miller, 1 July 1949.
[576] Herbert Hoover's presidency (1929–1932) and Franklin D. Roosevelt's presidency (1933–1945).
[577] *Journal of the Senate*, December 8, 1932, p. 50.
[578] *Journal of the Senate*, 1933, p. 45.
[579] Wendell S. Guyon to R. J. Hinton, 17 October 1944.
[580] Report of Field Examiner, XC-2,602,946, 313/21/ra, 12-02244-F.

committee action was taken on S-214.[581] The fate of S-214 thus reported appears to be inconsistent with Effie's understanding that S-214 had been passed by both houses of Congress and the Committee on Pensions, but was pocket-vetoed by President Roosevelt.[582]

If Effie's understanding was accurate that S-214 was pocket-vetoed after receiving both the blessing of Congress and of the Committee on Pensions, it explains and supports her later statement that she was advised by Senator Borah's successor Senator Thomas[583] to await a change in the Roosevelt administration before attempting to pass any subsequent private legislation. Unfortunately for Effie, that possibility never materialized due to the extension of the Roosevelt administration into 1945 and the subsequent passage of the Legislative Reorganization Act of 1946, Section 131 of which banned private pension bills entirely.

Regardless of the ultimate fate of S-214, the Committee on Pensions sought information about the status and viability of the claim asserted by S-214, which resulted in an April 28, 1937, letter from Frank T. Hines, administrator, to Senator George McGill, chairman of the Committee on Pensions, detailing the alleged deficiencies in the original Application as reflected in the Rejection Letters and the history of the file thus far (1937). It also raises the following additional alleged deficiencies:

[1]   no evidence of Grandpa Guyon's death was provided;

[2]   no claim was filed by Effie;

[3]   Finch and Arrasmith affidavits don't specifically say they served with Grandpa Guyon, and in any event their pensions arising from service in Captain Emmett Wilson's Company of Oregon Volunteers were granted by special acts of Congress;

[4]   there is no record of Captain Emmett Wilson's Company of Oregon volunteers in the

---

581 Ibid.

582 Effie M. Guyon to Senator Henry Dworshak, 26 January 1948, 313/21/ra, 12-02244-F; a discussion of the pocket veto and its effect is found in the United States Supreme Court's opinion in *The Pocket Veto Case*, 279 U.S. 655 (1929).

583 John W. Thomas (1874–1945) was appointed to the United States Senate in 1928 to fill the vacancy caused by the death of Frank R. Gooding and won a special election to finish the term. He was again appointed to the Senate in 1940 to fill the vacancy caused by the death of William E. Borah and again won a special election to finish the term. In 1942 he was elected to a full term, but died in office.

department of Idaho war service or the State of
Oregon; and the General Accounting Office has
no record of service of such an organization; and
[5] no evidence has been produced to show Grandpa
Guyon served in any active Indian hostilities
recognized or later approved by Oregon or the
United States.

Because of the foregoing alleged deficiencies, Mr. Hinton's
recommendation to the Committee on Pensions was that "the widow of
this veteran is not shown to be entitled to pension under any existing
law."[584] As already stated above, Effie believed that S-214 had been
pocket-vetoed after being passed by the Committee on Pensions, although
that belief is clearly inconsistent with Mr. Hinton's recommendation and
the field examiner's report identified above.

Effie Persists

Effie was not easily dissuaded from her quest, and in mid-1944 she
wrote Idaho Senator D. Worth Clark concerning "the Lesinski bill
signed by the President."[585] Her letter to Senator Clark, which Senator
Clark forwarded to Mr. Hinton, also contained the following
statement:

All the affidavits are now in the hands of the Committee
on Pensions, and as long as the Committee gave their OK
to the special bill which Senator Borah introduced in my
behalf, I see no reason that I should not be entitled to a
pension.

Effie's argument concerning the effect of Congress' passage of S-214
appears to have merit. After all, Congress had given its blessing to the
claim, which recognized its sufficiency, and the fact it may have been
pocket-vetoed did not alter the decision of Congress. In other words, the

---

[584] Hines to McGill, 28 April 1937, 313/21/41, 12-02244-F.
[585] This likely refers to the "Lesinski Pension Increase Act" of June 6, 1940, ch. 246, 54 Stat. 237,
which increased pension benefits "to veterans of the Regular Establishment entitled to pensions
under the general pension law on account of service-connected disabilities incurred in or aggravated
by service prior to April 21, 1898." It does not pretend to create a pension entitlement not already
existing.

pocket veto was not a final decision on the merits. Effie's assertion was that once S-214 was given the approval of Congress, the rights thus created were vested[586] and could not be taken away without due process of law. Effie's argument seems to have escaped Mr. Hinton, whose review of her claim was clearly limited to whether the information requested in the Rejection Letters from 1931 had been supplemented and says nothing of the vested rights issue. The vested rights issue was raised by Effie in later correspondence at least once, but appears never to have been officially considered—or determined.

What confuses Effie's argument somewhat is her attempted reliance upon the Lesinski Bill, which did not create an independent basis to assert entitlement to a pension not already granted. It may be that Effie was simply grasping at straws; more likely is that the language of the bill seemed to promise relief, but in reality did not.

The Veterans Administration Remains Unpersuaded

Mr. Hinton's response dated July 6, 1944, to Senator Clark makes several observations, including the following:

> Inasmuch as Mrs. Guyon has never filed a claim for death pension, a statement as to her entitlement to such benefit may not be made.
>
> [and]
>
> A letter was addressed to the veteran on November 27, 1931 for additional evidence relating to his alleged service for use in connection with his claim, but no response was ever received to that letter; therefore, it does not appear that death pension would be payable in this case.

Hinton's statement that Effie had never filed a claim must have astounded her. She had been advised by Idaho Senator Borah that after Grandpa Guyon's death in early 1934, she had an independent right to Grandpa Guyon's pension by virtue of being his widow, and she had successfully obtained congressional approval of that claim in the form of S-214. In Effie's mind, congressional approval of S-214 was the decisive

---

586 "Fully and unconditionally guaranteed as a legal right, benefit, or privilege"; see *Merriam-Webster's Collegiate Dictionary*, 10th ed.

factor that should have resulted in her getting the pension, despite the fact that it may have been pocket-vetoed. That view of the facts and circumstances was not shared by Mr. Hinton.

Effie could easily have remedied Mr. Hinton's first complaint by filing her own formal written application, but that problem was only a minor one. The bigger problem was that, more than thirteen years after the original Application, the response of the government in the Hinton letter of July 6, 1944, was "We still don't have the Required Supplement." From the government's perspective, the only thing that had changed since 1931 was the death of Dr. Guyon. All the efforts expended by Effie in the meantime were for naught because, according to the government, the Application was flawed and would never be acceptable until the Required Supplement was provided.

The Ill-Fated First Widow's Application

Seemingly undaunted by the negative responses from the government to the Application and by her and Dr. Guyon's almost iconic run of bad luck in their efforts to secure the pension through a special act of Congress, the plucky matriarch of the Guyon family sought success in the fall of 1944 by filing her own written application as Dr. Guyon's widow, supplemented by her marriage certificate to Grandpa Guyon and Grandpa Guyon's Decree of Divorce from Maggie (the "First Widow's Application").[587]

It is likely that this action on her part was prompted by Hinton's letter of July 6, 1944, observing that she had never filed a claim in her own name concerning which a decision could be made.[588] The marriage certificate and the decree of divorce filed with the First Widow's Application were clearly to establish her widowhood to Dr. Guyon.

Mr. Hinton's September 20, 1944, response to the First Widow's Application was prompt and to the point.[589] The information detailed in the Rejection Letters from 1931 had still not been provided after thirteen years, and until it was, there could be no pension.[590]

---

[587] Application for Pension or Compensation by Widow and/or Child of a Deceased Person Who Served in the Active Military or Naval Service of the United States.

[588] It is implicit in Mr. Hinton's letter that any application necessarily would be based on the 1927 Act; no other known act of Congress contemplated such relief outside a special act of Congress.

[589] R. J. Hinton to Effie M. Guyon, 20 September 1944.

[590] For some unknown reason, it appears that the mindset of both Dr. Guyon and Effie was that the Supporting Affidavits contained all the necessary factual allegations to make the Application successful, while the consistent response of the government through Messrs. Morgan and Hinton was the opposite.

Aside from restating the requirements of the 1931 Rejection Letters, Mr. Hinton's September 20, 1944, letter failed to comment on the application form used by Effie, her inclusion of the marriage certificate and Grandpa Guyon's divorce decree, or any other matters, which added to the misunderstanding and confusion rather than diminishing them.

This confusion is in part demonstrated by a letter dated October 17, 1944, from my father to Mr. Hinton on behalf of Effie,[591] wherein my father voices his belief that the lack of information alleged by Mr. Hinton's letter of September 20, 1944, was due to the fact that Mr. Hinton did not have the Supporting Affidavits to review, rather than that the Supporting Affidavits themselves were deficient. It is on that basis that my father suggested that the information collected by Senator Borah, which included the Supplemental Affidavits, had somehow been misplaced. The tone of the letter implies that when the "proofs" [i.e., the five Supplemental Affidavits] are found, the First Widow's Application should obviously be successful.

The suggestion that documents collected by Senator Borah's office might have been lost prompted the Committee on Pensions to engage a field examiner to investigate the matter and recover any information that might have been collected or filed with Senator Borah's private bill S-214.[592] The field examiner's report concluded that no information was found that confirmed Grandpa Guyon's military service.[593] Effie was promptly notified and given one year to furnish additional information.[594]

Effie Resurrects the First Widow's Application

Despite the one-year cutoff, there was no further action reflected in the file until 1948. On January 26 of that year, Effie enlisted the aid of Idaho Senator Henry C. Dworshak, who, on February 3, 1948, requested Mr. Hinton's assessment of the status of Grandma Guyon's claim. Hinton promptly responded on February 16, 1948, explaining as follows:

> Under date of January 31, 1945, the widow was requested to furnish evidence showing that the veteran served as a member of the Armed Forces of the United States. This

591 Wendell S. Guyon to R. J. Hinton, 17 October 1944.
592 R. J. Hinton to Director, Dependents Claim Service, 24 November 1944; R. J. Hinton to Wendell S. Guyon, 21 November 1944.
593 Report of Field Examiner, 12 December 1944.
594 R. J. Hinton to Effie M. Guyon, 31 January 1945.

evidence was not furnished and the claim was disallowed for failure to furnish such evidence.

No other activity appears in the file until February 23, 1949, when Grandma Guyon wrote to Idaho Senator Bert Miller,[595] who promptly requested a status report on the claim. Mr. Hinton responded to Senator Miller on March 22, 1949, explaining that her claim was disallowed on January 31, 1945, "for the reason that the evidence necessary to complete the claim was not provided within one year from the date of the request therefor."

Mr. Hinton's March 22, 1949, letter also invites Effie to "file another application if she wants a formal decision," and states that "the proper blank form" is enclosed for her to do so.

There is no copy of the "proper blank form" included in Mr. Hinton's letter, but it is safe to say it was identical to the form Effie filed as her First Widow's Application. Unfortunately, the form on its face is limited to applications arising from service in the regular armed services and clearly does not apply to Effie, which Mr. Hinton either knew or should have known. Consequently, his ill-advised action further muddied the water.

In the meantime, the file reflects receipt of a letter on March 21, 1949 (the letter is dated March 16, 1949), from Earl E. Morgan, an attorney with Beatty, Clarke & Murphy of North Platte, Nebraska, to Idaho Senator Bert H. Miller on behalf of the pension claim of Effie M. Guyon. The letter is an obvious attempt to supplement Grandma Guyon's First Widow's Application and likely was read and considered by Mr. Hinton before his March 22, 1944, letter to Senator Miller.

The Morgan letter in its best light restates the claim that Grandpa Guyon served in the Bannock Indian War in July and August 1878, that his service was verified by the Supporting Affidavits filed in 1931, and that Grandpa Guyon's affiants Finch and Arrasmith both received pensions through special acts of Congress for the same or similar service rendered by Grandpa Guyon. The Morgan letter also perpetuates the myth and misunderstanding of Effie that the information in the Supporting Affidavits was sufficient to establish entitlement to the pension, despite the fact that the government had consistently notified her it was not, to

---

[595] According to Effie on February 23, 1949, at the time she believed a "new law" in 1946 provided an opportunity for her to successfully apply for the pension; she reported that Senator Dworshak had attempted to have it approved "before the last Congress adjourned, but was unable to do so."

say nothing of the fact that special acts of Congress, the mechanism through which Finch and Arrasmith were able to become pensioned, were banned in 1946.

The Second Widow's Application

In response to Mr. Hinton's March 22, 1949, letter, Grandma Guyon filed, under cover letter of Senator Miller dated April 18, 1949, an Application for Pension or Compensation by Widow and/or Child of a Deceased Person Who Served in the Active Military or Naval Service of the United States (the "Second Widow's Application").

The application form provided by Mr. Hinton that became the Second Widow's Application did nothing but increase confusion and misunderstanding. Effie clearly was not the widow of an active member of the armed services, and it is unclear why Mr. Hinton would even propose it in the first place. There appears to be no reason to suspect malevolence on his part, but one must wonder why someone as familiar with the file as he must have been would promote something so clearly unworkable.

Predictably, the response to the Second Widow's Application was much like the first, with the specific response that it "fail[ed] to show that your husband rendered any service in the military or naval forces of the United States."[596]

Mr. Hinton's response raised Effie's frustration level, if not her ire, as her pension claim had never been based upon Grandpa Guyon's service in the regular armed forces of the United States, and she promptly requested that Senator Miller set Mr. Hinton straight on that issue.[597]

Effie also recounted in some detail the history of the basis for her claim and again raised the vested rights issue and implored Senator Miller to do whatever he could to help her.[598]

In response, Senator Miller again attempted to help her by forwarding her letter to Mr. Hinton as follows:

> Senator Miller requests that the enclosed communication be carefully considered in conjunction with all of the evidence of record, and that he be furnished a report with respect to any possible entitlement the widow may have to death benefits.

---

[596] R. J. Hinton to Effie M. Guyon, 27 April 1949.
[597] Effie M. Guyon to Senator Miller, 16 June 1949.
[598] Ibid.

Mr. Hinton's response details the efforts of his office to search records, including those of the applications of Finch and Arrasmith, any records of the late Senator Borah, and any other records to which his office had access, but, predictably, ends with the following:

> As previously stated to the claimant in numerous letters from this office further action on the claim may not be granted until she submits additional proof of service on the part of her husband that may be confirmed as meeting the requirements of present legislation for purposes of paying death pension. Should not such evidence of pensionable service be available it will be necessary to disallow her claim when the period of time for the submission of such evidence has elapsed.
>
> It is regrettable that a more favorable reply to your inquiry may not be made however in view of the lack of any favorable success in the search for evidence which would make it proper to approve an award in favor of the claimant no other reply is possible.[599]

Chronologically, nothing else appears in the file except for a "Disallowance Memorandum" stating that Effie's claim under the 1927 Act was disallowed due to the following: "Evidence of record fails to show that Edwin F. Guyon rendered compensable service during the Indian Wars."[600]

Lessons Learned or Not Learned

Based on the language of the Act itself,[601] it seems almost incomprehensible that the pension was <u>not</u> authorized. As the reader has

---

[599] R. J. Hinton to Senator Miller, 1 July 1949.

[600] Disallowance Memorandum, VA Form 8-523, 7 November 1953.

[601] Anyone who knows English and reads the 1927 Act knows what it *says*. The more pressing question to ask is, what did Congress *mean* as expressed in the 1927 Act? The answer to the question is that the intent of Congress is determined by applying court-created "rules of construction" to the language of the Act. The first such rule of construction is that if the intent of Congress may be discerned from the unambiguous language of the Act, then the inquiry is over and the Act is applied according to its literal terms. If the Act is ambiguous, i.e., subject to more than one reasonable interpretation, then information and evidence outside the language of the Act (i.e., "extraneous evidence") is considered, always with the ultimate objective of determining congressional intent. See, for example, *Russell Motor Car Company v. United States*, 261 US 514, 519 (1923).

246

seen, it is not difficult to lay blame at the feet of administrators who cannot escape the label of petty bureaucrats (or some other more pejorative term) because of their demands for information not in the language of the Act and arguably not contemplated by it.

On the other hand, the applicants are not without fault in the equation. Presuming that the Supporting Affidavits fully complied with the evidentiary requirements of the Act, they ignored the consistent statements from the government that the applications (there were three in total) were insufficient *notwithstanding the Supporting Affidavits.*

In a sense, it almost seems that the applicants and the government were carrying on separate written conversations with each other that the "other" never entirely understood. To express the problem in another way, the government made requests for information that was already provided or unnecessary, and the applicants responded with information that was either not requested or not pertinent.[602]

The reality is that the Application likely could *never* have been successfully supplemented as demanded by the government. The standard of proof required by the administrators under the 1927 Act was simply too high, and that was undoubtedly the reason for the special acts of Congress—to pension deserving veterans who were unable, for whatever reason, to meet the burden of proof required by the Government. However, even that option was denied the applicants, first due to Dr. Guyon's death, then because of the pocket veto of President Roosevelt, followed by the 1946 legislation that extinguished such special acts altogether.

It is the author's personal belief that the government bears the overall responsibility to be fair and to do justice, regardless of all other circumstances. Rather than recognizing this obligation, the government doggedly refused to recognize the information already submitted and continued to request information it must have known was impossible to acquire, even presuming that it was necessary or relevant in the first place. After all, the first application in 1931 was made over fifty years after the events supporting the applications occurred, and that application and its accompanying affidavits detailed all the information that was available.

---

[602] Although the events giving rise to the pension applications cover only the last few years of Dr. Guyon's life, the negative impact of the interim and ultimate denials of the applications on this struggling family, coupled with the overarching unfairness of the government in its treatment of this case, dictate that this relatively long story be told.

The sentiment that the government's denial of the application was improper was voiced in a rather poignant handwritten letter to Senator Borah in late 1931 by Charles E. Harris.[603] Harris's relationship with Dr. Guyon is not known, although his knowledge of the petition and the fact that he took time to write to Senator Borah suggest a friendship at least, and he may have been Doc's attorney. Referencing the E. W. Morgan letter of November 27, 1931, detailing the alleged deficiencies in Dr. Guyon's Declaration, Harris stated:

> It seems rather harsh to deny these old fellows something of a pension simply because they were unable to furnish all the information that would ordinarily be required for a Civil War or Spanish American War veteran. Both the doctor and myself are under the impression that the Act of March 3, 1927 was to provide especially for these men on the theory that they could not furnish much of the information that the other pension [illegible] required. There are not many of these old Indian War veterans left, and their time her[e] on earth is, to say the most, very limited.

Was There an Alternative?

What could have been done to secure a different result? It is true that hindsight is always 20/20, and this set of circumstances presents no exception to that rule. The easy answer is that upon the government's very first denial of the petition, Dr. Guyon should have filed a civil action in federal court seeking a judicial determination in the form of a court order that he was entitled to the pension.[604] Dr. Guyon appears to have clearly filled all the requirements set out in the statute, and we are left to wonder why he or Grandma Guyon never took legal action. Like the answers to many questions about his life, the answer is probably lost to history, and any attempt on our part to find it amounts to little more than speculation.

---

[603] Charles E. Harris to Senator Borah, 2 December 1931.
[604] United States district courts have constitutional authority under Article III to construe acts of Congress under Federal Question jurisdiction.

BIBLIOGRAPHY

Books

Baird, Charles Washington. *History of the Huguenot Emigration to America.* Vols. 1–2. New York: Dodd, Mead & Company, 1885.

Bruere, Robert W. *J. C. Penney, the Man With a Thousand Partners.* New York: Harper & Brothers, 1931.

Bonner, Thomas Neville. *Becoming a Physician: Medical Education in Britain, France, Germany, and the United States, 1750–1945.* Baltimore: Johns Hopkins University Press, 1995.

Brands, H. W. *The Age of Gold: The California Gold Rush and the New American Dream.* New York: Anchor Books, 2002.

Brimlow, George F. *The Bannock Indian War of 1878.* Caldwell, ID: Caxton, 1938.

Carlo, Paula Wheeler. *Huguenot Refugees in Colonial New York.* Brighton, UK: Sussex Academic Press, 2014.

Christopher, W. S. *Chemical Experiments for Medical Students.* Cincinnati, OH: Robert Clarke, 1888.

Cohen's 1853 New Orleans Directory, Including Jefferson City, Carrollton, Gretna, Algiers and M'Donogh. Woodridge, CT: Research Publications, 1980.

Currer-Briggs, Noel, and Royston Gambier. *Huguenot Ancestry.* Chichester, UK: Phillimore, 1985.

Dary, David. *Frontier Medicine From the Atlantic to the Pacific, 1492–1941.* New York: Vintage Books, 2008.

Duffy, John. *Sword of Pestilence: The New Orleans Yellow Fever Epidemic of 1853.* Baton Rouge: Louisiana State University Press, 1966.

Edwards, G. Thomas. *The Triumph of Tradition: The Emergence of Whitman College 1859–1924*. Walla Walla, WA: Whitman College, 1992.

Finnell, Arthur Louis, ed. *Huguenot Genealogies: A Revised Selected Preliminary List 2001*. Baltimore: Genealogical Publishing, 2001.

———, ed. *National Huguenot Society Bible Records*. Baltimore: Genealogical Publishing, 1996.

Forbes, Jeanne A. *Records of the Town of New Rochelle, 1699–1828*. New Rochelle: J. A. Forbes, 1916.

Forsythe, Mark, and Greg Dickson. *The Trail of 1858: British Columbia's Gold Rush Past*. Canada: Harbour Publishing, 2008.

French, Hiram T. *History of Idaho*. Chicago: Lewis, 1914.

Gardner, A. Dudley, and Verla R. Flores. *Forgotten Frontier: A History of Wyoming Coal Mining*. Boulder, CO: Westview Press, 1989.

Hughes, Thomas P. *American Ancestry: Giving the Name and Descent, in the Male Line, of Americans Whose Ancestors Settled in the United States Previous to the Declaration of Independence, A. D. 1776*. Baltimore: Genealogical Publishing, 1968.

Irwin, I. N. *1857/58 Sacramento Directory and Gazetteer*. Woodridge, CT: Research Publications, c1980.

Johnson, Richard Z., ed. *Illustrated History of the State of Idaho*. Chicago: Lewis, 1899.

Johnson, Walter. *Soul by Soul: Life Inside the Antebellum Slave Market*. Cambridge, MA: Harvard University Press, 1999.

Kaufman, Martin. *American Medical Education: The Formative Years, 1765–1910*. Westport, CT: Greenwood Press, 1976.

Kemble, J. H. *The Panama Route 1848–1869*. New York: Library Editions, 1970.

Lee, Grace Lawless. *The Huguenot Settlements in Ireland*. Baltimore: Genealogical Publishing, 2006.

Lotchin, Roger W. *San Francisco 1846–1856: From Hamlet to City*. Urbana, IL: University of Illinois Press, 1997.

Marteilhe, Jean. *Galley Slave*. Barnsley, UK: Seaforth, 2010.

O'Hart, John. *Irish Pedigrees; or the Origin and Stem of the Irish Nation, Vol. 2*. New York: Murphy & McCarthy, 1923.

Rasmussen, Louis J. *San Francisco Ship Passenger Lists*. Vol. 1. Baltimore: Genealogical Publishing, 1978.

Reinders, Robert C. *End of an Era: New Orleans, 1850–1860*. New Orleans: Pelican, 1989.

Rich, A. McKay. *The History of Montpelier, Idaho from 1864 to 1925*. Montpelier, ID: Bear Lake Publishing.

Rothstein, William G. *American Medical Schools and the Practice of Medicine*. New York: Oxford University Press, 1987.

Seacord, Morgan Horton. *Records of the Town of New Rochelle, 1687–1776*. New Rochelle: J. A. Forbes, c1941.

Steele, Volney. *Bleed, Blister, and Purge: A History of Medicine on the American Frontier*. Missoula, MT: Mountain Press, 2005.

Waksman, Selman A. *The Conquest of Tuberculosis*. Berkeley: University of California Press, 1964.

Wilde, Jens Patrick. *Treasured Tidbits of Time: An Informal History of Mormon Conquest and Settlement of the Bear Lake Valley*. Vols. 1–3. Utah: Keith W. Watkins and Sons, 1977.

Williams' Cincinnati Directory. Cincinnati, OH: Cincinnati Directory Office, 1890.

E. F. Guyon Correspondence and Documents

Brown, Maud Guyon. Papers. Private collection.

Guyon, E. F. Papers. Private collection.

Newspapers

Bear Lake County (ID) News.

Cincinnati Enquirer.

Dalles (OR) Daily Chronicle.

East Oregonian (Pendleton).

Idaho Statesman (Boise).

Montpelier (ID) Examiner.

New Orleans Times-Picayune.

Paris (ID) Post.
Utah Journal (Logan).

Wyoming Press (Evanston).

Other Publications

Cincinnati Lancet-Clinic 18 (1889, Jan–June).

Cincinnati Lancet-Clinic 24, no. 26 (1890, January 28).

Idaho Odd Fellow 13, no. 6 (1908, January).

Idaho Odd Fellow 16, no. 3 (1911, July).

Journal of the American Medical Association 31, no. 13 (1898, September 24).

Journal of the Senate, December 8, 1932.

Journal of the Senate, 1933.

Northwest Medicine 1.

Northwest Medicine 3, no. 6 (1911, May).

Northwest Medicine 16, no. 8 (1917, August).

Rich, J. C. Letter to the editor. *Medical Sentinel* 5 (1897): 345.

Riley, Glenda. "Women on the Panama Trail to California, 1849–1869." *Pacific Historical Review* 55, no. 4 (1986).

United States Census Records

Eighth Census, 1860, Fourth Ward, Sacramento City, Sacramento County, California.

Eighth Census, 1860, South Salem, Marion County, Oregon.

Ninth Census, 1870, Pendleton to Willow Creek Precinct, Umatilla County, Oregon.

Ninth Census, 1870, Fourth Precinct, Tenth Ward, San Francisco, San Francisco County, California.

Tenth Census, 1880, Alta, Umatilla County, Oregon.

Tenth Census, 1880, San Francisco, San Francisco County, California.

Twelfth Census, 1900, Montpelier, Bear Lake County, Idaho.

Fifteenth Census, 1930, Montpelier, Bear Lake County, Idaho.

Miscellaneous

Guyon, Edwin Fenimore. Interview with author, Victor, Idaho, September 15, 1990.

Gamage, et al. v. Masonic Cemetery Ass'n., et al., 31 F.2d 308 (USDC, ND Cal., SD, 1929).

Masonic Cemetery Ass'n, et al. v. Gamage, et al., 38 F.2d 950 (9th Cir. 1930).

Russell Motor Car Company v. United States, 261 US 514, 519 (1923).

70877303R00161

Made in the USA
San Bernardino, CA
08 March 2018